Genders and Sexualities in History
Series Editors: **John H. Arnold, Joanna Bourke** and **Sean Brady**

This series aims to accommodate and foster new approaches to historical research in the fields of genders and sexualities. The series promotes world-class scholarship that concentrates upon the interconnected themes of genders, sexualities, religions/religiosity, civil society, class formations, politics and war.

Historical studies of gender and sexuality have often been treated as disconnected fields, while in recent years historical analyses in these two areas have synthesised, creating new departures in historiography. By linking genders and sexualities with questions of religion, civil society, politics and the contexts of war and conflict, this series will reflect recent developments in scholarship, moving away from the previously dominant and narrow histories of science, scientific thought and legal processes. The result brings together scholarship from contemporary, modern, early modern, medieval, classical and non-Western history to provide a diachronic forum for scholarship that incorporates new approaches to genders and sexualities in history.

Sexual violence has become a major factor in the conduct of modern military conflicts. *Rape in War* is a response to the urgent need for historical approaches to the phenomenon. The collection challenges the often ahistorical narrative of sexual violence, exploring in detail the temporal, geopolitical, and ideological specificities of wartime rape during the twentieth and twenty-first centuries and throughout the world. The authors interrogate the dynamics of rape, forms of decision-making amongst perpetrators and their supporters, the relationship between rape in times of peace and war, and what this form of violence tells us about gender norms and practices. It addresses difficult issues related to the "memory" of sexual violation and its consequences. In common with all the volumes in the Gender and Sexualities in History series, the collection incorporates new scholarship in innovative ways. It is an exciting contribution to our understanding of violence in the past and today.

Titles include

John H. Arnold and Sean Brady (*editors*)
WHAT IS MASCULINITY?
Historical Dynamics from Antiquity to the Contemporary World

Heike Bauer and Matthew Cook (*editors*)
QUEER 1950s

Cordelia Beattie and Kirsten A Fenton (*editors*)
INTERSECTIONS OF GENDER, RELIGION AND ETHNICITY IN THE MIDDLE AGES

Chiara Beccalossi
FEMALE SEXUAL INVERSION
Same-Sex Desires in Italian and British Sexology, c. 1870–1920

Raphaëlle Branche and Fabrice Virgili (*editors*)
RAPE IN WARTIME

Peter Cryle and Alison Moore
FRIGIDITY
An Intellectual History

Jennifer V. Evans
LIFE AMONG THE RUINS
Cityscape and Sexuality in Cold War Berlin

Kate Fisher and Sarah Toulalan (*editors*)
BODIES, SEX AND DESIRE FROM THE RENAISSANCE TO THE PRESENT

Christopher E. Forth and Elinor Accampo (*editors*)
CONFRONTING MODERNITY IN FIN-DE-SIÈCLE FRANCE
Bodies, Minds and Gender

Dagmar Herzog (*editor*)
BRUTALITY AND DESIRE
War and Sexuality in Europe's Twentieth Century

Robert Hogg
MEN AND MANLINESS ON THE FRONTIER
Queensland and British Columbia in the Mid-Nineteenth Century

Andrea Mansker
SEX, HONOR AND CITIZENSHIP IN EARLY THIRD REPUBLIC FRANCE

Jessica Meyer
MEN OF WAR
Masculinity and the First World War in Britain

Jennifer D. Thibodeaux (*editor*)
NEGOTIATING CLERICAL IDENTITIES
Priests, Monks and Masculinity in the Middle Ages

Hester Vaizey
SURVIVING HITLER'S WAR
Family Life in Germany, 1939–48

Clayton J. Whisnant
MALE HOMOSEXUALITY IN WEST GERMANY
Between Persecution and Freedom, 1945–69

Forthcoming titles

Matthew Cook
QUEER DOMESTICITIES
Homosexuality and Home Life in Twentieth-Century London

Rebecca Fraser
GENDER AND IDENTITY IN ANTEBELLUM AMERICA FROM NORTHERN WOMAN TO PLANTATION MISTRESS

Julia Laite
PROSTITUTION AND REPRESSION IN THE METROPOLIS
Criminalization and the Shaping of Commercial Sex in London, 1885–1960

Melissa Hollander
SEX IN TWO CITIES
The Negotiation of Sexual Relationships in Early Modern England and Scotland

---

Genders and Sexualities in History Series
Series Standing Order 978–0–230–55185–5 Hardback 978–0–230–55186–2 Paperback
(outside North America only)

You can receive future titles in this series as they are published by placing a standing order. Please contact your bookseller or, in case of difficulty, write to us at the address below with your name and address, the title of the series and the ISBN quoted above.

Customer Services Department, Macmillan Distribution Ltd, Houndmills, Basingstoke, Hampshire RG21 6XS, England

---

Rape in Wartime

Edited by

Raphaëlle Branche
Assistant Professor, Université Paris-I

and

Fabrice Virgili
Director, UMR 8138 IRICE Université Paris-I, Panthéon-Sorbonne

palgrave
macmillan

First published 2012 by
PALGRAVE MACMILLAN

Palgrave Macmillan in the UK is an imprint of Macmillan Publishers Limited, registered in England, company number 785998, of Houndmills, Basingstoke, Hampshire RG21 6XS.

Palgrave Macmillan in the US is a division of St Martin's Press LLC, 175 Fifth Avenue, New York, NY 10010.

Palgrave Macmillan is the global academic imprint of the above companies and has companies and representatives throughout the world.

Palgrave® and Macmillan® are registered trademarks in the United States, the United Kingdom, Europe and other countries.

ISBN 978–0–230–36399–1

This book is printed on paper suitable for recycling and made from fully managed and sustained forest sources. Logging, pulping and manufacturing processes are expected to conform to the environmental regulations of the country of origin.

A catalogue record for this book is available from the British Library.

A catalog record for this book is available from the Library of Congress.

10 9 8 7 6 5 4 3 2 1
21 20 19 18 17 16 15 14 13 12

Transferred to Digital Printing in 2013

Contents

List of Tables and Figures

Tables

Figures

Notes on Contributors

Natalia Suarez Bonilla is Associate Professor at the University del Valle, Cali, Colombia. Her research focuses on analysis of the disruption caused by the Colombian civil war in daily life in terms of categories of perception of the world, instruments and the tools of cognitive skills. She has a PhD in sociology (EHESS-GSPM). Recent publications include "La qualification de l'ami et de l'ennemi révolutionnaire. Le cas de la Colombie", in Myriam Klinger Sebastien Schehr (eds), *Lectures du conflit.*

Raphaëlle Branche is Senior Lecturer in Modern History at Université de Paris-1-Panthéon-Sorbonne. She is a member of the Centre d'Histoire Sociale du XXe siècle (CNRS) and a junior member of the Institut Universitaire de France. Her research focuses on French colonialism and on violence committed by armed forces, both regular and irregular, in the nineteenth and twentieth centuries. Recent publications in English include "Sexual Violence in the Algerian War", in D. Herzog (ed.), *Brutality and Desire: War and Sexuality in Europe's Twentieth Century*; "Torture of Terrorists? Use of Torture in a 'War against Terrorism': Justifications, Methods and Effects. The Case of France in Algeria, 1954–1962", in *International Review of the Red Cross.*

Isabelle Delpla is Assistant Professor of Philosophy, University Montpellier III, and a member of the Research Center Triangle (UMR CNRS 5206). Her research focuses on international ethics and justice (e.g. *Le mal en procès. Eichmann et les théodicées modernes*, Hermann, 2011). Her work on postwar Bosnia deals with the Srebrenica massacre, the reception of the International Criminal Tribunal (ICTY) and the status of victims and witnesses (e.g. *Peines de la guerre, La justice pénale internationale et l'ex-Yougoslavie*, co-edited with M. Bessone, EHESS, 2010 and *Investigating Srebrenica*, co-edited with X. Bougarel and J.-L. Fournel, Berghahn, forthcoming in 2012).

Anne Godfroid is a doctoral student researching the Belgian occupation of the Rhineland under the joint directorship of Professors Pieter Lagrou (ULB) and Jean-Michel Sterkendries (Royal Military Academy, Brussels). She has worked since 2001 at the Royal Museum of the Armed Forces and of Military History in Belgium where she oversees the documentary collection (including photographs, drawings, prints and posters) and the library and archives. She has curated several temporary and permanent exhibitions.

John Horne is Professor of Modern European History, Trinity College Dublin, a Fellow of TCD and a Member of the Royal Irish Academy. He was the first Director of the Centre for War Studies at TCD, 2008–10. He is a member of the Executive Board of the International Research Centre of the Historial de la Grande Guerre, Péronne, which is a major museum of the First World War on the western front. He is the author of several books and over seventy chapters and articles, many relating to the history of war. Among his books are *State, Society and Mobilization in Europe during the First World War* (Cambridge, 1997); (with Alan Kramer), *German Atrocities, 1914. A History of Denial* (Yale, 2001); *A Companion to World War One* (Blackwell-Wiley) and *Vers la guerre totale: le tournant de 1914–1915* (Paris, Tallandier), both in 2010. He is currently working on a history of France in the Great War.

Adediran Daniel Ikuomola is Lecturer in the Department of Sociology at Adekunle Ajasin University, Akungba-Akoko, Ondo State, Nigeria. He obtained his PhD in sociology from the University of Ibadan in 2010. His primary research interests are deviancy and juvenile violence with an emphasis on lifestyle and self-control theories. His work has appeared in *Journal of Research in Peace and Conflict Review; Arts and Humanities; Culture and Development, and Social Research.* He is the author of *Crime and Violence as a Barrier to Gender Equality in Nigeria Politics.*

Maud Joly is a PhD student in History at Sciences-Po, Paris, and a former member of the Casa de Velázquez (EHEHI, Madrid). Her research work analyses "sexual violence" during the Spanish Civil War. Recent publications include "De la *corporéité* de la guerre: corps de femmes et *violence-spectacle* dans la Guerre Civile espagnole", in Sophie Milquet and Madeleine Frédéric (eds), *Femmes en guerres;* "Guerre Civile, violences et mémoires: retour des victimes et des émotions collectives dans la société espagnole contemporaine", in Luc Capdevila and Frédérique Langue (eds), *Entre mémoire collective et histoire officielle;* "Las violencias sexuadas de la guerra civil española: paradigma para una lectura cultural del conflicto", in *Historia Social.*

Pieter Lagrou teaches history at the Université Libre de Bruxelles. From 1998 to 2003 he worked at the Institut d'Histoire du Temps Présent (CNRS) in Paris and published on the legacy of the Second World War and comparative history. He is currently working on international justice and on European democracy. Recent publications include "Regaining the Monopoly of Force. Agents of the State Shooting Fugitives in and around Belgium, 1940–1950", in *Past & Present*.

Nayanika Mookherjee is a Reader of Social Anthropology in Durham University. She has published extensively on anthropology of violence, ethics and aesthetics. Recent publications include co-editing (with Christopher Pinney, 2011) the *Journal of the Royal Anthropological Institute* Special Issue, "The Aesthetics of Nation" and her book *The Spectral Wound: Sexual Violence, Public Memories and the Bangladesh War* (Duke University Press, forthcoming). Her current research explores adoption of "war-babies" (children born as a result of sexual violence during wars).

Regina Mülhaüser is a researcher at the Hamburg Foundation for the Advancement of Research and Culture. Her current research compares how different military actors in the Second World War dealt with sexual violence. She is the contact for the Working Group "War and Gender" at the Hamburg Institute for Social Research; and the International Research Group "Sexual Violence in Armed Conflicts". Other research interests include National Socialism, international law and post-Second World War memory politics in Europe and Asia. Her book *Eroberungen. Sexuelle Gewalttaten und intime Beziehungen deutscher Soldaten in der Sowjetunion* was published in 2009.

Marianna G. Muravyeva is Associate Professor of Law at Herzen State Pedagogical University of Russia. Her interests include gender history, history of violence against women, history of crime, human rights and gender and law. She has published on these issues extensively including: "Seksual'nye prestupleniia v evropeiskom voenno-ugolovnom prave rannego novogo vremeni" (Sex Crimes in Early Modern European Military Law), in *Dialog so vremenem: Al'manakh intellektual'noi istorii*; "Relations sexuelles, fornication et inceste spirituel entre kimovja (campari) dans la culture traditionelle russe", in Guido Alfani, Philippe Castagnetti and Vincent Gourdon (eds), *Baptiser. Pratique sacramentelle, pratique sociale (XVIe–Xxe siecles)*; "Forms and Methods of Violence against Women in Eighteenth-Century Russia: Law against Morality", in *Study Group on Eighteenth-Century Russian Newsletter*.

Norman M. Naimark is Robert and Florence McDonnell Professor of East European Studies at Stanford University. He is also Senior Fellow at the Hoover Institution and at the Freeman-Spogli Institute. Recently, Norman has worked on the history of violence and genocide, and on Soviet policies in Europe at the end of the Second World War and the beginning of the peace. He recently completed a short monograph, *Stalin's Genocides* (Princeton, 2010), which has been translated into a number of languages.

Tal Nitsán is doctoral candidate in Anthropology at the University of British Columbia and a scholar at the Liu Institute for Global Issues. Her research focuses on the intersections between gender, violence, law and society. Her current research explores women's organisations' campaign to eradicate violence against women in Guatemala. She is the author of *Controlled Occupation: The Rarity of Military Rape in the Israeli–Palestinian Conflict* (Shaine Center for Research in Social Science, 2007). Her contribution to this volume is an academic response to the public controversy her work on the Israeli–Palestinian conflict provoked.

Daniel Palmieri is Historical Research Officer at the International Committee of the Red Cross (ICRC). His work deals with ICRC history, the history of conflicts and of humanitarian action.

Nadine Puechguirbal is Women and War Advisor for the International Committee of the Red Cross (ICRC). Prior to taking up this role in July 2008, Nadine was Senior Gender Advisor for the United Nations Peacekeeping Operation in Haiti (MINUSTAH). She holds a PhD in Political Sciences at Université Paris-I (Panthéon Sorbonne). She is also a Senior Fellow at the UN-affiliated University for Peace in Costa Rica where she teaches in the Master's on Gender and Peace Building programme. She recently published an article entitled "Peacekeeping, Peace Building and Post-Conflict Reconstruction", in Laura Shepherd (ed.), *Gender Matters in Global Politics* (Routledge, 2010).

Amandine Régamey teaches Russian language and civilisation at Université Paris-I (Panthéon Sorbonne) and is an associate member of the Centre for Russian, Caucasian and Central Asian Studies (CERCEC EHESS/CNRS). She has been conducting research on the Chechen war since 1999, focusing on the representations of the war in Russian society and the army. She is the co-author with Anne Le Huerou of "Russia's War in Chechnya: The Discourse of Counterterrorism and the Legitimation of Violence", in S. Cohen (ed.), *Democracies at War against Terrorism* (Palgrave Macmillan, 2008).

Antoine Rivière is a doctoral student in history at the Université Paris-IV (Sorbonne). He is working on the subject of abandoned children and their mothers in Paris (1880–1920). Recent publications include "Archives de l'abandon. Les dossiers personnels des pupilles de l'Assistance publique parisienne (1880–1920)", in *La protection de l'enfance: écrits protégés, écrits ignorés. Les dossiers individuels de mineurs et de jeunes majeurs sous main de justice* (La Documentation française, 2010).

Alexandre Soucaille is Research Fellow at CNRS, Paris. He obtained his PhD in Social Anthropology at the Université Paris-X (Nanterre). His thesis was entitled "'It's not real India!' Les Adivasi face à la société indienne dans l'État du Jharkhand: ethnologie fragmentée d'une relation". He has extensively researched the Adivasis of Jharkhand, India, and is currently engaged in studying the domination structure of rape and status of "criminal tribes" in colonial and postcolonial India.

Katherine Stefatos is currently completing her PhD thesis at the Politics Department of Goldsmiths College, University of London. She holds a BA from the University of Athens in European and International Studies and an MSc in Gender and the Media from the London School of Economics. Her research interests include gender and political violence, nationalism and Modern Greek political history.

Fabrice Virgili is a historian and Senior Research Fellow at CNRS (IRICE-Université Paris-I-Panthéon-Sorbonne). His research is currently focused on gender and war. Recent publications include *Shorn Women: Gender and Punishment in Liberation France* (Berg, 2002); "Enfants de Boches: The War Children of France", in Kjersti Ericsson and Eva Simonsen (eds), *Children of World War II: The Hidden Enemy Legacy* (Berg, 2005), and the Preface to the French Edition of J. R Lilly, *Taken by Force. Rape and American GIs in Europe during World War II* (Palgrave Macmillan, 2007).

Acknowledgements

This book is partly the outcome of a conference organised in Paris in May 2009. During three days of intense debate the numerous and sometimes anonymous participants cultivated reflection, resulting in the texts published in this book. We particularly thank the presenters and participants whose contributions do not figure in this volume: Dara Kay Cohen, Malika El Korso, Claire Fourçans, Jane Freedman, Stéphanie Gaudillat-Cautelat, Michaelina Jakala, Delphine Lacombe, Julie Le Gac, Alisa Muratcuas, Akachi Odoemene, Valérie Pouzol, Zoë Waxman and Elisabeth Jean Wood.

The organisation of the conference would not have been possible without the warm support of the German Historical Institute in Paris and the personal commitment of its director Gudrun Gersman, her adjunct Stefan Martens and Margarete Martaguet. An international intellectual encounter of this scope requires the mobilisation of resources and the enthusiasm of many. We thank Isabelle Gasnault, Thérèse Lortolary, Sandrine Maras and Josette Mateesco at the Université Paris-I (Panthéon-Sorbonne) and the Centre National de la Recherche Scientifique (CNRS). Special thanks to Sylvie Le Dantec, who created the graphic design based on the artwork of Jean Lasne, *Éclatement*, whose reproduction was graciously granted by Jean-Bernard Sandler. Maryvonne Le Puloch diligently proofread all the texts.

Thanks to the financial support of Mrs Rama Yade, State Secretary in charge of Foreign Affairs and Human Rights, Mrs Badetz, Burnham and Puri-Léger have offered an exemplary simultaneous translation that has greatly enhanced the quality of the debates.

The conference and this volume have been financed by the Centre d'histoire sociale du XXe siècle (UMR 8058), the research unit IRICE, the Université Paris-I (Panthéon-Sorbonne), the CNRS, the Institut Émilie du Châtelet, the mayor of Paris, the International Committee of the Red Cross (ICRC), the Bibliothèque de Documentation Internationale Contemporaine (BDIC), the research unit Triangle/EA Université Montpellier III, the Institut Universitaire de France and the Regional Information Center of the United Nations in Paris.

Raphaëlle Branche and Fabrice Virgili

Writing the History of Rape in Wartime

Raphaëlle Branche, Isabelle Delpla, John Horne, Pieter Lagrou, Daniel Palmieri and Fabrice Virgili
Translated by Helen McPhail

> Rome had now become so strong that she had no need to fear any of her neighbours; but without women she would lose all in a single generation: without hope of offspring, the Romans were also without rights of intermarriage with their neighbours.
>
> – Livy, *History of Rome*, Book 1, XI

This is how Livy narrated the origins of Rome. Without the desired marriages, Romulus therefore organised games in honour of Neptune the Horse-god. As Livy continued,

> All the Sabines came, with their women and children. Roman households were opened to them, and as they saw the city, with its pleasing position, its ramparts, and its many houses, they were amazed at its rapid growth. The day came for the games and as all eyes and minds were concentrated on them, the plan was carried out as prepared: at the agreed signal, the youth of Rome rose up on all sides to seize the young girls. Most of them fell victim to the first abductor. Some of the most beautiful, reserved for the principal senators, were carried off into their houses by citizens charged to undertake this task. One among the others, far superior to her companions in height and beauty was, it seems, taken by the senator Talassius's group; as they were repeatedly asked where they were taking her, to protect her from all insults they cried out as they marched: "to Talassius" – hence the time-honoured phrase in the marriage ceremony. Terror threw the celebration into disarray, the parents of the young girls fled, stricken with grief; and as they cried out against this violation of the laws of hospitality, they invoked the god whose name had drawn them to

> the solemnisation of the games, as cover for treachery and sacrilege. The victims of the rape shared this despair and indignation; but Romulus himself visited each one in turn to explain that the blame lay with their fathers and their refusal to form alliances through marriage with a neighbouring people; and that it was as wives that they would share with the Romans in their fortune and their nation, and be joined with them through the sweetest knot that can bind mortals together, by motherhood. They should therefore soften their resentment and give their hearts to those whom Fate had made their masters. For many the sense of injury gave way to tender affection. Confidence in their domestic happiness grew stronger as, in addition to fulfilling their marital duties, their Roman husbands made every effort to replace for their wives the family and the country for which they grieved. To these words were added the abductors' gentle caresses, explaining the violence of their action by the force of their love, an all-powerful excuse for the women. (ibid.)

This narrative became part of the Roman canon while the expression "the rape of the Sabines" has become a standard phrase. Yet just as historians do not study wars through the prism of Cain's murder of Abel, so the reference to the abduction of the Sabine women does not represent the totality of acts of sexual violence any more than its analysis can do justice to the place occupied by rape in the dynamics of wartime. For in reality there is nothing to say that rapes are an inevitable or unchanging aspect of war, or that men assert themselves by conquering and appropriating women as a form of the victor's spoils. These apparently universal truths require historical scrutiny and discussion. Where rapes do occur in wartime, the male assertion of sexual dominance is of course likely to be at work. But is it the only, or even the main, factor at work? If, however, there are significant variations in the manner, scale and temporality of rapes in wartime, how should we understand and explain these?

Going somewhat against the idea that rapes are a universal feature of war is the way in which they have assumed particular prominence in some recent conflicts, at least as a deliberate strategy. Typical of these conflicts has been the blurring of boundaries between civilians and the military, between male and female roles. As with bombing that deliberately targets civilians, so rape seems to have become a weapon of war specifically aimed at non-combatant women.

A longer-term historical view allows us to question whether the importance assumed by rape in recent wars is quite so novel as it might seem without having to lapse into the universalist claim that it is the same in all conflicts. Nonetheless, the contemporary public awareness of rape in wartime, and the denunciation of its horror, indicates a particular sensibility to the issue, and this has been reflected in legal developments. Three factors at least explain this new-found visibility: first, feminist assertions concerning women's bodies; second, the particularities of the conflicts that accompanied the break-up of Yugoslavia; and third, certain internal developments in the social and human sciences. As to the first of these, the demand for women's control over their own bodies has been at the heart of feminist claims since the 1960s. Questions about divorce, contraception and abortion helped focus attention on violence against women, such as rape, genital mutilation, harassment and marital violence. From that time on, the gendered or sexual aspects of violence in wartime have attracted attention in a new way, and this new sharpness of focus affected attitudes to the wars in ex-Yugoslavia (1991–95). In contrast to the rapes committed on a large scale in Bangladesh in 1971, or in Guatemala throughout the years 1960–96, and which to this day remain little known, the significance of rape in a contemporary European conflict produced very different levels of visibility. So much was this the case that rape is now seen as one of the defining characteristics of the wars in ex-Yugoslavia and the weapon par excellence of "ethnic cleansing", occasionally even relegating massacre to second place. All this has echoed new preoccupations in history as a discipline and in other human sciences. For over this same period the study of wars, which had long been confined to military, political and diplomatic history, grew to include their social, cultural and gendered dimensions. Historians began to engage with what had long been considered (in Alain Corbin's words) "obscene objects"; like their colleagues in other disciplines, they reflected on practices whose inherent violence seemed increasingly apparent to almost everyone.

Rape and male domination

Susan Brownmiller published the seminal book on rape, *Against Our Will: Men, Women and Rape,* in 1975. A touchstone for later scholarship, it established a clear line of argument: rape expresses the power of domination exercised by men over women. The differentiation between men/torturers and women/victims strengthened this general interpretation, which wartime only seemed to amplify. Even today, the equation of rape with innate male domination runs through public and academic debate on this form of violence.

While not ignoring questions about the continuities between war and peace, the present volume takes its inspiration from two trends in historical scholarship – the promotion of gender as a category of social analysis and a concern to explore multiple facets of wartime violence. Together these provide a framework for looking at rapes not as a universal attribute of war arising from male domination but as the point where the gendered nature of experience encounters the various forms of violence that make up war. In other words, the question of the presence and nature of rape in times of war is not assumed but posed as a question, as something that needs documenting and explaining.

It also requires some definitions. Rape should not be limited to the forced use of the victim's body for sexual fulfilment, for just as important is how it subordinates the victim, whether a man or woman, to the aggressor. Rape asserts the power of the assailant and consequently the impotence of the man or woman who endures it. The performance of rape may extend beyond the individuals concerned and be aimed at their communities of origin. Nadine Puechguirbal shows how the rapes committed during the civil war in Somalia against Bantu Somali women by Somali attackers were intended not only to demonstrate the power of one ethnic group over another, which was considered inferior for social and racial reasons, but also to demonstrate the inability of the male kin of the victims to defend their honour. Wartime rape, in other words, produces a relationship of inequality between two kinds of men: those who assert their physical and societal virility by committing the assault and those for whom this same act represents a symbolic castration owing to their inability to protect their wives, sisters or mothers. By extension, rape can become the symbol of one nation's dominance over another and the sense of impotence may extend to a whole society.

Yet tensions exist between several possible readings of wartime rapes. They can be seen particularly clearly in the wars in ex-Yugoslavia when two kinds of denunciation of sexual violation coexisted with, or even contradicted, each other. The rapes of Bosniac women by Bosnian Serbs could be seen as an expression of male domination over women, but equally plausibly as an attempt to assert nationalist supremacy by one "ethnic" group over another. Feminist, political or even patriotic readings of rape were thus in mutual contradiction. Among the victims of rape, women whose husbands or sons had been killed or tortured stressed a patriotic reading that played down differences of gender in order to make men and women equal victims of the same Serb barbarity. This plurality of possible readings – patriotic or gendered, but also ethnic or social – is stressed among others by Katherine Stefatos in her chapter on the Greek civil war of 1945–49, when violence against "Red" women expressed and reinforced the reorientation of the national community towards conservative values.

Whatever the outcome, whether the domination entailed by rape is gendered, social, ethnic or national, it is certainly through the gender of the victim – male or female – that this form of power is exercised. But to ask questions about the politics of rape in individual incidents is to change the scale of analysis. What goes on in the face-to-face confrontation between aggressor and victim? For as with torture, another particularity of this kind of violence is the central involvement of the bodies of those concerned. Norman Naimark underlines the importance of personal narratives in recognising the mass rapes committed by the Red Army in Germany in 1945. The victim was forced to see, smell and touch the "other", while for the perpetrator, both the male erection and physical desire are the essential pre-condition of the assault. The consent and eventual satisfaction of the victim are often evoked after the event in order to justify the act and to valorise the manliness of the aggressor and of the group or organisation to which he belongs.

Another particularity of rape is the possibility of pregnancy, which has potentially devastating consequences in wartime. Some rapes are committed with the intention of procreation, with pregnant women forced to take their pregnancy to term. The result is a "time-bomb" that is detonated much later, sometimes in circumstances that have changed completely, and which leaves a physical trace of the original rape in the postwar world. Yet in other cases, the rapist has no purpose other than the relief of desire, the assertion of conquest and the imposition of power.

Rape in wartime: a new crime?

Despite the contemporary sensitivity to rape in wartime, its condemnation and translation into legal terms is nothing new. Rape has been explicitly proscribed in the great majority of civil and military criminal codes from the beginning of the modern era, starting with the jurists Gentili and Grotius, as described by Marianna Muravyeva. In the *Lieber Code*, the founding legal text on the conduct of war which was published in 1863 by the Federal government during the American Civil War, rape figures among the acts of "Wanton Violence" liable to capital punishment and even, in case of disobedience following intervention by an officer, summary execution. The Geneva Convention IV of 1949 included rape among acts prohibited in relation to the civilian population, stipulating in Article 27 that "women will be specially protected against any attack on their honour, and notably against rape".

This fairly consistent condemnation of rape in wartime illustrates its specificity in relation to other types of military violence. The laws of war are founded on the principle that some acts which are forbidden in peacetime, such as murder, become legitimate in wartime if they are committed according to certain criteria. Other acts have only been legally forbidden in recent times and not necessarily in a consistent manner, such as the collective execution of civilians, the bombing of non-military targets and torture, all of which could also be justified in terms of shortening the conflict, collateral damage or obtaining vital information. None of this applies to rape. As Gentili observed, if a woman bears arms, she may be killed but not raped. Such an act must always be prohibited. Nor can rape be justified by reference to any principle or extenuating circumstance. There is no political or utilitarian justification of rape as a legitimate military practice, just as no rape is committed by virtue of unintended, collateral damage. Its judicial legalisation by forced marriage does not aim to make it an acceptable military practice but rather to eliminate it, as in India after the rapes committed during the partition in 1947 mentioned by Alexandre Soucaille in his chapter about the violence of the militias formed by some landowners of Eastern India against the Naxalite revolutionary movement at the beginning of the twenty-first century.

For this reason, from a legal and judicial point of view, it cannot be claimed that wartime rape has constituted a blind spot when considering the violence of war. On the contrary, rapes committed by the enemy have often been the acts that best lend themselves to an irrefutable charge of barbarism and which (because the perpetrators could not argue military necessity) have made it possible to prove that enemy behaviour was genuinely criminal. Unlike the executions of civilians, deliberate arson and destruction, the rapes committed during the German invasion of Belgium and France in 1914 could not be justified by charges of sniper activity. Similarly, in Brussels in 1950 during the trial of Max Boden, who had been responsible for the deportation of Belgian Jews from the camp at Malines, the Tribunal focused its indictment on sexual misdemeanours perpetrated by the accused. This avoided the problem of establishing torture and complicity in the deportation as criminal acts, something that would have required retroactive qualification since their legal prohibition only occurred with the new Geneva Conventions of 1949. The specificity of rape in these contexts is that it constitutes a crime or misdemeanour under "ordinary" Common Law, independently of the circumstances of war.

From this point of view, the jurisprudence of the International Criminal Tribunals for the Former Yugoslavia (ICTY) and for Ruanda (ICTR) marked a turning point since they included rape as a crime against humanity in the former case and an aspect of genocide in the latter. At the ICTY, the new importance attached to rape resulted in a disproportionate number of charges being brought for acts of sexual violence against men when in reality the majority of victims remained women. At the ICTR, one of the reasons for rape being considered a component of the crime of genocide was the number committed with a machete, resulting in the death of the raped woman. In other times, the same deed could have been defined as murder: its qualification as rape reflects the seriousness that sexual violation has gained compared to other forms of wartime violence.

This new attention to rape in situations of war and conflict has been accompanied by greater attention to sexual crimes generally and by a considerable increase in the number of convictions in both national and international courts of law. It arose from the perception that rape was being used as a form of strategy in contemporary conflicts and it then contributed to a retrospective re-evaluation of the role of rape in former conflicts at the level both of public opinion and scholarly research. Thus although rape was not the object of verdicts during the Nuremberg Trials of 1945–46, recent historiography has questioned the image of the Nazis holding back from rape for racial motives, as Regina Mühlhäuser shows here in a pioneering study of all forms of sexual violence practised by the Wehrmacht on the Eastern Front. Nonetheless, this enhanced sensitivity to rape in wartime has its limits. For courts can do no more than pass judgement on a few perpetrators, and it is not reflected at all in policies of civil compensation for victims.

Committing rape in wartime

Without arguing that there is no continuity between rape in war and peace, the two certainly represent very different contexts. Does war facilitate rape, and if so, in what ways? The nature of wars (international, civil, revolutionary), their duration and their particular dynamics are among the fundamental parameters that determine the phenomenon. What are the moments most favourable to rapes being committed? Is it the invasion of enemy territory, its occupation or the moment of retreat? Are the interior or the rear more given to rape than the front? Are there some places where such acts of violence are particularly likely to occur, such as places of internment? In fact the study of rape in wartime emphasises its place in a much larger repertoire of sexual violence that includes being stripped naked, forced prostitution, the shaving of women's heads, sexual mutilation or blows and wounds aimed at the sexual parts of the body.

Understanding the decision to resort to rape also requires a grasp of the mechanics of decision-making in the groups concerned. Who authorised the rape and defined its manner? Who committed it? What are the effects of this kind of violence on the various actors, victims as well as aggressors, and more broadly on the different circles to which they belong? Then the question of the rapists' freedom of action needs to be considered. What margin of manoeuvre do individuals have? On what repertoire of violence do they draw when they act? What are they able to do and what are the things that stay forbidden? How should we assess the role of this particular act of violence within the totality of the acts of war?

The recognition of the rapists' point of view is important for understanding what is at stake in a rape. The perpetrator is usually part of a hierarchical structure whose association with the violence in question has a considerable influence on the latter's meaning for the individual rapist. From a crime punishable under military regulations or the criminal code to an act that is encouraged and even publicly celebrated, the range of possible attitudes is broad. Only through the precise analysis of the identity of the rapists, their margin of autonomy and the way they commit their deed can the place of rape in the unfolding violence of a given war be understood. For example, it is important to know where the rape is conducted (in private or in public) and when (day or night), just as it is relevant to know whether it is a single or collective act and whether there are witnesses. All such evidence is part of the scene of the crime and vital for describing and understanding the latter.

Likewise, rapists are men but it can happen that women take part in the assault, either directly or indirectly. It is important to appreciate who carries out the rape, and how, in order to situate the rape in relation to the larger meaning of the war. Likewise it is just as important to consider the status of the victims – whether civilian or military, women soldiers or irregulars – or, again, their age. Frequently the victims are not only young women: being old or a child is no protection against the assault.

In certain conflicts, racism or the use of ethnic criteria becomes a major factor in determining who are the victims and who the perpetrators. In other cases, rape derives from structures of social domination that are played out in wartime conflicts. Indeed, while the precise analysis of the repertoire of violence requires particular attention to the local setting (e.g. the actors' situations, their degree of acquaintance, the acts performed and the words used), it must also be related to other frameworks. This interplay of scales of analysis suggests the many ways in which rape can be understood, according to whether it is viewed nationally – as with the case of Belgian troops occupying the former enemy after the First World War, studied by Anne Godfroid – or locally. Natalia Suarez Bonilla adopts this perspective in relation to Colombian villages targeted by paramilitary groups during the civil war.

War imagined

Among the things that distinguish rapes in wartime from those perpetrated in peacetime is their imaginary dimension. Peacetime rape tends to be experienced according to a dichotomy between the fantasies of the rapist, which are psychosocial and rarely acknowledged outside the act itself, and the social stigmatisation of the victim, which is traditionally expressed in terms of the honour of the family, clan or community. Because of the shame often associated with the crime, or of the historically subordinate position of women, the level of rapes reported even today remains much smaller than the number of rapes committed.

In wartime, on the other hand, the space for imagining rape is greatly extended because it is incorporated into scenarios of violence that have their own language. In particular, the act and the fear of rape provide an extended symbolic and even a metaphorical register for talking about the community and nation at a moment of threat. Through its collective dimension and the fear that it generates, rape is seen as a threat to society as a whole and, in this way, it helps to weld the community together through condemnation of the enemy. What in peacetime is psychologically repressed, dealt with only indirectly or limited to legal proceedings, becomes in wartime the source of collective emotions, of feelings of aggression and vulnerability, or a summons to resistance. This does not prevent individual cases of rape being glossed over or ignored because of the difficulty or even the impossibility of pursuing the guilty enemy and also because they are only one form of violence amongst many. And although some of the latter may be connected to rape, they often appear to be more serious, such as torture, deportation or massacre.

Several characteristics relating to the discourse and image of rape in wartime arise from this relationship between the reality of the violence and its place in the collective imagination. First, rape can play a key role in the process of societal mobilisation for war. It crystallises fear of the enemy and serves to demonstrate its relentless barbarity. The very notion of rape becomes a metaphor for invasion and then occupation. Whether real or imaginary, tales of rape link the violation of the family sanctuary to that of the nation, ethnic group or race in ways that are rare in peacetime. Republican fears of rapes committed by the "Moroccan troops" during the Spanish Civil War, analysed here by Maud Joly, condense the nightmare of the nationalist invasion of Republican zones, just as happened with the explosion of images and accounts of rapes committed by German troops in Belgium and in France in 1914, which expressed the profound feeling of national violation in these two countries.

Furthermore, the imaginary dimension of rape is not limited to populations that are conquered or under threat. In order to reinforce domination the invader may equally make use of the fear of rape and its symbolism. In the case of wars of "ethnic cleansing", rape is projected as a desire for biological domination through arbitrary control of the bodies and reproductive capacity of the targeted population. This was true of the Pakistani army during the 1971 war of independence in Bangladesh, examined by Nayanika Mookherjee. The claim that the new nation was modern in its outlook made it possible, once the war was over, to overcome the traditional taboo concerning the female victims of rape by making them heroes of the nation.

In the case of asymmetric wars between conventional and guerrilla forces, the hidden enemy of any age and either sex who resists the regular male soldier may be invested with an imagined sexual deviance – hence the legend among Russian soldiers in the 1990s of Chechen women snipers, discussed by Amandine Régamey. Even without going as far back as the supposed *pétroleuses* of the Paris Commune, the fantasy of these murderous and castrating women – who were indistinguishable from the rest of the population but who supposedly used their sharp-shooting skills to aim at the genitals of the Russian soldiers – was rooted in the traditions of elite women snipers in the Red Army during the Second World War. The imagined threat that they posed provoked gendered forms of revenge, resulting in the rape of Chechen women, who were seen as potential enemies.

In other cases, however, where the goal of the invaders or the occupier is less clear-cut, large-scale rapes may be virtually passed over in silence, particularly if the "violated" community is too scattered and broken to react collectively. The difficulty felt both by the victims and also by their families, society or nation in speaking about their fate results in a silence very similar to that experienced in peacetime. Shame, the fear of family sanctions, the agony of giving birth to the "child of the enemy" – all contribute to this. On the other hand, a highly verbal and prolix narrative of rapes may flourish in wartime retailed by men to express their own failure to prevent the rape of "their" homes and womenfolk. As an expression of masculine impotence, such accounts make the woman victim the object of fantasies of revenge against the enemy. It is but a short step for the desire to punish to be displaced onto women themselves, once rape has opened the way to accusations of familiarity with the occupant. But the war only has to take a different turning, and rape disappears from public discourse, leaving the silence of the perpetrators and victims.

This silence can also affect male victims. The fact that rapes in wartime are a violent assertion of "virility" does not alter the fact that there are many forms of masculinity – dominant, subaltern, deviant – some of which are also open to fantasies of subjugation by rape. In Bangladesh once again, the new state's willingness to acknowledge women as the victims of rape stood in marked contrast to the silence surrounding Bangladeshi men who were violated by (West) Pakistani soldiers, and who, in doing so, confirmed much older colonial stereotypes in respect of "effeminate" Bengalis. In such ways, the upheavals of war display the fragility and reversibility of gender.

Thus although women are the vast majority of rape victims, men also suffer sexual violation. Their absence from the statistics of international organisations can be explained in part by the fact that abuses frequently occur in captivity, when victims are removed from their own community. Enclosed locations (prisons, police stations, detention centres etc.) are suitable places for male rape to be committed, generally by other men, whether during interrogations or as part of the daily humiliation of prisoners. Added to this is the silence of victims over a fate that suggests homosexuality, and thus their intimate gender identity.

Conversely, the aggressor may not always be male. On certain occasions women undertake, or at least accompany, acts of sexual violence against male or female victims, especially where objects are used in the violation as a form of torture. The example of the prison at Abu Ghraib showed that American women soldiers committed acts of sexual torture against Iraqi detainees. There is also the question of the reactions of women who form part of the social milieu of the male perpetrators of rape. Little was heard from Serb women opposing the acts committed by their husbands, brothers or sons in Bosnia. The rejection of raped women or of their children by their family or community is not exclusively a masculine response. While female solidarity with the victims can be found in such situations, the opposite may also happen, with rape victims stigmatised by other women because of the overriding significance of the conflict and its consequences.

Nonetheless, there is no gainsaying the turning point already referred to in contemporary sensitivities towards acts of sexual violence in wartime. Greater legal visibility has resulted in a much more consistent focus on rape, thus increasing the chances of successful prosecutions, and has also enlarged the space in which such crimes can be recognised and reparation made.

Consequences

Apart from brutally perpetrating a forced sexual act, rape penalises its victims by its long-lasting consequences. First, the effect of rape as an attack on the physical integrity and intimacy of the victim endures long after the act is finished, making the process of psychological and emotional healing difficult, and making forgetting impossible.

To the hidden suffering of rape victims is often added ostracism, stigmatisation or the silence of the community in which they live. Rape is still frequently considered a shameful crime that soils society as a whole; it breaks familial and social links and excludes its victims, forcing them into isolation. The study "Aujourd'hui je ne suis plus de ce monde" ("Now the World Is without Me"), published in 2010 by the NGO *Oxfam International* on sexual violence in the Democratic Republic of the Congo, illustrates by its very title the fate that awaits certain rape victims, who are henceforward banished from the collective future of their society.

Abandoned by their spouses and those close to them, victims find themselves alone and faced with the practical consequences of their assault, such as sexually transmitted diseases. These consequences accentuate the victims' solitude, and may even provoke new forms of it. A striking example is that of the Italian women raped by colonial French troops during the Second World war in Lazio, in Italy (the *Marocchinate*). Many of them were also infected with venereal diseases, infecting in their turn their husbands or fiancés, and, during the 1950s this created a genuine problem of public health in this part of southern Italy. Although it wished to intervene by supplying medical assistance to the sick of both sexes, the International Red Cross was finally dissuaded from doing so by the Italian government itself – which had no wish to risk damaging its relations with France through a revival of attention to this tragic episode of the war. Today, because of AIDS, infection through rape may sooner or later be the equivalent of a death sentence for its victims, so that the assault carries a double jeopardy for the victim.

Pregnancies are another consequence of rape and contribute further to isolating the victims, who have to bear this obvious sign of dishonour. The births do not resolve the situation because the opprobrium may be transferred to the children, who are seen as the offspring of the enemy. The repercussions of rape are thus transmitted across the generations. In the absence of abortion or infanticide, abandonment of the newborn has often been seen as the only means of wiping out the visible trace of the sexual abuse. Nonetheless, in looking at what happened to French children born of rapes perpetrated by German soldiers in 1914, Antoine Rivière also shows the importance of the state's protective role in relation to the children as well as to their mothers.

Albeit more rarely, the child born of the rape may be socially accepted as such and his first name can then serve as a marker to recall the conditions of his conception. The cases of children born as a consequence of sexual assaults committed during the civil war in Nigeria (1967–70) are symptomatic of this response. Acknowledgement is not always synonymous with acceptance, however, and as Adediran Daniel Ikuomola shows, because of their first names alone the sons and daughters of the rapes are often subjected to the same exclusions as their mothers. Traces of these forms of violence in postwar societies vary, as periods of silence alternate with speaking out, and as emphasis on the phenomenon is followed by marginalisation. Yet whether or not it is spoken about, there is often widespread knowledge of what has occurred. It is up to historians to find the traces and to reconstruct the narrative.

A history to be written

Archives, narratives and evidence are often elusive when it comes to naming and studying rape. The expressions used, whether those of ordinary speech or of legal or journalistic language, range from the dramatic (such as "outrages") to the more neutral when they do not simply tail off in a row of dots. Words often serve as an invitation to turn a deaf ear to rape just as the eyes may be averted.

Whether it has taken place in peace or war, speaking of rape is not an easy matter. In titling this book *Rape in Wartime* we wanted first and foremost to draw attention to the specificity of rape during collective conflicts, for the first pre-condition for writing a history of rape, after finding its traces in the archives, is to call it by its true name. Establishing statistics is also a major difficulty for wartime. Historians have to count – to establish the quantitative dimension of their subject. But the circumstances of wartime render this a very uncertain process, and the problem is compounded by the way in which distorted claims of rape may be part of the war itself and then of its subsequent memory. How can one count afterwards what was not accurately counted at the time? The dead leave a body and thus break off the administrative, civil or military record that followed them in their lifetime. Even here there can be huge difficulties in establishing accurate mortality figures at the end of a war. How much more difficult is it to enumerate acts of violence the imprint of which remains intimate and largely inaccessible to the armies of those who establish figures – doctors, police, judges, government officials and so forth? And even when the victims let it be known what they have undergone, when they narrate or complain, who can say what proportion of the totality they represent?

And yet the repeated occurrence of rapes is undeniably part of the definition of this form of violence in wartime. Identifying a certain number of individual cases for which there is hard evidence owing to the contingencies of police archives is quite different to analysing the claims on all sides that large numbers of rapes were committed – claims found in political archives, the press and in private correspondence or personal diaries. A critical spirit is vital. For the symbolic meanings of rape and the ways in which it may be used to define and denounce the enemy mean that it is a potentially valuable propaganda tool, with the scale of the rapes exaggerated as required. Confronted by this set of constraints the historian must work very hard to establish even a rough order of magnitude for the reality of rapes in wartime. The difficulty in answering the question "how many" no doubt explains in part the fluctuating place of rape in the history of warfare. But this also comes from the difficulty of finding even qualitative traces in the archives. However, recent works show that if the historian is determined to pose the question, this often leads to the discovery of sources that allow answers at least to be proposed. This has been true of rapes during the invasions that accompanied the outbreak of war in 1914, the violent entry of the Soviet Army into Germany in 1945 or the rampage of Moroccan units of the French army during the Italian campaign of 1943, among others.

A common feature of the various chapters published in this book is the determination to use the human and social sciences in order to illuminate the place and meaning of sexual violence in war. Rape varies in relation to the nature of different wars and their historical context. Nothing can be taken for granted about the place of rape in war; virtually everything has still to be established.

Hence our wish is to present a state-of-the-art study and to suggest avenues of research, conceptually as well as pragmatically. This book is part of a current wave of interest in the topic, generally focusing on recent conflicts.[1] Yet, as analysed by Joanna Bourke in her classic work, *Rape: Sex, Violence, History* (Virago 2007), there is still a great deal to do.[2] The aim of our project is to broaden the perspective on recent conflicts from gesture to memory, from facts to imagined realities.

However, working on rape is also an experience that involves the researcher intimately, and in ways often linked to his or her own sex – as shown by Tal Nitsán, who relates her experience of writing about the explosive issue of the supposed absence of sexual violence by the Israeli Defence Force in the occupied territories of Palestine. The challenge is to combine sensitivity with scientific rigour, in research as in writing. Each individual reacts with his or her own subjectivity and the troubling nature of the relationship with the subject matter is present at each stage, from the discovery of facts to the search for complementary sources, from the construction of the analysis to writing it up. This is also why writing about rape means taking into account in advance the emotions and reactions that investigating the evidence is likely to arouse. Because the answer is personal, it is illusory to think that there can be a single appropriate perspective valid for everyone. Yet the ideal of the right degree of distance is still a collective goal worth working towards. Although each individual makes the choices that are appropriate to him or her, two requirements appear essential: not to use euphemisms, for rape needs to be addressed in plain language, and not to indulge in rhetoric that can all too easily set up emotional or ideological blocks to finding its real meaning.

The search for the right degree of distance was attempted in the present case by the use of a collaborative approach to the issues and to writing about them. This book and the conference in which it originated are the fruit of meetings and exchanges over several years by six researchers, all of whom had experience of working on the violence in war in different places and periods and using different sources. The choice of a collaborative approach was a response to the psychological and personal difficulties of working on rape. It allowed for an open discussion of the different biases arising from the gender of the researchers, male or female, and of the various influences and insights that came from the periods and subjects of their prior studies. The result was a plurality of approaches, which prevented any one national focus or epistemology from dominating and which necessitated a certain pragmatism in constructing the book. There was certainly no pretence to exhaustiveness. No attempt was made to include studies of the full range of rapes in wartime, or even the best-known episodes. Neither the rapes of Nanking in 1937 nor those of the war in Bosnia in 1991–95 are dealt with. Our aim was simply to state the existence of the subject as a matter for reflection in the historical and social sciences, and to break new ground in showing how it might be explored. The diversity of the approaches adopted, like the variety of episodes and periods considered, is an integral part of this exploration.

Notes

1. See Elizabeth Jean Wood, "Sexual Violence during War: Toward an Understanding of Variation", in Ian Shapiro, Stathis Kalyvas and Tarek Masoud, eds, *Order, Conflict, and Violence,* Cambridge University Press, 2008, pp. 321–51, and "Armed Groups and Sexual Violence: When Is Wartime Rape Rare?", *Politics and Society* 37 (2009), pp. 101–29. And, more recently, Elizabeth Heineman, *Sexual Violence in Conflict Zones: From the Ancient World to the Era of Human Rights,* University of Pennsylvania Press, 2011, and John Roth and Carol Rittner, *Rape: Weapon of War and Genocide,* New York, Paragon, 2012.
2. See Dagmar Herzog, *Brutality and Desire: War and Sexuality in Europe's Twentieth Century,* Basingstoke and New York, Palgrave Macmillan, 2009, including chapters by R. Branche and R. Mühlhäuser.

1
Categorising Rape in the Military Law of Modern Russia

Marianna G. Muravyeva

With the release of Colonel Budanov, who killed a 17-year-old Chechen girl and allegedly raped her, on parole in February 2009, the Russian government closed the discussion on one of the most controversial issues of the "Russian military operation" in Chechnya, that is that of the conduct of the Russian troops in the republic. Although Budanov was clearly guilty, his main defence strategy was based on the assumption that Elsa Kungaeva was a sniper of the Chechen guerrillas and as such was considered an enemy combatant, and so what he did was quite justifiable.[1]

Alberico Gentili (1552–1608) would have disagreed with Budanov and his supporters: "It is not lawful to do this wrong [rape], even if it is sometimes lawful to kill women ... If a woman fights, why should she not allow war to be made upon her? ... But there is no reason why she should suffer so signal an insult [as rape]."[2] So Gentili insisted that rape should be prohibited during wartime and peace, and this prohibition should not be limited by the civilian population. To ground his argument Gentili made references to Seneca, Statius and Alexander of Imola, claiming that because women are too weak to bear arms and participate in wars, they should be treated the same as the old, disabled, children and clergy; on the other hand if a woman fights she should be treated as a man.[3] Gentili was among those who continued a long tradition of banning the rape of women during wartime in legal theory, but the reality of war never actually came close to the recommendations of lawyers such as Hugo Grotius, Samuel Puffendorf, Christian Thomasius, Emmerich van Vattel and many others who developed the concept of "just war". Discussing the problem Pierino Belli (1502–75) insisted that the privilege of the "ignorance of the law" does not refer to crimes, "for nature herself admonishes them that what you would not like done to yourself you should not do to others".

Ancient rulers were perfectly aware of that and honoured this principle. Even Totila (d. 552), the king of the Goths (Ostrogoth), being a barbarian and non-Christian, still executed an armour bearer who raped a maiden. But Belli was complaining about the present situation: "But at the present time, how few there are – even common and ordinary soldiers – who do not have an eye upon the mother or daughter of the family, plotting to defile her, and, though guests, leaving no stone unturned until the thing is accomplished!"[4]

Hugo Grotius summarised the discussion and it was his analysis that appeared to influence further legal thought in most European countries, Russia included.[5] Grotius places the question of whether ravishing women is against the Law of Nations within the framework of lawful/unlawful during combat. Common practice since Roman times, Grotius says, suggests some consequences which are not the result of war per se, but might be recognised as lawful, such as inflicting harm on enemies of the state, on their person and property. Grotius points out that there are two opinions about rape:

> they that permit it, respect only the Injury done to the Body of an Enemy, which by the Law of Arms they think should be subject to all Acts of Hostility. But others, with more Reason, look not to that Injury alone, but also to the Act of Brutality, which being neither necessary for the Security of those who commit it, nor proper for the Punishment of those against whom it is committed, should be as much punished in War as in Peace; and this last is the Law of Nations, if not all, yet of the most civilized.[6]

But in terms of punishment it is necessary to distinguish between the commanders and regular soldiers, and in the case of commanders one should distinguish between excusable and inexcusable reasons for committing a crime. At any rate, Grotius supported the idea that in cases of bloodshed and other mass actions committed for just and lawful reasons, the death penalty should be withdrawn as, quoting Caesar, *"Neither does anyone provoke you to severe Punishments, or fearful Judgments, which rather tend to depopulate a State, than to correct the Guilty."*[7] Grotius also specified the particular rules of conduct during wartime, that is, children and women must be excused by their tender age and sex. Only in the case of the gravest crimes against God could women be executed, as in the case of *Midianitish* women (Numbers 31:18), who were slain for their personal crimes, but virgins were spared.[8] This last point actually demonstrated that, following the Roman and medieval traditions,

Grotius allowed protection only to "pure" women, thus withholding mercy from the vast majority of them.

The rape of women became a symbol of any unjust war and inappropriate combatant behaviour in the seventeenth and eighteenth centuries. European military law, which began to be formed in the period, paid a great deal of attention to rape as a war crime and imposed strict punishments for it. Military Codes of German emperors (Maximilian I, Maximilian II, Ferdinand III), Swedish Kings (Gustav Adolfus and Charles IX) and Prussian kings (Frederick Wilhelm and Fredrick II), enacted in the sixteenth to eighteenth centuries, all specified the death penalty for rape.[9] Russian military law was no more tolerant.[10]

The first army regulations

Russia represents a good example of a country whose military law is little known, while the country itself was constantly conducting wars during the seventeenth and eighteenth centuries. The major military efforts were directed against its neighbours: Poland (Rzec Pospolita), Sweden and Turkey (the Ottoman Empire). Russia was famous for its extremely "barbarous" behaviour towards the civilian population on one hand, and strict regulations of sexuality due to the Orthodox influence on the other.[11] Foreigners, cruising the lands of Muscovy in the seventeenth century, recognised the details of Russian "barbarity", two of which were quite disturbing to them – the spread of sodomy and the low status of women. Putting sodomy aside for the purposes of this discussion, women were treated badly; they were sold, heavily beaten, systematically raped by their fathers and fathers-in-law;[12] noble women were locked in special houses (*terem*), and all were severely punished for the murder of their husbands (buried alive up to their shoulders and left to die without food and water).[13] Almost every traveller would describe the violent sexual behaviour of Russian Tsars towards the wives and daughters of their subjects. Swedish diplomat Petrus Petrejys (?–1622) portrayed Ivan IV in the following manner: "He was a vile barbarian, an extortioner and a tyrant, great skinflint, blasphemer, rake, a man of a wild, unjust and proud character, rapist of women ... he was an instigator of the dangerous and unjust wars against his neighbours".[14] Taking these reports into account, one can ask how Russia could not be considered a barbarous country whose "national spirit" resulted in the spread of deviant and violent sexuality.

It was in the seventeenth century that the first military regulations were formed and a "European" model of the army was attempted. The

Code for Artillery (*Ustav ratnykh pushkarskikh del*) appeared in 1621, aimed at regulation discipline and warfare among the *pushkari* (gunners). According to this code the gunners would be punished by death for pillaging and plundering the private lands of the civilian population, for billeting churches, breaking down mills, killing and raping pregnant women and mothers and other cruelties towards the civilian population.[15] On the other hand, the code also regulated the everyday sexual behaviour of the gunners, helping the state to discipline them. The code punished adultery and fornication by depriving rank and sending a gunner from his cannon in dishonour. The prosecution differentiated wartime from peacetime. During wartime the proceedings were held by the commander-in-chief (*golova*) based on the reports of the colonels (*voevoda*). In peacetime all the cases were referred to the special departments (*prikazy*) that represented the government. Here the military was treated as a distinct social group but it was subjected to state law. So the military codes had their jurisdiction only during war as such and in the camps and garrisons. It is also clear that there was a division between rape committed during actual military actions and the "immoral behaviour" of military men in camps and garrisons. The first was treated as a capital crime (the same as for murder, desertion, treachery etc.) and punished by death. The second invoked dishonour punishments for less important crimes.

The Code for Artillery was not very effective, as further legal processes showed. In 1647, two years before the enactment of the famous Russian Law Code (*Sobornoe Ulozhenie*), the government undertook another attempt to regulate army behaviour and introduce some discipline. In the introduction to the new military code (*Uchenie i hitrost' ratnogo stroenija ljudej – The Discipline and Skills of Military Men*) the author writes extensively about unruly army behaviour, the unchastity of soldiers and officers, the spread of drunkenness, lechery, blasphemy and other vices: "and now contrary to it [the purity and piety of old warriors] there is blasphemy and insults against God, drunkenness, swearing, lechery ... and they dishonour women and behave unjustly. And you hear how they dare say that these actions are common military habits and permitted for military men because they are not monks in a monastery".[16] The author even refers to Ottoman military discipline, offering it as an example of an effective army. This manuscript laid the foundation for the special chapter in the subsequent Law Code (*Sobornoe Ulozhenie*) of 1649. Russian Tsar Alexei Mikhailovitch (1645–76) was quite concerned with army discipline and ineffectiveness. Different state departments (*prikazy*) had been collecting reports from the borders about plundering and rape committed by soldiers, especially on the Russian–Polish border, and passed these to the tsar. The new Law Code, intended to regulate all aspects of Russian life, thus contained chapter 7, "Of Military Men". Starting with announcing peace and friendship between Muscovy and its neighbouring states (Poland, Lithuania, Germany and others), this chapter prescribes both administrative and military procedures for the Muscovite service class.[17] The state concern for servicemen behaviour runs through several articles: art. 2 – no inflicting harm and pillaging while going into and leaving state service; art. 3:24 – no harming crops; art. 32 – no fighting in camps between soldiers and officers; art. 6:22 – punishment for pillaging; art. 30 – punishment for murder, robbery and pillaging, and rape. Article 30 explicitly stated that "if those military men going into the tsar's service or leaving the service start ... plundering or murdering ... or raping women ... then they should be punished by death".[18] It's worth noting that there are two other mentions of rape in the code: the rape of a serf woman by her owner (which should be ruled according to canon law) and the rape of a noble mistress of the house by an intruder and his accomplices (death penalty). All of these together underline the importance of rape as a marker for public disorder and the importance of crime according to its public damage.

As the *Sobornoe Uozhenie* was intended to become universal law throughout the country, norms regarding rape also were to be applied universally in all army divisions. The prohibitions against the rape of women and doing "wrongs to people", which were traditionally included in the special tsar's orders addressed to the commanders at the beginning of each war, from now on acquired a legal basis. These writs specifically stated "not to do wrongs to them [the civil population] and to their wives and children" and to send the perpetrators to the special court where judges would "try them justly without any indulgence".[19] That these norms were actually applied we can see from court cases coming to the attention of the judges of *Razrjadnyi Prikaz* (military state department). In the year of 1668 (during the Russian–Polish war) there were four such cases. In one of them the judge ordered an investigation of the gang rape of tavern service women in Perejaslavl' committed by a squadron of *reiters* (horsemen) under the command of Christian Gogolschen. It was an important precedent as usually foreign officers were excluded from Russian jurisdiction and were subjected to the jurisdiction of their commanders who ruled according to German Imperial law or the law of the country from which they came.[20]

However, Muscovite authorities were more concerned with mercenary troops pillaging Muscovy's lands rather than those of Lithuania or Poland. In the epoch of mercenary armies many European military commanders paid enormous attention to disciplining the armies as they were dangerous not only to the enemy but also to the homeland. The Muscovy military department (*Razrjadnyj Prikaz*) was overwhelmed with cases of robbery, rape and plundering committed by different regiments in the Muscovy home territories, especially around garrisons and camps. Thus during the Swedish war of 1656–58 the government had to fight on two fronts at the same time: one being the enemy (the Swedish army) and the other being its own troops, as Moscow had to find additional resources to capture those troops (including Cossacks) who plundered and pillaged Courland and nearby territories.[21] The same happened during the Russian–Polish war of 1654–67 (the so-called Thirteen Years War). The greatest threat came from the army of boayarin Khovansky (executed in 1682 for anti-tsar rebellion), who was then commander-in-chief of the Novgorod regiment. His troops regularly pillaged not only conquered lands, but borderlands and Muscovite territories as well. The situation went out of control when the army was defeated by Poles in 1661 and the withdrawing troops (no more than 1000 out of 20,000 survived) literally plundered their own lands. Other reports came from Vitebsk, Smolensk, Polotsk and other border cities.[22] In this situation mass rape became part of pillaging strategies and never came to the military court as a separate charge, but was always included in an array of accusations: robbery, disorderly behaviour, mass murder and rape. A certain silence about mass rape arose, the charge absorbed in "disorderly army behaviour". This was unacceptable, but predictable.

When Peter the Great tried to discipline the army

Peter the Great (1682–1725) did reform Russian law and military law in particular. He made several attempts to introduce new military law. *The Rules of Military Conduct* (*Sheremetjev Articles*), created in 1702, continued the seventeenth-century tradition of prohibition against the rape of women "under the threat of death or cruel punishment according to the degree of guilt".[23] The alternative offered (according to the degree of guilt) became a novelty for military law and opened a window of opportunity to those who considered rape a means of warfare. The *Concise Code of 1708* (*Menshikov code*) reinforced the death penalty for rape.[24]

The ambiguity of Russian military law's attitude towards rape is clearly seen from a rape case in 1711, when different groups of officers expressed different verdicts. Two dragoons raped a teenager girl, Christina, close to Revel (Lifljandia). The *kriegsrecht* (military court) was formed from one major (the chief judge), one captain, one lieutenant and one under lieutenant, then several sergeants, corporals and soldiers (one from each regiment). The sentence according to the law should have been the death penalty. But the sentences given by the court members ranged between the following:

1. soldiers: whipping by the rod mercilessly;
2. corporals: to run the gauntlet (through the battalion once);
3. sergeants: to run the gauntlet (through the regiment once);
4. under lieutenants: to beat the major perpetrator (Chernyshov) with a knout and send him to hard labour (Siberian mines); to run the gauntlet (through the regiment ten times) for the accomplice;
5. the captain: to hang;
6. the major chief judge: death penalty (no specification).

The commander-in-chief, Field Marshal Prince Boris Sheremetijev confirmed the death penalty according to the *Menshikov code*, but suggested shooting instead of hanging.[25] None of them except Sheremetjev referred to any law; the majority of low rank suggested disciplinary penalties rather than capital punishment in such cases, certainly treating rape not as a capital crime but rather as a habitual crime committed during war. The officers by sentencing the culprits to death certainly showed their acceptance of the law and willingness to observe army discipline with harsh punishments. We can also see that the punishment was becoming harder as the rank of the judge became higher. It is unclear whether it had something to do with solidarity, but the soldiers definitely thought of rape as an offence, and as a disciplinary matter rather than a capital crime. Officers decisively defined it as a capital crime. This might suggest who actually committed rape.

Peter the Great attempted to put an end to the ambivalent attitudes towards rape. His Military Code of 1716 although modelled on the Swedish *Kriegsartikul* (Military code) was not a mere translation of it. Peter worked on the text and made extensive amendments, which might show his intentions in terms of disciplining the army. It is interesting that chapter 20, "Of Sodomy Sin, Rape and Fornication", had been amended most profoundly. This chapter defined (non-)conventional sexuality. It consisted of the following sexual offences: bestiality (sex with animals, art. 165 – corporal punishment); buggery, including rape (art. 166 – corporal punishment/death penalty in the case of rape); rape (art. 167 – death penalty); kidnapping and rape (art. 168 – penal labour for life/death penalty); adultery (art. 169–70 – punishment according to the circumstances of the case and the degree of guilt); incest (art. 173–4 – death penalty/church penance); bigamy (art. 171–2 – reference to the church court); prostitution (art. 175 – deprivation of rank and expelling from the regiment); producing illegitimate children (art. 176 – imprisonment and church penance in addition to the obligation to provide for the child and his mother or marriage); obscenity in speech and songs (art. 177 – no specified punishment).[26] The list of crimes underlines the essence of these offences: they were considered crimes against nature rather than against the victim's person. They also aimed to discipline the army rather than protect the female population. These offences reflected what the state regarded as model sexuality within the disciplined army environment. Moreover, they suggested this model was to be universal in society, the model of the heterosexual marital procreative relations unit.

Article 167 stated that if a woman, old or young, married or unmarried, in enemy or friendly territory, is raped and she reports it, the rapist is to be beheaded or sent to the galleys for life, according to the degree of force used. Article 168 adds that if an honest wife, a widow or a maiden is secretly abducted and raped and she sooner or later reports it, the rapist is to be punished by death – beheaded. These two articles do not say anything new in European military law as they translate the Swedish Military Code into Russian, except that the alternative punishment for rape which Peter added himself meant that less force was used for the less capital crime. What was new was a commentary, which totally differed from the Swedish text. It starts with a reference to nasty women and how they try to use false accusations of violence in order to cover their unchaste behaviour and whoredom. Then the Code prescribes that a judge should not believe such a woman, but should conduct a very accurate examination, including witness statements, and consider whether she raised a hue and cry. These rules apply to all women (even if they are chaste) if the rape took place in the forest. If there are no witnesses the Code prescribes to pay attention to the material evidence: (1) if the victim's or perpetrator's robe is torn apart; (2) if there are bruises on them both; (3) if a woman reports very quickly. Upon the last circumstance the Code states that "very quickly" means during the day, and if she does not report that very day, but on the following day or later, she must be suspected of *wanting it*. Otherwise, if the evidence is in place the judge has authority to torture or adjure the accused (depending on his social position; noblemen were almost always adjured). What we see is a clear pattern of the rationalisation of rape used in other European countries, for example in England, as if Peter had carefully studied Judge Hale.

Another interesting comment deals with whores. The Code states that, first of all, a whore could be raped, second, the rape of a whore should be punished as severely as the rape of an honest woman, because violence is violence even committed against a whore and a judge should look into the case but not consider the personality of the victim. This comment is very revolutionary and valuable as it was supposed that in terms of discipline military men should not rape anybody as rape was a form of disrespect to the will of another person and could be interpreted as potential inclination to disobey a commander's orders.

In spite of his own "enlightened" views Peter used the custom of war quite effectively. Thus in 1708 while fighting Ukrainian resistance he ordered his favourite Men'shikov to arrest the wives and children of hetman Kochubei and some of his supporters, which Men'shikov was happy to do. Peter specifically ordered him not to touch the women, which suggests that Peter kept in mind the possible implications of such actions.[27]

Peter consolidated Russian military law and enacted royal ordinances regarding military actions in any territory, ordering soldiers not to touch women during invasions and travelling enemy lands.[28] But in spite of the reforms military courts still did not differentiate mass rape from pillaging in general and did not prosecute it as a separate charge. The only way to get prosecution was to submit an individual complaint, which was according to the Military Code and other laws.

The structure of military courts did not encourage justice either. Seventeenth-century military courts were independent bodies; they consisted of regimental judges appointed by their commanders with one or two representatives from *Razrjadnyj Prikaz*. The decisions they made had to be validated by the commanders-in-chief. Peter's reforms of the military courts did not make any real difference to the system, although they did become more collegial and accountable to the military authorities.[29] These courts were intended to proceed with individual rather than collective complaints. The poor state of the court records does not allow us to represent the full picture of rape cases, but extant records give an impression that once the complaint was admitted by the court the verdict would be in favour of a complainant. However, the punishment prescribed by the law, the death penalty, was rarely given and after the ordinance of 1744, which prescribed the substitution of the death penalty with hard labour, punishments were awarded according to this law. Here lies the biggest discrepancy between state law and court practice. Court practice from the state military courts gives evidence of corporal punishment for rape rather than the death penalty, which highlights the treatment of rape as a disciplinary matter rather than a capital crime. Out of 53 cases from the eighteenth-century military courts, 16 (a third of all the cases) involved child-rape (the youngest girl raped was two-and-a-half years old), but only five had the death penalty as a punishment (four were substituted by hard labour and exile). The rest of the punishments included corporal punishment (running the gauntlet or beating by a knout), deprivation of rank and church penance.[30]

Russian military regulations and the international laws of war

Russia continued to align its military law with the rest of Europe in the nineteenth century moving toward creating international humanitarian law and universal rules of war. Russia actually played quite an active role in establishing international humanitarian law and the first Geneva Convention. However, in the nineteenth century, having participated constantly in wars and other conflicts, Russian military law was as strict as in the eighteenth century, punishing most war offences (looting and rape in particular) by death.[31] Russian military law also followed the general trend of European military law, which divided all offences into those against military service and general offences. The latter group was left under the jurisdiction of the general criminal courts even in cases when military men were involved. Rape was listed among those crimes. But the death penalty still stayed intact if rape was committed during wartime.[32] The laws and customs of war as taught to rank-and-file military suggested careful treatment of civilians, which was in tune with the international law of the age, especially after the First Geneva Convention (1864) and Hague Convention (1899). One popular book for the military insisted that "insults, offences, and atrocities against local inhabitants of the enemy land are strictly prohibited",[33] and another author stated that "it needed to abstain from the offences against women's honour and chastity, as well as from the offences against old age, always respected everywhere".[34] This is a rare mention of the necessity not to commit rape. The scattered statistics from Military and Naval courts of the period suggest the prosecution for rape was 2–3 cases per year, which is low enough and concerns mostly garrisons and quarters.[35]

It was the First World War when sexual assault crimes were first thought to be a war crime as they were committed on a very large scale and classified as a tool of mass destruction. The War Crimes Commission of the First World War explicitly mentioned rape and forced prostitution as violations of the laws and customs of war. They were two of the enumerated offences, ranked high on the list of war crimes. However, the Commission failed to influence the final trials of war criminals on these charges.[36] Russia did not participate in concluding peace talks due to the October Revolution of 1917 and the ongoing civil war. The Bolsheviks, who gained power, started the whole new legislation process based on class struggle and revolutionary justice against exploiting classes. The newly formed Red Army was supposed to have high morals as they were fighting for their own people and a better future against reactionaries and capitalists. This idea did not work in practice and rape was used on both sides, reds and whites, to subjugate the local population to certain political rule. Atrocities on both sides were committed for different reasons, not necessarily political or economic. Whites, consisting mostly of military generals and officers, proceeded traditionally by issuing regular ordinances prohibiting looting and rape of the local population under threat of the death penalty.[37] Reds issued revolutionary orders to treat the population "correctly": to avoid unnecessary killings and looting and rape of the local population.[38] Both reds and whites launched special committees to investigate the war crimes of the other side and the proceedings of these committees are full of almost identical episodes of mass rape and forced prostitution of the local population aggravated by the fact that they were all committed by fellow countrymen.[39] Thus a Special Committee, created by General Denikin to investigate the crimes committed by reds, included a report about the rape of young women between 16 and 25 in Ekaterinburg by local reds. Twenty-five women were raped and some of them killed afterwards. One 16-year-old girl, a student of a local gymnasium, was gang raped by a group of reds over 12 days and finally shot down after other torture.[40] Other reports from different places are full of such details. Although white commanders insisted on following the law in the form of military courts, in reality (opposite to the revolutionary tribunals of the reds) the rank-and-file practised rape as well.[41]

The Red Army

New Soviet military law embedded into the Criminal codes of 1922 and 1926 maintained the pre-revolutionary division between crimes against the military and general crimes committed by the military during peace and wartime. Looting became a military crime while rape continued to be a general crime to be punished under the general criminal law in general state criminal courts. The Criminal Code of 1926 had a vague definition of "illegal violence against the civil population" committed during wartime and punished by no less than three years imprisonment, and in aggravated circumstances by execution of a firing squad (art. 193.18). This article was further supported by the special *Regulations of Military Offences* of 1927 (the new edition of 1924). Article 28 of the *Regulations* stated that general crimes committed by the military during wartime are punished under this article but not under the Criminal Code, which stipulated the death penalty in aggravated circumstances.[42] It was this understanding that constructed the basics of military law through the Second World War and Nuremberg Tribunal. During the Second World War all criminal cases in the regions under martial law would be tried by military tribunals under military administration. Military courts (called tribunals as well) remained the main source of justice in the army but now were all under the purview of the immediate commander. It was commanders of all army levels who were responsible for prosecuting crimes against the local population.[43]

The mutual accusations of war crimes by Germany and the Soviet Union started right from the beginning of the Great Patriotic War (the Russian name for the German attack on the Soviet Union). On 27 April 1942, V. V. Molotov, Soviet foreign minister, published a note on atrocities and violence against the local population of occupied Soviet territories. This document, intended mostly for propaganda purposes, carefully picked out the most outrageous acts of German soldiers, describing in detail mass murders, tortures, humiliations, killing of women and children, and, of course, rape and forced prostitution. Thus, the document records that in the Belorussian village Kholmy (Mogilev region) Nazis arrested six girls of 15–17 years old, raped them, cut out their breasts, put out their eyes and finally killed them by tying them to a tree.[44] Germans also launched propaganda against the Soviet Union and collected their own documents about war crimes of the Soviet army. The Wehrmacht War Crimes bureau exposed the crimes against German prisoners of war as well as other war crimes committed by Soviet soldiers in 1944 and 1945. In Eastern Prussia when Germans temporarily regained some territories, the bureau reported that hundreds of German civilians had been slaughtered and most women raped.[45]

The Second World War proved rape to be instrumental in warfare. All participants used this tool upon civilians. Nazi war crimes, including rape, were exposed during the Nuremberg Tribunal. The rapes committed by the Soviet army were not spoken about for some time, but were definitely exposed in the 1960s and then 1990s, when the Soviet Union and Russia underwent serious domestic political problems accompanied by liberal reforms. Soviet and then Russian historiography has tended not to mention the behaviour of the Soviet soldiers in the "liberated" territories and especially in Germany and Hungary. On the contrary, Western historiography, especially after the collapse of communism, exposed Red Army rapes in Germany and Eastern Europe as a part of blaming Stalinism and the communist past.[46] This memory war is still fought in present-day Russia when the government tries to create the glorious narrative of the past as a part of new national identity. The evidence is very scattered and mostly based on memoirs and oral history done by researchers as the archives of the Second World War in Russia are closed and won't be opened for quite some time, so to receive any statistical data is not possible at the moment. The authors (apart from those in denial insisting that all relations with local women were consensual) stress two central moments: the brutality and barbarity of the soviet soldiers (mostly described by Beevor as a part of the appeal to Western audiences) and the motivation of revenge taken by soviet soldiers on German women.

Norman Naimark pointed out the difference in the Soviet troops' behaviour in different countries. Thus in Bulgaria the Red Army's actions were almost exemplary; pillages, looting and rape were relatively absent. It might have had something to do with the leadership and general discipline as well as with the centuries of friendly relations and genuinely open welcome from the Bulgarian population.[47] The notion of revenge, pressed by Soviet propaganda, played quite an important role in creating the atmosphere of hatred toward the enemy, including the civilian population. Naimark paints quite a distressing picture of the soviet army's behaviour in Germany, especially in East Prussia.[48] However, to say that it was approved by the commanders as a means of warfare is quite problematic, because there is plenty of evidence that officers tried to stop rape and military courts prosecuted rape, although not effectively.

Svetlana Aleksievich, whose book *The War's Unwomanly Face* was based on interviews with women combatants and was finally published without censorship in 2005, reports conflicting memories of Soviet women-combatants about the rape of German women. One woman, a corporal, recalled that

> five German girls came to our commander. They cried ... The gynecologists examined them: there were wounds there. Lacerations.

> Underpants all in blood ... They were raped during the whole night. Soldiers were queuing ... Our battalion was drawn up. The girls were told: look closely, if you recognize anybody, we will shoot them immediately, despite the rank, shame on us. But they sat there crying. They did not want ... did not want more bloodshed. That's what they said ... Each of them was given a loaf of bread. That's all the war.

Male veterans revealed their actions as well with regret. One of Aleksievich's male interviewees said,

> We are advancing ... First German villages ... We are young. Strong. Four years without women. There is vine in the cells. Food. We caught German girls and ... Ten men raped one ... There were not enough women, population fled from the Soviet army, we took young. Girls ... Twelve–thirteen years old ... If she cried, we beat her, gagged her with something. She is in pain, but we laugh. Now I do not understand how could I ... A boy from an intelligent family ... But it was me ... The only thing we were afraid was that our fellow women would know about it. Our nurses. We were ashamed ...[49]

Whatever explanations were used, mass rape was not unique to the Soviet army during the Second World War. Rape traditionally constituted a part of the warfare behaviour of all armies involved in the war and it took another fifty years after the end of Second World War to finally recognise rape as a war crime punished under international criminal law.

During the past four hundred years Russian military law constructed rape as a war crime along with regulating the army's conduct towards the civilian population within the framework of the European process of regulating warfare. It was quite important for the country as the government introduced the crime of rape through military law into the state criminal system and turned it into a capital crime. Rape of women, this necessary marker of any early modern and modern war, although a grievous crime, was not viewed in terms of bringing harm to a woman's person or as a sign of interpersonal violence; it was not even about women. The lawmakers' efforts concentrated on the general disciplining practices of the army where sexuality became the most obvious and effective tool to keep order and control human behaviour. At the same time the sentencing strategies allowed the army command and government officials to manipulate the conquered territories and use rape as a political tool on newly acquired lands.

Notes

1. See materials on the case in the mass media: *Delo polkovnika Budanova: materialy*, www.goryachiy.narod.ru/2001/; *Delo polkovnika Budanova: poslednjaja ekspertiza*, www.npar.ru/journal/2003/; Alexandr Minkin, "Ludi gorazdo lutshe, chem o nikh dumajut", www.memo.ru/hr/hotpoints/N-Caucas/ch99/ and many others.
2. A. Gentili, *De Jure Belli Libri III*, Hanoviae, 1612, II, ch. 21, pp. 423–4.
3. Kelly Down Askin, *War Crimes against Women*, Cambridge, MA, Martin Nijrhoff, 1997, pp. 26–7.
4. P. Belli, *De re militari et bello tractatus*, ed. E. C. Nutting, Oxford, 1936, I, par. VII, ch. 3:14.
5. Peter I ordered the translation of Grotius into Russian in 1712 – see the manuscript at the Manuscript Department of the National Library of Russia (St Petersburg), National Library of Russia, f. 550, F.II.36.
6. Hugo Grotius, *The Rights of War and Peace*, ed. and with an introduction by Richard Tuck, from the edition by Jean Barbeyrac, Indianapolis, Liberty Fund, 2005, III, 4:19.
7. Grotius, III, 11:3, 17.
8. Grotius, III, 11:9.
9. See the collection in *Corpus Juris Militaris*, Leipzig, 1723.
10. On rape in the European military law, see Marianna Muravyeva, "Seksual'nye prestuplenija v evropejskom voenno-ugolovnom prave rannego novogo vremeni", *Dialog so vremenem: Al'manakh intellektual'noj istoriji* 29 (2009), pp. 248–70.
11. See Eve Levin, *Sex and Society in the World of the Orthodox Slavs, 900–1700*, Ithaca and London, Cornell University Press, 1999.
12. This was called *snokhachestvo*, a custom described by ethnographers in the Russian peasant communities when a father-in-law would rape (or force permanent sexual relations upon) his daughter-in-law despite his son's protests. Being treated as incest in the law, *snokhachestvo* was prosecuted by the state and canon law from the seventeenth century onwards.
13. See the accounts of Russia by foreign travellers in Francesca Wilson, *Muscovy: Russia through Foreign Eyes, 1553–1900*, London, Allen & Unwin, 1970.
14. Petr Petrei, *O nachale vojn i smut v Moskovij*, Moscow, 1997, p. 238.
15. "Ustav ratnykh pushkarskikh i drugikh del, kasajuschijsja do voennoj nauki", in M. Rosengeim, *Ocherk istoriji voenno-sudnykh uchrezhdenij v Rossijindo konchiny Petra Velikogo*, St Petersburg, 1878, pp. 257–67.
16. *Uchenie i hitrost' ratnogo stroenija ljudej*, 1647, National Library of Russia (NLR), f. 536, F.115. P. 15rev-16.
17. On Muscovite service class in the seventeenth century, see Richard Hellie, *Enserfment and Military Change in Muscovy*, Chicago, University of Chicago Press, 1971.
18. "Sobornoe Ulozhenie 1649 goda", in A. G. Man'kov, ed., *Akty zemskih soborov*, Moscow, 1985, pp. 83–256. There is also an English translation, which can be used for reference: Richard Hellie, ed. and trans., *The Muscovite Law Code (Ulozhenie) of 1649, Part 1: Text and Translation*, Irvine, CA, Charles Schlacks, Jr, 1988.

19. See, for example, writs to Shein and Ismailov, Prozorovsky and Kondyrev (1632); Veljaminov and Isupov, Debeert (1633): *Akty, sobrannye v bibliotekakh i arkhivah Rossijskoj imperiji Arkheograficheskoju ekspeditsieju Imperatorkoj Akademiji Nauk*, St Petersburg, 1836, III, nos 206, 207, 223, 224.
20. K. Petrov, ed., *Opisi arkhiva Razrjadnogo prikaza*, St Petersburg, 2001, p. 264.
21. See the correspondence of *Razrjadnyj Prikaz: Opisanie dokumentov i bumag, khranjaschihsja v Moskovskom Arkhive Ministerstva Justitsiji*, Moscow, 1899, XI, st. 270, 276.
22. *Opisanie dokumentov*, XII, st. 122, 132, 162, 164, 262.
23. NLR, f. 550, Q.II.30, p. 12.
24. "Artikul kratkij", in Rosengeim, *Ocherk istoriji*, p. 299.
25. Rosengeim, *Ocherk istoriji*, pp. 87–8.
26. "Artikul Voinskij", in A. G. Man'kov, ed., *Zakonodatel'stvo perioda stanovlenija absolutisma*, Moscow, 1986, pp. 358–60.
27. D. O. Maslovskij, ed., *Severnaya vojna. Dokumenty, 1705–1708*, St Petersburg, 1892, p. 74.
28. See, for example, the orninances from the Russian–Turkish war of 1739: D. O. Maslovskij, ed., *Stavuchanskij pokhod. Dokumenty 1739 goda*, St Petersburg, 1892, nos 2, 28, 31, 39, 40, 42.
29. On the military courts organisation in Russia, see Rosengeim, *Ocherk istoriji*; F. I. Kalinychev, *Voprosy voennogo prava Rossiji v period obrazovanija feodal'no-absoljutistskogo gosudarstva (vtoraja polovina XVII veka)*, Moskva, 1950; N. A. Petukhov, *Istorija voennyh sudov v Rossiji*, Moskva, 2003, pp. 3–101.
30. See the collection of cases in RGVIA, Russian State Military Historical Archive, f. 8.
31. *Polevoe ugolovnoe ulozhenie dlja rossijskoj dejstvujuschej armiji*, St Petersburg, 1812, pp. 19–21.
32. *Svod voennykh postanovlenij. Vol. VI. Voenno-ugolovnye ustavy*, St Petersburg, 1869, art. 279, p. 66.
33. N. F. Kol'devin, *Zakony voennogo vremeni*, St Petersburg, 1877, p. 6.
34. M. V. Piunovskij, *Zakony i pravila vojny po mezdunarodnomu pravu*, St Petersburg, 1877, p. 37.
35. See *Otchet po voenno-morskoj sudnoj chasti*, St Petersburg, 1872–1902.
36. Kelly Dawn Askin, *War Crimes against Women. Prosecution in International War Crimes Tribunals*, The Hague, Martinus Nijhoff Publishers, 1997, pp. 42–5.
37. See, for example, order no. 7 (14/28 Aug. 1918) by Denikin: V. Zh. Tsvetkov, *Belyj terror – prestuplenie lil nakazanie?*, www.dk1868.ru/statii/TstvetkovS.htm. The author gives the reference to the State Archive of Russia: GA RF, f. 6532, op. 1, no. 1, ff. 218–19.
38. See, for example, the order (10 June 1918) by new revolutionary commander Mironov for Ust'-Medveditskij forces, www.dk1868.ru/history/mironov/13.htm.
39. "Krasnyj terror v gody grazhdanskoj vojny. Po materialam Osoboj sledstvennoj komissiji", *Voprosy Istoriji* 7–10 (2001).
40. "Krasnyj terror", *Voprosy Istoriji* 8 (2001), pp. 14–15.
41. V. P. Buldakov, "Revolutsija, nasilie i arkhaizatsija massovogo soznanija v grazhdanskoj vojne: provintsial'naja spetsifika", *Belaja gvardija* 6 (2002), pp. 4–11.

42. *Ugolovnyj kodeks RSFSR*, Moskva, 1926; *Polozhenie o Voinskikh Prestuplenijakh*, Moskva, 1928.
43. V. M. Chikvadze, *Sovetskoe voenno-ugolovnoe pravo*, Moskva, 1948, pp. 432–7. On Soviet legal attitudes to the war crimes during the Second World War, see George Ginsburgs, "Laws of War and War Crimes on the Russian Front during World War II: The Soviet View", *Soviet Studies* 11:3 (1960), pp. 253–85.
44. See *Vneshnaja politika Sovetskogo Sojuza v period Otechestvennoj Vojny*, Moskva, OGIZ, 1944, I, p. 226.
45. A. de Zayas, *Nemesis at Potsdam*, Lincoln, University of Nebraska Press, 1988, pp. 61–9. See the same author's work on the work of the bureau: *The Wehrmacht War Crimes Bureau, 1939–1945*, Lincoln, University of Nebraska Press, 1989.
46. See popular accounts, such as Cornelius Ryan, *The Last Battle*, New York, Simon and Schuster, 1966, and Antony Beevor, *Berlin: The Downfall, 1945*, London, Viking, 2002. For research on Red Army rape, see Norman M. Naimark, *The Russians in Germany: a History of the Soviet Zone of Occupation, 1945–1949*, Cambridge, MA, Belknap Press, 1995; James Mark, "Remembering Rape: Divided Social Memory and the Red Army in Hungary 1944–5", *Past and Present* 188 (August 2005), pp. 133–61.
47. Naimark, *The Russians in Germany*, p. 70.
48. Naimark, *The Russians in Germany*, pp. 69–140.
49. Svetlana Aleksievich, *U vojny ne zhenskoe litso*, Moskva, 2005, http://lib.ru/NEWPROZA/ALEKSIEWICH/zhensk.txt.

2

The Unquestioned Crime: Sexual Violence by German Soldiers during the War of Annihilation in the Soviet Union, 1941–45

Regina Mühlhäuser

Naum Epelfeld was 13 years old when the German army invaded Berdychev (Ukraine) on 5 July 1941. Fleeing from air raids, he and his family found shelter in the cellar of a nearby hospital. "Everybody sensed that terrible things were about to occur", he remembered after the end of the war.

> Night fell. There was no light. We sat in the dark, huddled against each other, and talked in whispers. Suddenly we heard people entering the hospital building, heard orders barked in a foreign language. The noise of breaking glass and the crack of gunshots impressed themselves on my mind. It all became clear to us. The Germans were taking Berdychev. After a while two soldiers entered the cellar where we were hiding. They lit their way with flashlights and said something, but nobody understood them. Then they started to approach the people sitting on the floor and to shine their light on their faces. Eventually they stopped in front of a girl and a woman, led them into an empty room, and raped them. The girl – she was our neighbour's daughter – was named Guste. Guste Glosman was fourteen or fifteen years old. Soon afterward, she was shot together with her parents. That was how the occupation began for me. The worst part of my life.[1]

Epelfeld describes a situation directly after the invasion of the city. The Germans entered every place they believed to be entitled to, which included the penetration of women's bodies – a symbol of victorious trespassing. In many wars, the "sexual conquest" of the enemy women appears to be a reward for and booty after the military success. Ruth Seifert has pointed out that it is one of the unwritten rules of war to allow the victor to perpetrate violence against women in the short, unsettled periods directly after combat.[2] In the case described here, however, the occurrence of sexual violence might appear somewhat as a surprise, since Nazi racial ideology denoted sexual contacts between men who considered themselves to be "Aryan" and women who were classified as Jewish as "racial defilement" – officially a crime that was strictly forbidden.[3] In Epelfeld's account, it is not clear if the soldiers actually knew that the women they attacked were Jewish. Other narratives, including ego-documents by German soldiers, however, clearly demonstrate that the men were aware of their trespassing of the boundaries of Nazi racial ideology.[4]

To date, it is widely assumed that soldiers who violated the Nazi racial laws were harshly punished. Indeed, many people presume that German men who were committed to Nazi ideology exercised "racially aware" self-restraint. And while the German war of annihilation is one of the best researched examples in the field of wartime violence and genocide studies, the phenomenon of sexual violence (and more generally, sexuality and sexual practices) has remained largely absent.[5] This might, on the one hand, be due to the fact that sources are scarce and complicated to interpret. On the other hand, it presents a delicate challenge to develop a vocabulary and a form of presentation that neither trivialises the issue nor evokes a voyeuristic view. In addition, the deficit of research can be grasped as one effect of the affect-laden response that the entanglement of war, violence and sexuality tends to generate. The interdependency that sexuality and violence get into during war is ultimately deemed an inevitable fact that does not need to be questioned or investigated until the acts committed are recognised as particularly brutal or clearly a strategy of war.[6]

In the first comprehensive study on sexual violence by German soldiers during the Second World War, published in 2004, historian Birgit Beck concludes that rape by soldiers of the Wehrmacht cannot be considered a military strategy for the following reasons: first, to date no document is known that ordered German men to perpetrate sexual violence; and, second, the military laws defined "sexual violation" (*Notzucht*) as a crime against military discipline – which in some cases actually led military judges to sentence rapists to serve prison terms.[7] Sources on the two other German military formations in the Soviet Union, the SS and the police, confirm these findings. Officially, the SS and policemen were forbidden to engage in sexual contacts (rape as well as prostitution and consensual relations), in particular with women who were considered to be "racially inferior".[8]

To conclude that acts of sexual violence during the German war of annihilation in the Soviet Union were especially scarce would, however, be premature. If nothing else, one would ignore innumerable testimonies of eyewitnesses which indicate the occurrence of various forms of sexual violence in every phase of the war – at the front lines as well as in the occupied territories and during the different stages of the "final solution".[9] In the following chapter, I thus want to take a closer look at some of the different forms of sexual violence German soldiers, SS and policemen perpetrated during the war in the Soviet Union. What kind of acts occurred, who was targeted and what meaning did these acts obtain in relation to the war effort? In the second part, I will turn to the question of how the military leadership dealt with these acts. Did their regulations promote or limit sexual violence? To conclude, I will argue that the military leadership opened up "spaces of opportunity" in which the perpetration of sexual violence could become a normal part of everyday warfare.

Different forms of sexual violence

My analysis of sexual violence during the war and the occupation in the former Soviet Union is based on oral testimonies and written accounts of victims, spectators and perpetrators as well as on Nazi documents. Some describe acts which they have experienced themselves or witnessed directly, others report crimes they know from hearsay. Inevitably, all of these sources are shaped by contemporary ideas of heterosexual violence as well as by gendered conceptions of guilt and shame.[10] In many cases, the sources do not display a lot of reliable details and furthermore there are no possibilities to prove if a story happened exactly the way it is told. Indeed, we have to take into account that eyewitnesses deliberately conceal details (for instance because they consider them to be too intimate) or exaggerate the degree of violence (whereby they stress that the victims were at the mercy of the German men and it was beyond any possibility for them to exercise resistance). In addition, some stories are most definitely based on rumours, passed on in order to scandalise the behaviour of the Germans, to avert suspicion, to distract oneself with "sex-and-crime-stories" and so forth. Despite these reservations, I do assume that the testimonies – as a collective body of evidence – refer to real occurrences: for every account there are many others who describe quite similar forms of sexual violence. I am thus not so much concerned with every single account in itself; rather, I am looking at the multitude, at the ensemble of the sources.[11]

Overall, the acts could be directed against Jewish women (or women whom the Nazis categorised as Jewish), but also against non-Jewish local women (who could see themselves as enemies or sympathisers of the Nazi regime) and against women whom the Nazis designated as "ethnic German", that is "of German descent".[12] The variation in degree and intensity of sexual violence against women of different groups can hardly be established, because many sources do not disclose information on the origins of the victims.

In Naum Epelfeld's account, cited at the beginning of this chapter, sexual violence appears as a form of violence that accompanied the German army's invasion of new territory. Indeed, similar descriptions can be found in numerous accounts about the conquest of cities.[13] In the first months after the German invasion of the Soviet Union, sexual violence seems to have been a tool that soldiers and SS-men implemented when they searched houses or interrogated people. Numerous witnesses testified that members of the Wehrmacht and the SS forced female (and sometimes male) inhabitants to strip when they entered a house.[14] On the one hand, coerced nakedness meant a degradation of the victims, on the other hand, it implied a specific defencelessness in front of the armed men in uniform. In some cases, women in underwear were forced to bend down and pretend to clean the stairs of their house, while German policemen were watching.[15] Instances like this reveal the linkage between sexual fantasies and acts of violence.

In different situations members of Wehrmacht, the SS or the police also conducted body searches, including the search of bodily orifices. Military regulations did indeed instruct the soldiers to body-search the inhabitants for firearms or secret messages. However, these instructions did not include the acts that some German men performed: the touching of the victim's breasts, the squeezing of their nipples or other sexual violations. Testimonies on similar forms of sexual violence are numerous and reveal that the men occasionally interpreted the regulations "obstinately"[16] according to their own interests. In a situation in which the (often very young) men felt bored and afraid, acts of verbal, voyeuristic and physical sexual assault could offer them a possibility to affirm their own superiority and power and to ease their feelings of distraction and stress.

Numerous testimonies describe German soldiers touching women with their hands and their weapons. To beat them on their breasts or their sexual organs was apparently a method for intimidation and torture.[17] If this happened in their own private walls, the victim's feeling of exposure could be intensified. While sexual torture of men – as Sheila

Meintjes has demonstrated – is implemented to generate "sexual passivity" and thus eliminate bodily strength and political power; similar acts against women serve to "activate" female sexuality and to relegate women to their societal position as sexual objects.[18]

Coerced undressing, the search of bodily orifices, sexual torture and other forms of sexual violence were also perpetrated in situations in which women and men were imprisoned – at police-stations, in prisons, military buildings and camps. The perpetrators were German men and local collaborators. In their book on the "final solution" in Riga, Andrej Angrick and Peter Klein document rapes by officers of the Arajs-commando, a Latvian formation that collaborated with the German Security Police. The Jewish survivor Ella Medalje, who had been interrogated in the Arajs headquarters in summer 1941, testified in front of a court in Hamburg in the 1970s:

> One night when we were already preparing our bedding on the floor, the door opened and two Perkonkrust-people with torches entered. They shone every woman in the face and examined them. Then they ordered the women whom they selected to follow them in a row. After some time, one woman returned in a horrible emotional condition, and the Perkonkrust-people took away another woman. In this manner, they brought six or seven women upstairs, where they stood in the study of the commander ... On the next day, these six or seven women were seated on a truck that stood in the courtyard and transported somewhere. I can only assume that they were shot.[19]

Women who were kept imprisoned could be raped in the presence of other prisoners or in isolation. Even if they were, as in Medalje's account, ordered to leave their cell, the other prisoners knew or suspected what happened to them. In addition to the humiliation, the victims thus feared that their being raped could become public outside the walls of the prison. For their fellow prisoners, on the other hand, their knowledge probably triggered feelings of shame as well as the fear to be next. Rape could indeed become a direct threat as well as a symbol of power and a non-verbal means of communication between the perpetrators and the persecuted.[20]

In confinement, some women furthermore experienced gang rape. While Soviet propaganda frequently exploited corresponding fantasies,[21] testimonies on this are extremely rare. The absence of narratives does, however, not necessarily indicate that gang rape was uncommon. It might also be due to the fact that the feelings of terror and shame which victims as well as witnesses experienced were particularly strong. At any rate, it is safe to assume that some of the soldiers who participated in gang rapes would not have raped a woman on their own initiative. Joshua Goldstein has demonstrated that the pressure to comply is a very important factor in cases of gang rape. Indeed, the fulfilled act frequently seems to strengthen the allegiance and loyalty within small units. Goldstein argues that collective delinquency causes the individuals to lack any sense of responsibility. On the contrary, Miranda Alison assumes that the bond between the men results precisely from their awareness of shared responsibility.[22]

Recent research furthermore suggests that gang rape in times of war is frequently perpetrated in a hierarchical order. The highest-ranking officer is the first to enter the woman's body; the subordinate soldiers respect his performance and wait until they are allowed to follow. In the life-threatening situation of combat, when men are extremely dependent on one another, gang rapes confirm the inextricable bonds between them and the reliability of their hierarchies. With a mixture of lust and willingness to destroy, the men meet one another in the body of a woman. In this process, they reaffirm their masculinity and sexual potency.[23]

Sexual violence could also serve to intimidate women who trespassed the traditional gender roles and carried arms as soldiers of the Red Army or guerrilla fighters. Today it is estimated that one million women served in the army and the guerrilla groups, about half of whom carried weapons and fulfilled military service at the battlefront.[24] A former German soldier, who was interviewed at the exhibition "War of Annihilation – Crimes of the Wehrmacht 1941–1945" in Vienna, perceived the picture of a woman with arms as an extremely unsettling experience, even 50 years after the end of the war:

> "What we found horrifying was ... a formation of broads, here even women were in war. That was upsetting, really upsetting for us ... Yes, I mean, that a woman – that was completely against our order, against our soldierly understanding. Once we experienced that, well there was ... God ... at the side of a street ... a Russian woman in uniform, her pants were pulled down, and her legs spread apart, and so they laid her on the street. That was an expression, which among the ferocious privates ... somehow, since we were men among us, well, it could somehow turn into hatred, rage, an incomprehension. Without further ado. One has to understand that."
>
> "Does that mean she had been undressed?"
>
> "No, no. She was shot."

This former soldier appeared largely unaffected by the crimes documented in the exhibition. The only crime that he spoke of by himself was related to the dislocated female body – and here he instantly demanded understanding for the perpetrators, because the "formation of broads" was "against our order". Indeed, during the Second World War women in the Red Army had broken into the exclusive male domain military. For the masculine soldierly self-image they posed a specific irritation and provocation. The nature of the military – as a site of the production of cultural masculinity and thus as a site of the stabilisation of gender-specific power relations – was jeopardised.

Above all, the public display of the raped woman, as depicted in the account of the former soldier, demonstrates that the acts of sexual violence were often not only directed against the victims. The exposed female bodies were supposed to be seen, they were a visible proof for the occurrence of sexual violence and the lack of power of the victims. Thus sexual violence communicated different messages to various groups: (1) It demonstrated the powerlessness of the spectators. Consequently it was a tool to frighten and discipline the local population. (2) Furthermore the female bodies affected the self-conception of the local population, in particular of the men who had not been able to protect "their" women. In that, it appeared as a message of victory. (3) Last but not least the dead female bodies (as well as the photographs of them that some German soldiers took and later put in their albums) communicated a message to the comrades in the male society Wehrmacht/SS: they demonstrated the unflinching aggressiveness of the perpetrators.[25]

Military regulations

The Nazi authorities knew about these crimes. In a rather brief language, often in the form of a list, local military commanders or civil bureaucrats reported cases of rape and gang rape in line with looting, theft of cattle and excessive consumption of alcohol. On 10 August 1941, not even two months after the German invasion of the Soviet Union, the command of the 9th Army reported that the number of sexual crimes in the combat zone had risen significantly.[26] In response, military commanders issued guidelines in which they urged the soldiers to exercise "restraint with respect to the other sex". Some commanders demanded rigorous action against German soldiers' "running wild and lack of discipline".[27]

In fact, however, the military leadership generally faced a dilemma. On the one hand, sexual violence was considered to be undesirable, because it jeopardised the military discipline, health and reputation of the forces, and furthermore violated Nazi racial ideas. On the other hand, sexual violence was deemed a normal, virtually unavoidable part of war. Since male virility was, moreover, presumed to be an expression of strength and ultimately beneficial for the war effort, most military commanders did not see themselves in the position to strictly enforce the bans on sexual contacts.

Military doctors did indeed establish that a man would be mentally and physically strengthened by heterosexual satisfaction. Wehrmacht commanders moreover acted upon the assumption that military-organised (comparably safe, cheap and easily accessible) opportunities to seek sexual satisfaction would bind the individual soldier to the army and strengthen the cohesion of the small military units.[28] Consequently, the Wehrmacht High Command tried not to ban, but to control and regulate soldierly sexuality by handing out condoms, establishing "sanitation houses" (*Sanierungshäuser*) for hygienic disinfection after sexual intercourse and by organising military brothels.[29]

Compared to desertion, unauthorised leave, self-mutilation or sedition of military strength, the Wehrmacht did not assess sexual violence as a "primary crime". Narratives of former soldiers indicate that a rapist could become subject to disciplinary action by his commanding officer. Furthermore, a number of soldiers were court-martialled. In general, however, disciplinary consequences seem to have been the exception. Unreported cases were certainly much more numerous.[30]

If, however, a case of rape did end up in front of a Wehrmacht court in the occupied territories of the Soviet Union, the judges imposed comparatively light sentences. While soldiers sentenced as sex-offenders at the Western front often remained in prison for many years, their counterparts at the Eastern front usually escaped with sentences of between a couple of months and two years.[31] According to Birgit Beck, this difference was mainly due to the methods of racial warfare at the Eastern front. The Barbarossa Decree from 13 May 1941, which regulated the activities of German court martials in "the East", had established that no criminal offences committed by German soldiers against Soviet civilians were to be punished. Exceptions should only be made when military discipline or the security of the troops required it, for instance in cases of "serious actions that are caused by a lack of self-restraint".[32] Sexual violence in combat, however, was seldom regarded as "serious action", and even less so if the victim was designated as "racially inferior". In accordance, rapists at the Eastern front were not punished for harming the "gender honour" of a woman (a term that was important in some cases at the Western front), let alone for violating her physiological and psychological integrity. Rather, the final verdicts in rape cases usually elaborated that the defendant had harmed the reputation of the Wehrmacht.[33]

David Raub Snyder has emphasised that the penalty at the courts of the different military divisions varied and that a couple of courts imposed high sentences at the Eastern Front despite the Barbarossa decree. Ultimately, however, most men did not have to serve their entire prison sentence. Commanding officers generally granted parole after only a few months in prison, with most decisions by commanders ultimately based on the criterion of the individual soldier's willingness to subordinate himself to military order. Even men who faced multiple charges of rape (as well as homosexual activity or child molestation) could rejoin the *Wehrgemeinschaft* fairly soon after being convicted. Especially after the initial victories stopped and the German military situation grew more and more difficult, the Wehrmacht did not want to provide convicted soldiers with food and shelter in the safety of a prison while other men risked their lives at the front lines.[34]

How the SS leadership dealt with sexual violence has not yet been researched comprehensively. However, the documentary paper trail indicates that SS men often did not fear to be punished. For instance, some SS men in Minsk declared in 1943 publicly that the regulations on "racial defilement" were suspended "in the East" – and even though this was by no means true, they did not have to face any disciplinary consequences.[35]

Furthermore, members of the SS, the police and the Wehrmacht seem to have had the opportunity to cover up their trespassing of racial boundaries. Leading criminal assistant Walter Thormeyer, for instance, who was employed at the commander of the safety police in Kraków, Poland, was denounced for sexual contact with a "Jewish spy". Upon this accusation, he shot the woman in question, claiming she had been an "unreliable agent".[36] The case against Thormeyer was closed and he was exempted from punishment – an example that demonstrates that at least some German men in the occupied territories of the Soviet Union acted upon the assumption that they had complete power over the "enemy women".

Even though we cannot deduce that the Wehrmacht and SS promoted sexual violence strategically, the sources demonstrate that sexual violence was an integral part of German warfare. And while the Wehrmacht did establish measures to discipline and punish soldiers, these were seldom enforced. It is exactly this lack of enforcement that opened up "spaces of opportunity" (*Gelegenheitsräume*)[37] in which sexual violence could become an accepted and normal part of the everyday situation of war and combat. Indeed, Wehrmacht sexual politics in the Soviet Union were not only repressive, but – using a term of Michel Foucault – also productive. Through the provision of condoms as well as opportunities for hygienic disinfection and prostitution, the Wehrmacht High command offered the men comparably safe and easily accessible opportunities to seek sexual satisfaction.

If we do not limit our analysis of sexual violence during the war in the Soviet Union to acts of rape, but furthermore consider acts of enforced undressing, coerced nakedness, sexual torture, sexual blackmail, sexual enslavement and other crimes, we will get a much better idea of the impact of sexual violence on military strategies and war efforts. To document and analyse these forms of violence will change our ideas of the gendering of the war in a more general way. Among other things, it will demonstrate that men not only have the power to commit sexual violence, but are also vulnerable and experience sexual violence on a regular basis.

The history of sexual violence by German soldiers in the "occupied Eastern territories" cannot be explored sufficiently with a one-way top-down approach. Drawing on the work of Elizabeth Jean Wood, it is important to examine the interaction between the military leadership, the small units and the individual soldiers. The actors often harboured different ideas about gender, sexuality, race and violence, which furthermore were not static, but could differ in the different territories and stages of war. Correspondingly, sexual violence cannot be grasped as a crime that always happened in the same manner. Indeed, we have to examine the different forms of sexual crimes, the varying motives of the perpetrators and the different consequences for the people who became victims.

Notes

1. Naum Epelfeld, "Möge mein Gedächtnis das Vergessen verhindern...", in Boris Zabarko, ed., *"Nur wir haben überlebt". Holocaust in der Ukraine. Zeugnisse und Dokumente*, Berlin, Dittrich, 2004, pp. 110–29 (111); my translation.
2. Ruth Seifert, "Krieg und Vergewaltigung. Ansätze zu einer Analyse", in Alexandra Stiglmayer, ed., *Massenvergewaltigungen. Der Krieg gegen die Frauen*, Frankfurt am Main, Fischer, 1994, pp. 87–112 (93).
3. See among others Cornelia Essner, *Die "Nürnberger Gesetze" oder die Verwaltung des Rassenwahns*, Paderborn, Ferdinand Schöningh, 2002, p. 219.
4. See for instance the transcript of a wiretapped conversation between petty officer Helmut Hartelt and sailor Horst Minnieur, detained in a British POW

camp in 1943, cited in Sönke Neitzel and Harald Welzer, *Soldaten. Protokolle vom Kämpfen, Töten und Sterben*, Frankfurt am Main, S. Fischer, 2011, pp. 164–5.

5. Elizabeth D. Heineman, "Sexuality and Nazism. The Doubly Unspeakable?", *Journal of the History of Sexuality* 11:1–2 (2002), pp. 22–66; Doris L. Bergen, "Sexual Violence in the Holocaust. Unique or Typical?", in Dagmar Herzog, ed., *The Holocaust in International Perspective (Lessons & Legacies, vol. 7)*, Chicago, Northwestern University Press, 2006, pp. 179–200.
6. Gaby Zipfel, "Ausnahmezustand Krieg? Anmerkungen zu soldatischer Männlichkeit, sexueller Gewalt und militärischer Einhegung", in Insa Eschebach and Regina Mühlhäuser, eds, *Krieg und Geschlecht. Sexuelle Gewalt im Krieg und Sex-Zwangsarbeit in NS-Konzentrationslagern*, Berlin, Metropol, 2008, pp. 55–74 (55).
7. Birgit Beck, *Wehrmacht und sexuelle Gewalt. Sexualverbrechen vor deutschen Militärgerichten 1939–1945*, Paderborn, Ferdinand Schöningh, 2004, pp. 72, 335. For a summary of her findings in English see Beck, "Sexual Violence and Its Prosecution by Courts Martial of the Wehrmacht", in Roger Chickering, ed., *A World at Total War. Global Conflict and the Politics of Destruction, 1937–1945*, Cambridge University Press, 2005, pp. 317–31. David Raub Snyder makes a similar argument in *Sex Crimes under the Wehrmacht*, Lincoln, University of Nebraska Press, 2007, pp. xi, 135.
8. Andrej Angrick, *Besatzungspolitik und Massenmord. Die Einsatzgruppe D in der südlichen Sowjetunion 1941–1943*, Hamburg, Hamburger Edition, 2003.
9. On the variety of sources see Wendy Jo Gertjejanssen, "Victims, Heroes, Survivors. Sexual Violence on the Eastern Front during World War II", PhD dissertation, University of Minnesota, 2004; Monika Flaschka, "Race, Rape and Gender in Nazi Occupied Territories", PhD dissertation, Kent State University, 2009; Regina Mühlhäuser, *Eroberungen. Sexuelle Gewalttaten und intime Beziehungen deutscher Soldaten in der Sowjetunion*, Hamburg, Hamburger Edition, 2010.
10. Accounts of sexual violence generally follow a gendered "rape script". For a critical analysis see among others Sharon Marcus, "Fighting Bodies, Fighting Words. A Theory and Politics of Rape Prevention", in Judith Butler and Joan W. Scott, eds, *Feminists Theorize the Political*, New York, Routledge, 2002, pp. 385–403, particularly p. 392.
11. For a more detailed description of my approach and the difficulties of testimonies on sexual violence see Mühlhäuser, *Eroberungen*, p. 28.
12. On the Nazi category of "ethnic German" see Doris Bergen, "The Nazi Concept of "Volksdeutsche" and the Exacerbation of Anti-Semitism in Eastern Europe, 1939–45", *Journal of Contemporary History* 29:4 (1994), pp. 569–82.
13. Compare for instance Jakob Littner, *Mein Weg durch die Nacht*, Berlin, Metropol, 2002, pp. 52, 54.
14. See for instance Faye Schulman, *A Partisan's Memoir. Woman of the Holocaust*, Toronto, Second Story Press, 1995, p. 65.
15. See among others Republic of Poland, Ministry of Foreign Affairs, ed., *German Occupation of Poland, Extract of Note Addressed to the Allied and Neutral Powers*, New York, Greystone Press, 1941, p. 21.
16. On the concept of "obstinacy" see Alf Lüdtke, *Eigen-Sinn. Fabrikalltag, Arbeitererfahrungen und Politik vom Kaiserreich bis in den Faschismus*, Hamburg, Ergebnisse, 1993, p. 377.

17. See for instance "In Bialystock, zum Druck vorbereitet von Rachel Kownator", in Wassili Grossman and Ilja Ehrenburg, eds, *Das Schwarzbuch. Der Genozid an den sowjetischen Juden*, Reinbek, Rowohlt, 1994, pp. 385–95 (395).
18. Cited in Louise du Toit, "Feminismus und die Ethik der Versöhnung", in *Mittelweg 36* 16:3 (2007), pp. 4–29 (16).
19. Testimony of Ella Medalje, 15. 1. 1979, Office of Public Prosecutor, Hamburg, Germany (StA Hamburg), SB 37, 141 Js 534/60, Bl. 6310., cit. in Andre Angrick and Peter Klein, *"Endlösung" in Riga, Ausbeutung und Vernichtung 1941–1944*, Darmstadt, Wissenschaftliche Buchgesellschaft, 2006, p. 81. *Perkonkrust* (thundercross) is the name of a Latvian fascist organisation founded in 1933. We do not know if Medalje's attribution is correct. To date, many eyewitnesses use *Perkonkrust* as a more general term for collaborators (ibid., p. 80).
20. Seifert, "Krieg und Vergewaltigung", p. 101.
21. A remarkable example is Genia Demianova, *Comrade Genia. The Story of a Victim of German Bestiality in Russia Told by Herself*, with preface by Ronald Scarfe, London, Nicholson & Watson, 1941, pp. 54–9.
22. Joshua Goldstein, *War and Gender. How Gender Shapes the War System and Vice Versa*, Cambridge University Press, 2001, p. 365; Miranda Alison, "Wartime Sexual Violence. Women's Human Rights and Questions of Masculinity", *Review of International Studies* 33:1 (2007), pp. 75–90.
23. Rolf Pohl, "Massenvergewaltigung. Zum Verhältnis von Krieg und männlicher Sexualität", *Mittelweg 36* 11:2 (2002), pp. 53–75 (67).
24. Susanne Conze and Beate Fieseler, "Soviet Women as Comrades-in-Arms. A Blind Spot in the History of War", in Robert W. Thurston and Bernd Bonwetsch, eds, *The People's War. Responses to World War II in the Soviet Union*, Chicago, University of Illinois Press, 2000, pp. 211–34 (212).
25. On the multilayered communicative functions of violence see Jan Philipp Reemtsma, *Vertrauen und Gewalt. Versuch über eine besondere Konstellation der Moderne*, Hamburg, Hamburger Edition, 2009. He argues that every act of violence addresses not only the victim, but furthermore a third party, an (actual or imagined) spectator or the general public, who perceives the destructive dimension of violence as an expression of the state of society. It is important to explore this "triadic constellation" of violence in order to understand the perpetration of violence not merely as an irregular exception, but as a form of social acting.
26. AOK 9/Abt. Ic, Armeebefehl, Betr.: Überwachung der Disziplin, 10. 08. 1941, National Archive and Record Administration (NARA), RG-242 314/679, p. 649.
27. AOK 11, geh., gez. von Manstein, 20. 11. 1941, printed in *Der Prozess gegen die Hauptkriegsverbrecher vor dem Internationalen Militärgerichtshof Nürnberg vom 14. November 1945–1. Oktober 1946 (IMT)*, 42 vols, Munich and Zurich, 1947, vol. 20, p. 700.
28. Mühlhäuser, *Eroberungen*, p. 175.
29. See Wendy Jo Gertjejanssen, "Victims, Heroes, Survivors: Sexual Violence on the Eastern Front during World War II", PhD dissertation, University of Minnesota, 2004, p. 180; Mühlhäuser, *Eroberungen*.
30. Beck, "Sexual Violence"; Christian Thomas Huber, *Die Rechtsprechung der deutschen Feldkriegsgerichte bei Straftaten von Wehrmachtssoldaten gegen*

Angehörige der Zivilverwaltung in den besetzten Gebieten, Marburg, Tectum, 2007, p. 95.

31. Beck, *Wehrmacht und sexuelle Gewalt*, p. 247.
32. Hitler, *Kriegsgerichtsbarkeitsbefehl, 13.05.1941*, printed in *Deutsche Besatzungspolitik in der UdSSR*, ed. Norbert Müller, Köln, Pahl Rugenstein, 1980, pp. 64–6 (65).
33. Beck, *Wehrmacht und sexuelle Gewalt*; Raub Snyder, *Sex Crimes*.
34. Snyder, *Sex Crimes*, p. 138.
35. Hans-Heinrich Wilhelm, *Die Einsatzgruppe A der Sicherheitspolizei und des SD 1941/1942*, Bern, Peter Lang, 1996, p. 479.
36. Klaus-Michael Mallmann, "Mensch, ich feiere heut' den tausendsten Genickschuß. Die Sicherheitspolizei und die Shoah in Westgalizien", in Gerhard Paul, ed., *Die Täter der Schoah. Fanatische Nationalsozialisten oder ganz normale Deutsche?*, Göttingen, Wallstein, 2002, pp. 109–36 (123).
37. On the concept of *Gelegenheitsräume* see Bernd Greiner, *Krieg ohne Fronten. Die USA in Vietnam*, Hamburg, Hamburger Edition, 2007.

3

The Victimisation of the Body and the Body Politic during the Greek Civil War, 1946–49[1]

Katherine Stefatos

During the Greek Civil War (1946–49) and the years to follow, thousands of citizens, among them a great number of women, were persecuted, confined and terrorised in a series of incidents of continuous political violence and oppression. This essay argues that throughout this politically and socially turbulent period (1946–74), the phenomenon of political violence against the female dissidents took an explicitly gendered form not only in its implemented practices such as rape and sexual abuse, psychological terror, political imprisonment and exile, but also as a means of re-traditionalising gender roles and power relations as "natural" and "given". This essay will try to bring forward the downplayed gendered characteristics of sexually related violence, especially rape, during the Greek Civil War (1946–49) and analyse it within the nationalist ideology and the ascribed traditional gender roles through which the mechanisms of terrorisation were institutionalised and legitimised. The research question, based on postgraduate work, is situated within a wider theoretical debate on the interconnectedness between gender, political violence and nationalism. It also brings together interdisciplinary theoretical insights and methodological contributions from politics, history and gender studies through the employment of a series of sources, such as interviews, memoirs and archival material.

As part of my PhD research I have conducted so far 32 semi-structured interviews along with numerous informal conversations with former partisans, guerrilla fighters, political prisoners and exiles (mainly women, but men as well) during the Greek Civil War (1946–49) and the military dictatorship (1967–74). The majority of the political detainees live in Athens but originate from different regions of Greece, have basic education and with regard to political belief are mostly leftist (Communist or European Left). The interviews and discussions were conducted in Athens, in central and northwestern Greece, in the Aegean islands and in former exile islands (Makronisos, Trikeri, Ai Stratis, Yiaros) during pilgrimage trips with political detainees.

The interviews were usually taped, with the permission of the political dissidents, and detailed notes were made afterwards. I was brought into contact with the informants by other researchers, people who work in archives and organisations for the preservation of historical memory, but also by friends and acquaintances. Also important was the experience gained while working at the Museum of Political Exiles of Ai Stratis in Athens, not only in terms of establishing contacts but also in achieving a deeper understanding of the period and of the experience of confinement. Among other things, such as the issue of trust, what should be revealed and to what degree to an "outsider", the question of my own political placement also arose as significant in a number of instances during the interviews. The narration of my grandfather's personal story of political incarceration often helped to establish a climate of trust with the informants.

The issue of violence, especially the sexual nature of abuse, was not raised directly, but incidents of sexual assault – including rape – arose during the interview. However, when rape cases were narrated, the disclosure usually involved the experiences of other women (acquaintances, co-prisoners) and not of the narrator. Even though it has been argued by feminist scholars that victims need to narrate their stories in order to heal,[2] I made a conscious decision not to directly raise the issue of sexual violence in an effort to avoid further traumatisation. Additionally, I believe that women are in a position to renegotiate their experiences on their own terms as well as to adopt the appropriate coping mechanisms.

According to the historian Tasoula Vervenioti there are less than 100 memoirs written by women guerrilla fighters and/or political inmates.[3] The published and unpublished memoirs by former partisans and political detainees proved to be a valuable source of information, but as in the oral testimonies, rape as a personal experience is rarely mentioned. In fact, when rape cases are reported in women's written accounts, the discussed incidents refer to sexual assaults against their comrades. There is the exception of the author Regina Pagoulatou who in her memoir describes her attempted rape at the Trikeri exile camp.[4] It is worth pointing out that her memoir was originally published in 1974 in New York, where Regina permanently resided.

As part of my research on sexual assault, rape and terrorisation during the 1940s, the archival resources that were consulted consist of newspapers, political documents, correspondence and photographs. This essay is mainly based on the Contemporary Social History Archives (ASKI), which proved to be particularly useful. ASKI were founded in 1992 in Athens and their aim is to preserve and promote archival material of contemporary Greek history. The main archives examined were of the United Democratic Left (EDA), personal archives of former inmates such as the poet Victoria Theodorou, but especially Ilias Staveris's archive and the material he collected in relation to the Women's Movement.

The League for Democracy in Greece, a political group founded in 1945 in order to support the Greek political dissidents and their persecuted families, contains a body of important archival resources concentrating on modern Greek history and is located at the King's College London Archives. The Modern Greek Archives of the League for Democracy contain information on the persecution, internment and abuse of women. Rape cases are also included.[5] Additionally, reported cases of rape that took place between 1945–47 are documented on the Memorandum submitted by the Greek Democratic Army to the United Nations in March 1947, published in 1987.

In the Greek Literary Archive (ELIA) in Athens I was able to research the newspapers of the period (mostly the Greek newspaper *To Vima*) in order to locate recorded incidents of rape and the way they are described. The rape of the teacher Pepi Karayianni is one of the few cases that was not only made public but was also reported in the non-leftist press. As mentioned earlier, the Museum of Political Exiles of Ai Stratis in Athens, which opened to the public in 2006 in an attempt to preserve the historical memory of exile and imprisonment in Greece, holds valuable archival and photographical material, as well as artwork produced by inmates in former exile sites and camps, ranging from the early 1920s until the fall of the military junta in 1974.

When it comes to the scholarly output of modern Greek studies, and the Greek Civil War historiography, there has been a noteworthy expansion of the research spectrum through innovative and interdisciplinary research techniques and methodological tools. Despite the interdisciplinary trends, there are still some major research gaps and issues which remain political taboos and are poorly examined.[6] As aptly pointed out by Antoniou and Marantzidis, violence and gender are among the neglected issues not only in the postwar academic literature, but also in the public dialogue. The anthropologist Riki Van Boeschoten argues that when it comes to gender violence during war or conflict in the contemporary Greek setting, "we are faced with an almost complete void".[7] In fact, Van Boeschoten's paper on the trauma of war rape provides a powerful argument about the conditions that have led to the under-representation of war rapes in the case of Greece. Her account remains the only published work so far linking sexual violence to the experiences of women in the Greek Civil War, and situated within the political context of war rapes in the former Yugoslavia (1992–95) and in the Greek Civil War (1946–49).

At this point it is necessary to mention the greatly influential work of Tasoula Vervenioti[8] who has extensively explored the participation of women in the Greek Resistance and the Democratic Army. She was the first to provide a history of the women partisans and guerrilla fighters, but also their experiences as political detainees in the postwar Greek society. In addition to Vervenioti's work, Janet Hart's analysis is important in providing an insight into women's active engagement in the Resistance Movement and the role of gender in social and political movements.[9] However, there are two key parameters excluded from Hart's work. The first one is the dynamics of violence and its impact on women's lives; the second is the reconstruction of gender roles as a vital component of the nationalist project. The historian Margaret Poulos has also attempted to connect the experiences of female warriors in the Greek Revolution of 1821 and the partisan women during the Resistance and the Civil War to notions of citizenship and national identity.[10] Poulos emphasises the symbolism of female warriors and their employment in both the nationalist and feminist discourse in order to investigate the construction of a feminist identity and female agency.

Nevertheless, the female traumatic experience during and after the conflict is still treated rather reluctantly within the contemporary academic discussion. There is a troubling silence regarding the gendered constructions of political violence and nationalism, closely connected to the revival of traditional assumptions that project a trivialised gender identity. The experiences of the politically active women need to be engendered and situated within a wider academic debate in order to reveal the gender-based organisation of power within the nationalist project. Within the "acceptable" national history,[11] the role of nationalist ideology in terms of nurturing gender quotas and normalising sexual intimidation, terrorisation and rape needs to be recognised as crucial.

Women in postwar Greece

The Greek Civil War officially began in 1946 and was the outcome of a highly polarised, socially and politically unstable period, tightly connected to the brutal German, Italian and Bulgarian Occupation (1941–44). The struggle between the leftist and rightist forces started in 1943 and escalated to a fratricidal civil conflict. The governmental forces, backed by the United Kingdom and the United States, created an anti-Communist apparatus, facilitated by paramilitary rightist bands. This phenomenon of terrorisation, sexual intimidation and abuse, torture and murder took on vast proportions between February 1945 and February 1946 and was characterised as the "white-terror". The last act of the civil war drama was played out in the summer of 1949 with the Communist defeat on the mountains of Western Macedonia, leading the country into long-term instability. Particularly for the leftist population, the termination of the Civil War resulted in widespread persecution, repression and abuse, as the Communist Party remained outlawed until 1974 and its members and sympathisers were treated as social and political pariahs.

Women of all ages, backgrounds and levels of political awareness were politically persecuted, transported by government forces to detention centres and concentration camps (usually on remote islands) and in many cases sexually assaulted as a punishment or correctional practice for holding "incorrect" or "suspicious" political beliefs. The suffering of women in its specific qualities and deep personal and social effects has been marginalised or downgraded by the official rhetoric, the public dialogue and by the female victims themselves, even after the end of the seven-year dictatorship (1967–74).

Throughout the 1930s and early 1940s, Greek society relegated women to the private sphere as a means of ensuring family structure, continuity and stability through modesty and virginity, but especially the moral code of honour. The concept of *timi* (honour) was particularly pivotal within Greece's family milieu and societal structure and served as the mechanism of the exclusion of women from the social and political arena.[12] Especially until 1952 when women gained the right to vote, their political status as citizens was literally non-existent. The Resistance Movement and the subsequent civil war political conditions gave the opportunity to women to become actively engaged within the political realm through their participation in political organisations without violating the pre-existing gender hierarchies.[13] In fact, Margarita Kotsaki, a former political detainee, states in her memoir *A Life Full of Struggles* that the Greek woman, before her participation in the Resistance movement, "was neglected, an inferior gender in relation to men – persuaded that she was destined only for the house, the household, the closed life, that she has no rights".[14]

The Communist-led Resistance organisations, the National Liberation Front (EAM) and the United Panhellenic Organisation of Youth (EPON) offered grounds for claims of equality and emancipation. Undoubtedly, under these circumstances, women gained a relative autonomy and, to some extent, equality, albeit for a short period and under conditions of extreme hardship and fear. The complexity and difficulties involved in women's participation and mobilisation became evident especially in the context of the Greek Democratic Army (DSE). Women's participation has been remarkable both in terms of numbers and contribution, especially in the last phases of the civil strife.[15] Margaret Poulos argues that the Democratic Army considered the recruitment of women as instrumental due to a substantial lack of human resources, and that women joined the Democratic Army as a reaction to the brutal violence perpetuated by the rightist groups.[16] Within this context, Eleni B. in her interview also mentioned that as her family was already politically labelled, since her father was a partisan who was murdered during the Occupation, she joined the DSE in order to escape from the rightist terrorist bands that roamed the villages. She states characteristically that "the paramilitaries raped, sheared women, murdered. My mother was informed by the villagers that they would come after me, so I decided to flee to the Mountain with the guerrillas."[17] However, as the line between coercion and consent, voluntary participation and recruitment is blurred and since the Communist leadership aimed for female mobilisation without challenging social consensus and gender hierarchies, a consequential patriarchal rhetoric was adopted.[18]

As argued by feminist scholars, activists and researchers interested in the experiences of women in times of war, female activism and mobilisation often challenge the boundaries of what is "private", and the long-existing patriarchal structures.[19] For traditional Greek society, the political struggles of women gave an impetus for equality and emancipation claims. Yet, soon after the crisis is over, the restoration of the traditional gender roles is expected. Similarly, within the Greek context, the widening of these contestations entailed a significant cost; the political persecution and reintegration to the private domain was articulated by the state, but the Communist Party on its own required a mandatory return to pre-existing gender roles through paternalistic attitudes.[20]

The psyche and the body: sexual victimisation in the Greek Civil War

During the Greek Civil War, the oppressive regime in power not only targeted political dissidents but also the civilian population, especially during the early (1946–47) and late (1949) stages of the conflict. In most cases, civilian women had no direct links with either the Democratic Army or the Communist Party, but they were still massively assaulted and terrorised as a means of preventing their recruitment by the Democratic Army.[21] During the period of "white terror" (1945–46) and the early stages of the Civil War (1946–47) women were gang-raped, forced into prostitution, mutilated, sexually assaulted in public places or in front of their relatives, had their heads shaven and were stripped naked.[22] The terrorisation continued and intensified in 1949 and women, primarily from northern Greece, joined the Democratic Army out of a fear of being raped, exiled or imprisoned, even executed, and not just because of their ideological beliefs.[23]

Approaching rape in the Greek Civil War: victims and perpetrators

One of the main objectives of the overall research is to argue that mental and psychological abuse, sexual insinuation and oppressive techniques are equally disturbing and traumatic experiences for women political prisoners, as Eleni, a former political exile, disclosed:

> During the Resistance and while exiled I couldn't bear the psychological violence. I couldn't put up with it. I'll tell you something ... when you are beaten, after the first lash, after a while the body gets used to the beatings and it becomes numb. But, when it comes to psychological violence and the threat of rape, you cannot handle it.[24]

The psychological terrorisation along with the sexual and physical abuse was implemented in order to create a climate of social disruption and political degradation. However, a gender analysis of the role of sexual abuse and political terror presupposes recognition of the actuality of violence perpetuated by the State, including that performed by groups neither directly controlled nor restrained by the State during war or armed conflict.[25] In that respect, the arguments provided by feminist scholars are important. Crawley in particular, based on Pettman, states that during war, "bodies, boundaries, violence and power come together in devastating combination". On these grounds, Crawley continues: women's bodies "become the site for signifying the dominance of one group over the other".[26]

Thus, violence against women, regardless of whether it is sexual or physical, has to be re-conceptualised as an assault, not only on women's bodies and psyches, but also on the body politic, since this violence is primarily an exercise of political power and dominance.[27]

In oral testimonies, rape is frequently referred to as a common practice of right-wing paramilitaries, especially during the 1945–47 period; still, there are no official statistics of the actual number of sexual assaults.[28] According to the Memorandum submitted by the Democratic Army to the United Nations in March 1947, 211 rapes were recorded within the year 1945–46, but there are whole regions that are not included, such as Athens, the islands and other parts of mainland Greece, while the reported cases refer to violations that took place until March 1947.[29] Undoubtedly the actual number is much higher, since the codes of shame and honour were deeply established and most of the cases were unreported.[30] On these grounds, the archival records indicate the mass rape of 300 young refugee women in 1945 in a camp at Ioannina, who were later forced into prostitution, in an effort to prevent their recruitment by the Democratic Army.[31]

The assaulters were in most cases members of paramilitary groups and the gendarmerie who were often acting with complete anarchy. On some occasions the perpetrators of sexual assaults were army officers, former high-ranking officers of the National Army, but nationally minded (*ethnikofrones*) citizens and locals often acquaintances of the victims facilitated the assaulters.[32] The inhabitants mostly out of fear specified the "suspected" houses of those who had some possible links with the Democratic Army or were of a leftist family background. The politically "suspicious" houses carried black round markers so that the National Army could more easily seek retaliation.[33] When it comes to retaliation rapes by the Communists, according to Riki Van Boeschoten, there are no well-known cases, and this can be explained by the fact that the Democratic Army was reliant on the local communities and the local population both in terms of human and material resources.[34] However, and in a completely different context, during an interview with Eleni, a former political exile, she revealed that the husband of a Communist family with which she sought refuge when she was hiding to avoid arrest, attempted to rape her; she managed to escape from the window and was later caught by the police and sent into exile.[35]

It is difficult to argue that the sexual crimes committed were based on a specifically organised project directed by a central authority. The majority of the sexual assaults were, however, conducted by paramilitary units with the help of the rightist bands that were formed by the government in 1946, under the names MAY (Country Security Units) and MAD (Municipal Security Units).[36] A year later, those units were transformed into Tagmata Ethnofrouras (the National Defence Corps), closely connected to the Army.[37] The interrogation of women took place in police stations, or designated centres such as military camps where women all over Greece, often without any previous political involvement, had to face physical, psychological and sexual terrorisation. Nevertheless, we need to be aware of the silence and impunity, along with the general atmosphere of the period "in which rape as an instrument of national politics is made thinkable".[38] Wendy Bracewell analyses the hysteria over "nationalist" rape in Kosovo through the prism of Serbian nationalism in the 1980s, however in the Greek case, rape was mostly a form of political rather than of national or ethnic annihilation, as has been the case in other nationalist or war contexts.

Even though rape, sexual assault and torture was rampant and unregulated in the initial stage of the civil conflict – although still massive and extremely violent – in the following years and within the context of internment, the mechanisms of violence were materialised into a more organised, almost scientific form of abuse. The perpetrators of sexual assaults and political violence were not any longer only right-wing paramilitaries, police and army officers. Doctors who were either compliant or cooperating with the regime often facilitated the abuse of women, as well as the judicial system that further legitimised the persecution and harassment. Pepi Karayianni's case, a teacher raped while imprisoned and unconscious, exemplifies this collusion of the military, medical and judicial state apparatus. She was sentenced to death by the military judges under Law 509/1947 on charges that she was acting as a spy against the nation on behalf of a foreign country. Doctors were not only aware of the assault, but they dismissed the initial rape accusation because the victim refused to undergo a second medical examination. Furthermore, in a number of instances, doctors became the coercers or perpetrators of sexual assaults. Similarly, two doctors (one of them a military doctor at a local police station) raped Glykeria, a 22-year-old political detainee, using their medical instruments.[39]

Even though political intimidation through the sexual victimisation of female dissidents was principally exercised in the interrogation and detention centres, the threat of being raped or sexually abused in the concentration camps and prisons was a constant one. Women were continuously reminded that if they did not sign the Declarations of Repentance they would be beaten and harassed or their children would be taken away from them. As the journalist and political exile, Aphrodite Mavroede-Panteleskou, recalls

> What scared us the most was when they were taking us out (of the tents) in the dark. We didn't know what the purpose of these night

abductions was and we were shivering. We only knew that they were selecting the young women and an undefined fear of something dreadful was keeping us in distress.[40]

Similarly political prisoner and exile Anna Solomou describes in her memoir the mechanisms of terrorisation that were used against the female and male dissidents, wherein one could trace sexual humiliation and abuse.[41] Besides *bastinado* and *panagitsa* (a form of torture that entailed the tying up of the prisoner who stood for hours against a wall), Anna was threatened that if she did not reveal her comrades she was either going to be thrown out of the window or raped.[42] During their interrogation women were not only tortured by police officers, but there was one officer who was syphilitic and threatened to sexually assault them and transmit his disease in order to press a confession.[43] Despite the threats Anna did not say anything; that was a common practice among the dissidents. Similarly, Electra Apostolou, who was brutally abused and murdered during her interrogation, also stated, "every time I'm captured I don't worry at all ... as I no longer have memory, I don't have ears, I don't have a tongue...I don't even have one day of a past."[44]

As mentioned earlier rape in oral and written testimonies is not narrated especially when the writers refer to their own experiences. One of the few cases where incidents of rape are mentioned is in Regina's Pagoulatou memoir, in which she describes her attempted rape by a guard at the exile island of Trikeri.

> ... the door opened suddenly. The beam of the flashlight revealed the presence of my body, like a sculpture in the dark, and a soldier fell on me with force, switching off the beam. In his face I recognized the night guard ... the stench of wine filled the darkness. I was against the wall unmoving. "Orders! Orders that you not get away", he shouted and his hands gripped my body like pincers. My body became heavy, like wood, and I became one with the wall. "Don't, don't! For God's sake! Don't do it", I shouted and put my hands in front of my chest to keep him off, while his hot breath, heavy with wine and panting, warmed my nostrils and the smell made my inside churn ... "Don't do this to your sister!", I was shouting and crying. And with one hand against his chest, I raised my other hand and gave him a vigorous slap on his face. His legs became tangled with mine. He tried to bend my legs and to throw me down ... "I am your sister, soldier, don't you see me? Your sister ..." and my voice

> was pierced by the force of my own voice. I felt his hands loosen their grip, and a sob rose up in his chest ... How could I be such a wretch? ... They got me drunk and ordered me to come here. Forgive me woman. Forgive the beast that was ordered to go astray ... I felt like a living dead woman, frozen in my place.[45]

In relation to the prevailing silence, we need to be aware of the social norms and the gender biases that dominated Greek society in that period and to a large extent still exist. According to these norms, such matters were private. The atrocity of rape was considered private and women were to remain silent. It is worth pointing out that in the pamphlets of the period, but also in narratives and oral accounts, women themselves often adopt the recommended female attitude. Elisavet, during our interview when commenting on the fear of rape, avoided using the actual word "rape" and instead on employing the term "dishonour".[46] The Left also adopted a conservative rhetoric, often exclusionary, illustrated by the Memorandum of the Greek Democratic Army, but also in later historical accounts and testimonials.[47]

In this framework of analysis, Sharon Marcus stresses the need to approach rape as a *linguistic fact*, in relation to the ways "the violence of rape is enabled by narratives, complexes and institutions".[48]

Sexually assaulting the female body and the body politic: the coexistence of the "political" and the "ethnic"

Sexual violence in wartime is not simply attacking the female body; it is primarily intended to suffocate the political body. The legitimisation of violence against women is primarily an exercise of political power. In the Greek case, sexual violence was also transformed into a weapon of political repression, targeting women and men who were politically active, as well as the local population. The target was not only the physical body but also the disintegration of the community and social chaos. I seek to further project the argument provided by Jacobs and colleagues that conflict has a gender dimension and is, in many cases, sexualised.[49] This essay is aiming to stress the sexualised nature of violence within the context of the Greek Civil War. The sexualised element is not only detected as being related to physical coercion or to overtly sexual assaults but also located within the highly patriarchal system of gender and power relations.

Women's role as partisans and activists was degraded and their bodies were sexually targeted in order to turn them from dissidents into immoral women and legitimise their brutalisation.[50] In fact, as argued by Van Boeschoten, "all these forms of violence on the female body were clear transgressions of the social code of honour".[51] Pettman also stresses that this type of violence affects not only the body and psyche of the victim, but also the body politic "so that both person and society are so disintegrated they are paralysed and negated".[52] Within the context of the Greek Civil War, the state did not recognise the detainees of the Civil War as political prisoners and exiles. Political dissidents were deprived of any sense of self, especially the *political* self, while their political and gender identity was constantly contested, exploitable and at stake. Furthermore, within the nationalist project of rehabilitation, women's roles as guerrilla fighters and political dissidents were not only denied, but primarily trivialised. "The title *synagonistria* (fellow-combatant) – an honorary term of address throughout the Resistance – became a synonym for a woman of 'loose morals'."[53]

What Krog and other researchers interested in gender violence are arguing here is that the bodies of women in times of war, political instability and economic disparity are victimised both sexually and symbolically.[54] Psychological terrorisation and sexual victimisation use the vulnerable, sexualised body but also target notions of honour, chastity and virginity that were – and to a certain degree still are – very prominent in the patriarchal family and community structure of Greece. As Elisavet, a political prisoner, recently disclosed, "only the matter of honour, through rape or even the threat of it, would force me to give in and sign a declaration of repentance".[55] In a similar vein, political prisoner Margarita Kotsaki notes in her testimony that Vaitsa Plianka from Florina in northwestern Greece, imprisoned at the Averof Prisons before her execution, revealed to her co-prisoners that she was raped. She stated, "I didn't say anything sooner because I was embarrassed. Now that I'm going to die, I want you to know."[56]

Militarised rape bears the cultural significance of controlling and penetrating the "enemy" women of a different race, religion and – in the case of the Greek Civil War – political affiliation.[57] Rape, sexual abuse and intimidation are transformed into a political strategy.[58] Olympia Papadouka recalls the horrifying scenes that took place at the Female Averof Prisons between "the child of rape", as he was called by the women political prisoners, and his mother.[59] As the "child of rape" was a product of forced impregnation during the Greek Civil War, there were times that the mother beat the child and other times that she cuddled him, tormented by guilt and trauma.[60] Both the child and the mother were the victims of a violent mechanism, systematically executed by its agents in order to politically discredit the dissidents and disrupt social cohesion. The preceding case was not the only one; the leftist newspapers of the period reported a number of incidents of gang rapes resulting in the impregnation[61] of women who were captured by the gendarmerie or the army and were handed over to the paramilitary units formed by the government and closely connected to the army, which later conducted the sexual assaults.

Within the aforementioned socio-political context and the prevailing system of power relations, even the threat of sexually assaulting a woman was transformed into an equally horrifying weapon of repression. In cases of impregnation as a result of rape, the torment and guilt were tremendous, given the resulting social stigmatisation and family isolation. For instance, in the peripheral Lamia camp, a detainee had an affair with a guerrilla fighter and became pregnant. The guerrilla fighter was killed before having a chance to marry and hence the child would be illegal. For this reason she decided to give birth in the concentration camp and drown her own child in the toilets in order to avoid public outcry.[62] Similarly, once again at the Lamia prisons, an imprisoned woman was hiding her pregnancy, as she was a widow. Her pregnancy was a product of rape by members of the Country Security Units (MAY), but she did not reveal it to the Directorship of the prison or to her family in order to avoid the obloquy. When the woman gave birth, the boy was adopted and her husband's family disowned her due to the supposed adultery.[63]

Instability, hate, ethnic and nationalist differences all transform women's bodies into battlefields.[64] Rape, forced impregnation and institutionalised prostitution are common practices within many nationalistic regimes. During the Greek Civil War, the supporters of the Left and the Slavic-speaking women were singled out and sexually targeted. The vast majority of the victims of war rapes that took place in the villages of northern Greece belonged to the Slavic-speaking minority.[65] In the villages of Kastoria and Florina, in northwestern Greece, where the Slavic-speaking population was significant, the sexual assaults, rapes and mutilations were targeting mostly women who belonged to the ethnic minority. According to the DSE Memorandum, in the village of Ftelia 30 women and young girls where "dishonoured" (the term usually refers to rape) by the armed paramilitary groups.[66] Similarly in the village of Filiates in the area of Ioannina in March 1945, the terrorist band of EDES[67] "disgraced" 30 women of the *Tsam* minority.[68]

Vervenioti argues that female political dissidents managed to overcome the traumatisation of the "Bulgarian" designation more easily than that of the "whore".[69] The ethnic stigma, however, marked the Slavic-speaking women, who were simultaneously perceived as Communists, for decades to come, and provided the justification for their sexual abuse and socio-political marginalisation. It cannot, however, be argued that sexual victimisation was part of a strategy of ethnic cleansing,[70] despite the fact that the ethnic classification "justified" the sexual assaulting. As argued by Riki Van Boeschoten, it had more to do with the construction of the enemy in an ethnic key.[71] Even though rape has been described as an instrument of war and ethnic cleansing and as a method for procreating one's ethnic group,[72] within the context of the Greek Civil War it primarily became an ideological and symbolic component of sexual and political violence. Thus, in the Greek case, it was mostly the "ethnic" in the service of the "political" and not the other way around.

Sexual terrorisation of underage political prisoners

In an effort to address the political and gender aspects of a wider nationalist and repressive ideology, however, I believe it is important to take a look at the state oppression of the juvenile detainees who were imprisoned as political dissidents despite their youth. Political repression and nationalist rehabilitation were exercised, even against the underage political prisoners,[73] with a distinct ferociousness that targeted both their political and gender identity. The ideological and moral basis of their abuse can be traced within the nationalist ideology and the religious and paternalistic narratives of the period. The torture of the underage inmates was primarily where the gendered characteristics and nationalistic patterns coincided with the goal of political annihilation.

The strategy of eradication enacted against the juvenile political detainees comprised enforcement of malnutrition, dehydration, extensive beating, forced nudity, lewdness and rape. The aim of these extreme forms of harassment was not only the signing of the Declaration of Repentance and the renunciation of Communism, but primarily the exemplification, terrorisation and the moral and bodily mortification of the dissidents. The male political prisoners at the Prisons of Intzedin (Crete), along with 330 under-age male exiles at the notorious exile camp of Makronisos, denounced the burning of the genitals with cigarettes and anal penetration with instruments.[74] Besides the Directorship and the guards, former members of paramilitary groups with criminal records were also employed as torturers; in fact, they were the ones conducting evaluation, supposedly to figure out whether the prisoners were male or female, and under the influence of drugs they sexually assaulted the juveniles.[75]

In regard to the process of both corporal and psychological violence, the gendered characteristics are noteworthy. Sexual difference and hegemonic masculinity were accentuated and proven effective when it came to creating anxiety, fear and vulnerability among the juvenile detainees. The minors were usually naked during interrogation and torture; nudity, along with sexual innuendo, caused vulnerability and shame. Dignity was particularly important in Greek society; sexual assault against male and female prisoners was perceived as a violation of the traditional code of honour and was extended to the family and community. The sexual victimisation of men was aimed at feminising them by challenging their masculine identity. There is an actual and symbolic parameter within the abuse of men, since a sexual assault or a stroke on the genital area would lead not only to their feminisation and vulnerability but also to sexual incompetence.

Sexual abuse and harassment of young women, on the other hand, was a common form of torture and remained the ultimate fear for the prisoners, leading to their traumatisation and stigmatisation. On many occasions, the naked and tortured female body became the locus of sexual fantasy and desire for the torturers.[76] Women, through nakedness, sexual assault and humiliation, were transformed into the "disposable other";[77] even female body functions such as menstruation and gestation were trivialised by the tormentors. Sexual violence by state agents was normalised but it also underlined the dominant form of masculinity, as cultivated within gender power relations and the continuous process of militarisation.

Besides the gendered parameters in the oppressive and torturous mechanisms employed by the state and its institutions, the gender characteristics of their abuse often coincided with the goal of political rehabilitation. Under-age female internees were exposed to a series of degrading and profoundly political practices such as their transfer from the female Averof prisons to the Kallithea and Kastoros prisons (Athens), where criminal convicts and prostitutes were also held.[78] Women emphasise in interviews and memoirs their distress, not only from the fear of sexually transmitted diseases and the demoralising effect that their confinement might have on what they referred to as "public women", but mainly from the fact that they were perceived as common criminals and not as political dissidents.[79] Moreover, the stigma that they wanted to overcome was not only that of the "dishonoured" woman resulting from their rape or assault, but also that of the prisoner and the criminal.[80] The specific mode of harassment was clearly targeting and dishonouring both their gender and political identity. Female activism and political awareness were deliberately equated with promiscuity, despite the young age of the detainees, in order to provide legitimisation of their confinement and abuse.

With explicit nationalist patterns, "hellenisation" through coercion, confinement and torture were also a vital part of the state-operated project and even applied to the underage internees. Physical abuse and sexual and moral humiliation, through demeaning practices such as urinating on the prisoners, had an advantage over their ethnic purification.[81] Even though the Greek Civil War was not an ethnic conflict, the supposedly ethnic differences were emphasised and politicised, mostly on the basis of "otherness". Consequently, the underage inmates were not only transformed into the political "other", they also became ethnic aliens and traitors of the nation, religion and family. The recuperation of minors was progressed as mandatory, since they were young and thus easily transformed into pure and virtuous Greeks. Nationalist and ethnic proscriptions were employed in order to justify the maltreatment and torture of the underage dissidents. Therefore, the internment, repression and especially sexual violence against minors trespassed "political" lines through the projection of national and ethnic purification.

Conclusion

The aim of this essay was to argue that sexual victimisation, especially rape in armed conflict, needs to be re-conceptualised as a political strategy and also as an intended socially and politically constructed experience. Gender violence – as expressed through rape – as a means of political eradication was not an isolated event of Greek political history. Especially during the Greek Civil War, it was primarily a constituent element of a state-operated nationalist project. The overall national project of regeneration was to obtain the consensus of the submission of women through patriarchal patterns of control and silencing. Therefore, the bodies, actions and beliefs of women had to be controlled and punished in case they were in a position to challenge the prevailing gender and power hierarchies. Within this imposed system of power relations, the reconstruction of the *ethnos* (nation) was passing through the "bodies" of women.

Notes

1. An earlier version of this essay was published by the *Journal of Modern Greek Studies* 29:2 (October 2011), pp. 251–77.
2. Bina D'Costa, "Coming to Terms with the Past in Bangladesh", in Luciana Riciutelli, Angela Miles and Margaret H. McFadden, eds, *Feminist Politics*

Activism and Vision. Local and Global Challenges, Toronto, Inanna Publications and Education, 2004, p. 227.

3. Tasoula Vervenioti, "Mnimes kai amnisies ton arheion kai ton martyrion gia ton elliniko emfylio: I Athina kai i eparhia, i igesia kai ta meli", in R. Van Boeschoten, T. Vervenioti, E. Voutyra, V. Dalkavoukis and K. Bada, eds, *Mnimes kai lithi tou Ellinikou Emfiliou Polemou*, Thessaloniki, Epikentro, 2008, pp. 81–102.
4. Regina Pagoulatou, *Exile. A Chronicle, 1948–1950*, New York, Pella, 1999.
5. MGA/Info XVI/Women, "Rapes", "Maltreatments and Attacks".
6. For more on recent trends of 1940s Greek historiography, see Giorgos Antoniou and Nikos Marantzidis, "The Greek Civil War Historiography, 1945–2001: Toward a New Paradigm", *The Columbia Journal of Historiography Online* 1 (Fall, 2003), available at www.columbia.edu/cu/history, and "The Axis Occupation and Civil War: Changing Trends in Greek Historiography, 1941–2002", *Journal of Peace Research* 41:2 (2004), pp. 223–31.
7. Riki Van Boeschoten, "The Trauma of War Rape: A Comparative View on the Bosnian Conflict and the Greek Civil War", *History and Anthropology* 1:14 (2003), p. 43.
8. Tasoula Vervenioti, *I Gynaika tis Antistasis. I eisodos ton gynaikon stin Politiki*, Athens, Odysseas Publications, 1994; idem, "Left-Wing Women between Politics and Family", in Mark Mazower, ed., *After the War Was Over. Reconstructing the Family, Nation and State in Greece, 1943–1960*, Princeton and Oxford, Princeton University Press, 2000, pp. 103–14; idem, *Diplo Vivlio*, Athens, Vivliorama, 2003.
9. Janet Hart, *New Voices in the Nation. Women and the Greek Resistance (1941–1964)*, Ithaca and London, Cornell University Press, 1996.
10. Margaret Poulos, *Arms and the Woman. Just Warriors and Greek Feminist Identity*, New York, Columbia University Press, 2009.
11. D'Costa talks about the creation of an "acceptable" national history, through the elevation of certain narratives, "Coming to Terms", p. 227.
12. See Hart, *New Voices in the Nation*, and Michael Herzfeld, "Within and Without: The Category of 'Female' in the Ethnography of Rural Greece", in Jill Dubisch, ed., *Gender and Power in Rural Greece*, Princeton, Princeton University Press, 1986, pp. 215–33.
13. Also see Vervenioti, "Left-Wing Women".
14. Margarita Kotsaki, *Mia zoi gemati agones*, Athens, Sighroni Epohi, 1987, p. 40.
15. According to Vervenioti the proportion of women in the Democratic Army in 1949 had reached 50 per cent, in the combat units 30 per cent and in the services 70 per cent. Tasoula Vervenioti, "I mahitries tou Dimokratikou Stratou Elladas", in I. Nikolakopoulos, A. Rigos and G. Psallidas, eds, *O Emfylios Polemos. Apo ti Varkiza sto Grammo*, Athens, Themelio, 2002, p. 126. For more on the women guerrilla fighters of the DSE see the account of Kostas Gritzonas: *Mahitries tou Dimokratikou Stratou*, Athens, Filistor, 2001.
16. Margaret Poulos, "Gender, Civil War and National Identity: Partisans during the Greek Civil War 1946–1949", *Australian Journal of Politics and History* 46:3 (September 2000), p. 418. Also see, Gritzonas, *Mahitries*, and Vervenioti, "I mahitries".
17. Interview conducted 9 April 2009, Athens.
18. See Vervenioti, "I mahitries", p. 137.

19. Indicatively see D'Costa, "Coming to Terms", and Cynthia Cockburn, "The Gendered Dynamics of Armed Conflict and Political Violence", in Caroline Moser and Fiona Clark, eds, *Victims, Perpetrators or Actors? Gender, Armed Conflict and Political Violence*, London and New York, Zed Books, 2001, pp. 13–29.
20. In relation to the forced incorporation in the private sphere and the traumatic reintegration of leftist women into civil society, see Tasoula Vervenioti, "Left-Wing Women", pp. 112–13, 119, and Hart, *New Voices in the Nation*.
21. Ilias Staveris, a political exile, reports in his personal archive, which contains archival documents from the Women's Movement from 1945 until the late 1950s, that 120,000 women were terrorised and abused (he refers to different forms of violence, including confinement, sexual, physical, psychological abuse and the overall terrorisation of women with no links to the Communist Party) either by members of the paramilitary groups or by the agents that the state had appointed (officers of the army and the gendarmerie). Staveris Archive, Box 4, Contemporary Social History Archives (ASKI).
22. Van Boeschoten, "Trauma", p. 44.
23. This is the argument that Van Boeschoten, "Trauma", p. 43, and Vervenioti, "I mahitries", p. 137, put forward, but it also emerges in the memoirs of women who joined the Democratic Army. Archival research, especially in the Archives of the United Democratic Left (Box 140, 145, ASKI), with data on the profiles of the political detainees and the personal archive of Ilias Staveris (ASKI) and the Memorandum (1987) of the Democratic Army to the United Nations, submitted in March 1947, also points to that direction. Plousia, a political exile and former partisan, disclosed that if she managed to flee to the "Mountain" she wasn't going to be captured and sent into exile; the interview was conducted 1 June 2007 at Trikeri, followed by a number of informal discussions in Athens, especially on 5 March 2008. Plousia's co-exiles, Eleni and Nitsa, adopt the same viewpoint in relation to the necessity of joining the Democratic Army as a mode of rescue: interviews 1–3 June 2007 and informal conversation on 5 March 2008, Athens.
24. Interview conducted 1 June 2007, Trikeri Island, Greece.
25. See Moser and Clark, eds, *Victims*, and S. Jacobs, R. Jacobson and J. Marchbank, eds, *States of Conflict: Gender, Violence and Resistance*, London and New York, Zed Books, 2000.
26. Heaven Crawley, "Engendering the State in Refugee Women's Claims for Asylum", in Jacobs, Jacobson and Marchbank, eds, *States*, p. 95; Jan Jindy Pettman, *Worlding Women: A Feminist International Politics*, London, Routledge, 1996.
27. Crawley, "Engendering", p. 95.
28. Van Boeschoten, "Trauma", p. 43.
29. Memorandum, p. 395.
30. Van Boeschoten, "Trauma", p. 44.
31. See Ilias Staveris Archive, Box 4 (ASKI), EDA Archive (ASKI) and Olympia Papadouka, *Ginekies Filakes Averof*, Athens, Diogenis, 2006, pp. 181–5.
32. Kostas Gritzonas, Mahitries, pp. 26–7.
33. Pagona Stefanou, an underage political prisoner, talks about the markers on leftist houses in her memoir, Pagona Stefanou, *Ton Afanon*, Athens, Themelio, 1998, pp. 50–1.

34. Van Boeschoten, "Trauma", p. 52 n. 7.
35. Interview with Eleni conducted 1 June 2007, Trikeri island.
36. MAY stands for *Monades Asfaleias Ypaithrou* (Country Security Units) and MAD for *Monades Asfaleias Dimosyntiritoi* (Municipal Security Units). See Polymeris Voglis, *Becoming a Subject. Political Prisoners during the Greek Civil War*, New York and Oxford, Berghahn Books, 2002, p. 71.
37. The collaboration of the armed paramilitary bands with the Security Forces was confirmed by the Minister of Public Order, S. Merkouris, on 20 March 1946. See *Oi misoi sta sidera*, ed. Panayiotis Aronis and Vardis Vardinoyiannis, Athens, Filistor, 1995, p. 15.
38. Wendy Bracewell, "Rape in Kosovo: Masculinity and Serbian Nationalism", *Nations and Nationalism* 6:4 (2000), p. 582. Van Boeschoten discusses the impunity as a means of ethnic and political cleansing in relation to silence and invisibility; "Trauma", p. 51.
39. For the cases of Glykeria and Pepi see Papadouka, *Ginekies*, pp. 182, 247–52. For Pepi's case see the Modern Greek Archives (MGA/Info XVI/Women Prisoners) and the Greek Literary and Historical Archive (ELIA) (*To Vima*, 6 and 14 February 1947).
40. Stavros Avdoulos, *To Fenomeno Makronisos*, Athens, Ellinika Grammata, 1998, p. 186.
41. Anna Solomou-Teriaki, *Mia Zoi mesa stis Kataigides*, Athens, Paraskinio, 2004.
42. Solomou-Teriaki, *Mia Zoi*, p. 109.
43. Solomou-Teriaki, *Mia Zoi*, p. 111.
44. Staveris Archive, Box 4, ASKI.
45. Pagoulatou, *Exile. A Chronicle, 1948–1950*, pp. 133–4.
46. Interview with Elisavet conducted 17 July 2008, Livadeia, Greece.
47. The DSE Memorandum (1987) uses the word "dishonour" in a number of instances as well as Gritzonas, *Mahitries*, in his account of women guerrilla fighters. Van Boeschoten, "Trauma", p. 49, and Vervenioti, "Left-Wing Women", p. 113, also comment on the employment of the term "dishonour" in the Memorandum in order to comment on the patriarchal attitudes of the Left.
48. Sharon Marcus, "Fighting Bodies, Fighting Words: A Theory and Politics of Rape Prevention", in Judith Butler and Joan W. Scott, eds, *Feminists Theorize the Political*, London and New York, Routledge, 1992, pp. 385–403 (388–9).
49. *States*, ed. Jacobs, Jacobson and Marchbank, pp. 1–2.
50. Antjie Krog, "Locked Into Loss and Silence: Testimonies of Gender and Violence at the South Africa Truth Commission", in Moser and Clark, eds, *Victims*, p. 203.
51. Van Boeschoten, "Trauma", p. 44.
52. Pettman, *Worlding Women*, p. 102.
53. Vervenioti, "Left-Wing Women", p. 112
54. Krog, "Locked"; Crawley, "Engendering"; M. Turshen, "The Political Economy of Rape: An Analysis of Systematic Rape and Sexual Abuse of Women during Armed Conflict in Africa", in Moser and Clark, eds, *Victims*; Liz Kelly, "Wars against Women: Sexual Violence, Sexual Politics and the Militarised State", in Jacobs, Jacobson and Marchbank, eds, *States*.
55. Interview conducted 17 July 2008, Livadeia, Greece.
56. Kotsaki, *Mia zoi gemati agones*, p. 66

57. Turshen, "Political Economy", p. 59.
58. Cockburn approaches these types of assault as a deliberate political strategy ("Gendered", p. 37). Also see Turshen, "Political Economy", pp. 55–68, and Krog, "Locked", pp. 203–16.
59. Papadouka, *Ginekies*, p. 183.
60. The political prisoners Elli, Zoe and Mairi, detained at the female Averof prisons, narrated this incident during their interview. Interviews conducted on 20 November 2006, Athens.
61. A number of similar assaults are included in the memoir of the political prisoner, Olympia Papadouka, *Ginekies*, pp. 181–5. Additional information can be found in the Personal Archive of Ilias Staveris, Box 4 (ASKI).
62. Maria Karagiorgi, *Perimenontas tin Eirini*, Athens, Proskinio, 2005, p. 149.
63. Karagiorgi, *Perimenontas*, pp. 150–1.
64. Krog, "Locked", p. 203.
65. See the Memorandum, pp. 33, 45–6, 50, 85–7, and Gritzonas, *Mahitries*, pp. 26, 34–5.
66. See DSE Memorandum, p. 33, and Gritzonas, *Mahitries*, p. 24.
67. The National Republican Greek League (EDES) was a nationalist guerrilla force, formed during the Axis Occupation. The other communist resistance organisations accused EDES of collaboration with German and Axis forces in order to gain control. EDES, backed by British forces, escalated to a significant political force of the Right.
68. See Van Boeschoten, "Trauma", p. 44.
69. Vervenioti, *Diplo Vivlio*, p. 76 n. 51.
70. This is the argument that Van Boeschoten also makes when discussing rape in the Greek Civil War in comparison to the sexual atrocities that took place in the Bosnian conflict, "Trauma", p. 44.
71. "Trauma", p. 44.
72. Indicatively, see Turshen, "Political Economy"; Krog, "Locked"; Vesna Kesic, "From Reverence to Rape: An Anthropology of Ethnic and Genderized Violence", in Marguerite R. Waller and Jennifer Rycenga, eds, *Frontline Feminisms. Women, War and Resistance*, New York and London, Routledge, 2001.
73. The legal age of adulthood in 1945 Greece was 20.
74. Papadouka, *Ginekies*, pp. 218–19.
75. Papadouka, *Ginekies*, p. 219.
76. Polymeris Voglis, *Becoming*, p. 136; Margarita Kotsaki, *Mia zoi*, pp. 65–71; Papadouka, *Ginekies*, pp. 181–5; Staveris Archive Box 4 (ASKI).
77. Kesic, "Reverence", p. 33.
78. Vervenioti characterises this transfer as a substantially political one, *Diplo Vivlio*, p. 145; Papadouka, *Ginekies*, p. 226.
79. Elisavet, interview conducted 17 July 2008, Livadeia, Greece.
80. Polymeris Voglis, *Becoming*, p. 213.
81. Papadouka, *Ginekies*, pp. 218–23.

4

Mass Rape and the Inscription of Gendered and Racial Domination during the Bangladesh War of 1971[1]

Nayanika Mookherjee

Bangladesh has undergone a double and disrupted postcolonial trajectory. In 1947, Indian independence from British colonial rule resulted in the creation of a new homeland for the Muslims of India by carving out the eastern and northwestern corners of the country as two widely separated territories, known as East and West Pakistan respectively. In the formation of Pakistan, Islam was the sole principle of nationhood unifying these two widely disparate units, separated not only geographically but also by sharp cultural and linguistic differences. Ostensibly they formed a single nation state. But it is important to remember that the Islam of Bengal, bearing the imprint of different historical and social forces, was not the Islam of Pakistan. "Orthodox" Muslims in other parts of South Asia also interpreted the practice of Islam in Bengal as too Bengali, equating it to being Hinduised (Hindus constituted a sizeable minority in East Pakistan). Moreover, real military and administrative power lay in West Pakistan and successive Pakistani regimes, reluctant to rely on religious allegiance alone, embarked on a strategy of forcible cultural assimilation towards the Bengalis of East Pakistan. Soon after Partition in 1947, the Bengali language was targeted to be replaced by Urdu as the only state language so as to purge Bengali culture of its perceived "Hindu" elements. The ensuing protests became the Language Movement which the Pakistani government suppressed on 21 February 1952 by shooting dead three students who were demanding that Bengali should be kept as a state language along with Urdu. The promulgation of martial law by General Ayub Khan in 1958 and the subsequent Pakistani discriminatory policies further accentuated the systematic reduction of East Pakistan to the status of a colony. West Pakistani civil, military, economic and administrative control led to "enormous disparities in the social and economic development of the two regions".[2]

In 1966 the Awami League (initially the Awami Muslim League) formed by Maulana Bhasani and H. S. Suhrawardy) under Sheikh Mujibur Rehman formulated the Six Point Demands, which represented a secular programme of political and economic development for the whole country within a broad democratic framework and paved the way for the demand for autonomy. An upheaval against the Ayub regime in 1969 lent further support. In the ensuing elections held in December 1970, under the leadership of Yahya Khan, the Awami League – led by Mujibur Rehman – won overwhelmingly and it became clear that he would lead Pakistan. When the Pakistani government refused to transfer powers to the elected representatives, by announcing the postponement of the Assembly session on 3 March 1971, Mujib called upon the people on 7 March 1971 to launch the struggle for national liberation through a movement of Non-Cooperation. However, under the command of Tikka Khan, a premeditated Pakistani military crackdown, "Operation Searchlight", ensued from the night of 25 March 1971. This crackdown involved firing upon and attacking student hostels and the civilian population and triggered a nine-month war of liberation by East against West Pakistan in 1971 (the Bangladesh War).

In the course of the war, between one and three million Bangladeshis were killed, though the exact figure is impossible to establish.[3] Additionally, rape took place on a wide scale. Figures for the number of Bengali women raped by Pakistani soldiers range from 200,000 to 400,000.[4] After the war, many recalled the statement by Sheikh Mujibur Rehman that three million had died and 200,000 women had been raped as indicating the order of magnitude of the devastation brought by the war. However, there was more to the issue of rape than even these figures revealed. Recent scholarship has also highlighted how the non-Bengali "Bihari" communities (considered to be collaborators of the Pakistani Army) were attacked by Bangladeshi liberation fighters during and after the war, with many being killed and many women being raped. Also, oral testimonies that I have gathered suggest that Bengali Muslim men were raped by West Pakistani troops, although in what numbers it is impossible to say. This was in response to the attacks and repercussions of the Pakistani army and collaborators. India joined the war on Bangladesh's side in December 1971, although it was already involved in providing training in guerrilla and conventional warfare. Intense guerrilla activities were carried out by the *Muktis* (the Bengali guerrillas) led by General Osmany and conventional warfare was carried out by the Indian forces (for the final ten days). This culminated nine months later in the establishment of a People's Republic of Bangladesh on 16 December 1971. As the war was being waged and ten million refugees poured across the border into India, Bangladesh was suddenly catapulted from relative obscurity into the headlines of the international press. With Pakistan being backed by China and America – and with the possibility of Russia joining India in support of Bangladesh – the Bangladesh war had the potential to erupt into an international crisis in the Cold War context.

Unusually, instead of shrouding the issue of rape in silence, the Bangladeshi government following the war publicly referred to women from all socio-economic backgrounds who were victims of rape by Pakistani soldiers as *birangonas* ("war heroines") to prevent them from being socially ostracised, and attempted to rehabilitate them. However, the opposite was the case with male rape victims whose testimony remains confined to oral statements gathered by researchers. This chapter draws on my ethnographic research into the public memories of sexual violence of the Bangladesh war of 1971 and seeks to explore and account for the differences between what happened in the two forms of rape, of women and men, and the ways they were dealt with by officialdom and in public discourse.[5]

Public discourse on rape of women and men in wartime

Historically, few measures have been taken to address rape against women committed during armed conflict. In order to redress this imbalance, there has been a recent focus by organisations and literature concerned with human rights on documenting testimonies of sexual violence in order to contribute to the formulation of gender-aware policies from the local through to the national and international levels. This literature usually presumes that sexual violence during wars is shrouded in postwar silence, making it imperative for feminists and researchers to "recover", "witness" and "speak out" about it. However, during the initial weeks of my fieldwork in Bangladesh, I increasingly unlearned the presumption about the silence of the history of rape within the meta-narrative of the war of 1971. Instead, I found evidence of the constant invocation of the history of rape in state discourse and policies which eulogised the women raped as "war heroines", both in documents published immediately after the war in 1972–73 and again in the 1990s, in exhibits in museums and in newspaper narratives of "real" "war heroines" that drew on oral history projects.[6]

All this contrasted sharply with the accounts that I also came across by liberation fighters and social workers of instances of male sexual violence toward other men. The narrative thrust of these stories was that in order to establish the religious identity of Bengali Muslim men during the war in 1971, West Pakistani soldiers constantly checked whether Bengali men were circumcised. Proof of their Muslim identity would be confirmed by the absent piece of skin on their penis following which they would be spared and usually allowed to leave. To Pakistani soldiers, the non-circumcised penis would be proof of a Hindu man who might then be killed. Humiliation and gendering is intrinsic to both the processes of the rape of men and the checks on their penis. Nonetheless, they are not similar incidents and one incident does not necessarily lead to another. The narration of these two instances of violation of men primarily functions to highlight what is considered by the narrator as the "depravity" of the Pakistani soldier "who *even* did *this*". However, there are various instances when the violation of men would be mentioned in passing and would seem "thin" evidence to scholars. The repetitiveness of these accounts is what makes these pieces of "thin evidence" interesting to explore. In the documentation of sexual violence of the Bangladesh war, however, there is no reference to instances of male sexual violence vis-à-vis the reiteration of the violent encounter of the "war heroines".

The public silence relating to male rapes stands in marked contrast to the constant evocation of the rape of women. One of the oft-cited reasons for the latter is that Pakistani soldiers primarily wanted to improve the genes of the Bengali Muslim people and populate Bangladesh with "pure" Muslims, since Bengali Muslims were considered to be "Hinduised", "half Muslims" and "impure".[7] But what were the parallel reasons for the violation of Bengali Muslim men? While the principal focus of this chapter is the rape of men and the subsequent silence concerning this, the role of the racial and gendered processes at work are highlighted by comparison with the rape of women.

Sexual violence and gendering identity during wars

Throughout the 1980s and 1990s, feminist scholars revisited war and conflict to establish the link between patriarchy and militarisation.[8] Their findings revealed that although war has been neatly classified as genderless, it is in fact one of the most gendered human activities. If rape is always a matter of power and dominance, rape in wartime will be shaped both as an act and in its broader significance by the types of power that are at issue in the conflict – nationalism, religious identity, caste, ethnicity, sexuality and politics.[9] Dramatic episodes of rape against women during collective violence serve as an indicator of the place that women's sexuality occupies in an all-male, patriarchal arrangement of gender relations, between and within religious or ethnic communities. In this sense, rape in war is part of a violent dialogue conducted between men – this being the other side of "the matrimonial dialogue between men in which women are exchanged as signs".[10] As Stiglmayer has noted in the case of Bosnia, "not because they are women, but because the women are Muslim, Croatian, or Serbian they are raped. And yet because they are women, men are using against them their most effective weapon: rape."[11]

These feminist theorisations on wartime sexual violence have been significant in identifying the intersections of ethnic, national, religious or cultural identity with gender in order to explain whether and when women are likely to be raped during situations of conflict. Since women are raped in part for what they symbolise, it is necessary to understand the social and cultural values and representations in which power is located in order to account for the victims of rape and the situations in which the rapes occur. However, there has been little work on sexual violence towards men apart from some scholarship related to slavery[12] and the recent Abu Ghraib violations.[13] Male rape in wartime, however, suggests that the gendered representation of power and dominance targets men as well as women, and hence involves multiple definitions of masculinity.

Particularly useful in this regard is the work of Judith Butler and Marilyn Strathern.[14] To get away from the notion that femininity invariably connotes the female body, Judith Butler shows how bodies become gendered through the continual performance of gender. She proposes that "gender is an identity tenuously constituted in time, instituted in an exterior space through a stylised repetition of acts".[15] Rather than performance, she refers to performativity, which is citational – it entails citing past practices, referring to existing conventions and reiterating known norms. Performativity thereby makes it imperative to explore the processes through which the body is gendered. This is similar to Marilyn Strathern's idea of "embodiment", which examines how gendered difference is produced and experienced in social transactions and discourse whereby the action and end become the gendered activity. As a result the gendered activity is not linked to the male or female bodies, but to the process and final version of the activity. By gender she means "those categorizations of persons, artefacts, events, sequences and so on which draw upon sexual imagery – upon the ways in which the distinctiveness of male and female characteristics make concrete people's ideas about the nature of social relationships".[16]

In the case of the 1971 Bangladesh War, the gendered performativity of rape ensured the feminisation and subordination of the person who was raped and the masculinisation of the rapist through the exertion of power. The "gendering of inequality" is ensured through wartime rape which imposes anonymity and a "weaker" sexuality on the raped, whether a woman or a man.[17] It brings to the surface, savagely and explicitly, familiar forms of sexual violence that are now charged with racialised and gendered discourses and supplied with a symbolic meaning – a meaning conveyed by the canonical 200,000 female victims in Bangladesh. Beyond the woman herself, rape affects the family, community and nation. It also aims to emasculate men who are raped, along with men whose women are raped.[18] The link between sexuality and the state is central to this formulation of masculinity and femininity through sexual violation.

The Bengali Muslim gendered and racialised

As mentioned earlier, in the formation of Pakistan, Islam was the sole principle of nationhood unifying two widely disparate units, separated not only geographically but also by sharp cultural and linguistic differences. Bengali Islam bore the imprint of different historical and social forces and was infused with beliefs and practices which represented the popular culture of Bengal. Revivalist movements in the nineteenth and twentieth centuries had sought to revitalise and purify Islam in Bengal, campaigning against what they regarded as "innovations, accretions and deviations" of "Indianised", "half converts", "nominal Muslims" and therefore "unreliable co-religionists".[19] Successive regimes in Pakistan drew on these precedents when they embarked upon a strategy of forcible cultural assimilation of Bengalis into the new Islamic nation state.

The so-called explicit intentions explain the nature of rapes by the West Pakistani army against Bangladeshi women and the publicity they received. It could have been the inevitable "by-product" of poor discipline or of soldiers who were briefly "out of control". This episode of mass violation was part of a campaign to rescue "Islam in danger" and to populate Bangladesh with a new race of "pure" Muslims and to dilute, weaken and destroy Bengali nationalism.[20] The imposition of religious, territorial, racialised and gendered boundaries was primarily marked on women's bodies and the womb. Rape of women in Bangladesh was apparently justified by the notion of *maal-e-gonemat* (the booty of war).[21] It became the essential means to change the racial makeup of the "Hinduised Muslim". The *Kafer*, who were seen to be small-boned, short, dark, lazy, effeminate, *bheto* (rice and fish-eating and cowardly), half-Muslim Bengalis of the river plains were to be converted into broad-boned, tall, fair, wheat-eating, warrior-like, brave, resilient, manly Muslims of the rough topography of West Pakistan.[22] Thus tropes of food, landscape and physicality created a distinction between Bengali Muslims and the West Pakistani army. This arose from historical, racial, religious, cultural and ethnic differences between East and West Pakistan. Ultimately the distinction can be traced back to a racialised characterisation of the Bengalis that had been effected by the British in the later nineteenth century, and which the West Pakistani military elite might have internalised.[23]

The "unnatural" violation of Bangladeshi Muslim men

After the war, from 1972 onwards, Bangladeshi newspapers and the 15-volume manuscripts of the Liberation war provided vivid and horrific testimony to the mass rape of women.[24] The same sources, by contrast, contain no reference to the sexual violation of men. However, in interviews with liberation fighters, incidences of sexual violence of men during the Bangladesh war would be cited: "Men were also raped during the Liberation War which is totally unnatural to Asian culture and society. Here it is more natural to rape women during wars" (interview by author on 21 March 1998, liberation fighter, Sayedurrahman Mahtab).

The references to the rape of men would often be made in the course of the discussion of silences in the histories of the 1971 war. This is different from reference to the rape of women, which is often articulated as public secrets that need to be repeated *as secrets*. References to the male rapes are enveloped in a zone of taboo and *Muktijoddhas* (liberation fighters) would often add, "I don't know whether I should be saying this." The comment highlights the point that rape of women is "natural" to "here" (in Bangladesh) and by the same token is an uncomplicated expression of masculinity. According to a director of the rehabilitation programme for women in 1971,

> During wars there is a tendency to take opportunity in [the] case of an attractive woman. A man would kill a man as the man could otherwise kill him. But women cannot kill a man and above all if a man killed a woman that would be cowardice. But these men could express their masculinity by raping her and rape is like killing a

> woman. (interview by author, 5 September 1998, Mrs Fulrenu Guho, Director, Rehabilitation of Refugee Women in India in 1971)

By contrast, the rape of men, which is negated in "Asian culture", is seen as shameful for perpetrator and victim alike. Indeed, the rape of men becomes a means by which the "depravity" of the perpetrators is highlighted by the narrator since the rapists have indulged in an "unnatural" sexual act. Here, the rape of Bengali Muslim men by the Pakistani soldiers – who are "pure Muslims" – is an attempt to undermine the masculinity of Bengali men, who are thereby considered to be homosexuals and thus made powerless with respect to the dominant, heterosexual form of masculinity.[25]

The absent piece of skin

The practice of male rapes is part of the larger process by which Bangladeshi men were controlled and categorised by the West Pakistani army during the war. In interviews and press reports, individuals from various socio-economic backgrounds pointed out that the Pakistani army confirmed they were Muslims by inspecting whether they were circumcised, predominantly at check points, which became the terrain of anticipated violence and rape. As mentioned earlier, this checking of the male population was an attempt to reconfirm the Muslim identity of the "Hinduised" Bengali Muslims and to seek the unity of East and West Pakistan based on religious unity. People would be asked to get out of public transports, undo their *lungis* (a sarong like cloth worn by poor men most of the time and by richer men within their homes) or trousers, and would be checked by the roadside. Those found to be non-circumcised were deemed to be Hindus and might well be killed.

Circumcision was a sign that the man in question was Muslim. Yet it simultaneously confirmed his status in the eyes of West Pakistani soldiers as an imperfect Muslim. He embodied not only the political threat of the break-up of the nation by the creation of an independent East Pakistan but also the deeper threat to the gendered order of Pakistan owing to his supposed lack of virility through the stereotype of the Bengali man as lazy, effeminate, small and dark. Paradoxically, the already suspect feminised Bengali Muslim needed to be reconfirmed as a Muslim but in the process further feminised through violation. This contributes to Strathern's theorisation of how gendered difference is produced and experienced in social transactions and discourse. Here the action and process of violation, terror and humiliation is manifested as a gendered activity, of the feminisation and racialisation of men.

Processes of interrogation of masculinity and emasculation thus epitomise specific aspects of ethnicity. Heterosexual manhood is equated to a pure Muslim manhood, metonymic with the Pakistani administration's construction of "pure" Islam in West Pakistan. The ethnic selves of the Bengali Muslims, which are viewed as more impure than "pure" Muslims, are constructed as being ethnically inferior. They are not only inadequate effeminate males with impure practices of religion and hence of a lower sexuality, they are also less than human. This is exemplified by the animal-like connotations of the Bengali Muslim, who is considered to be lazy, untrustworthy and conniving. This contrived animality allows him to be framed in behavioural terms as someone given to ruse and stratagem, similar to the Hutu constructions about the Tutsis in Rwanda.[26]

I have followed Strathern's concept of "embodiment" to show that the action and end of rape is the gendered activity that constructs the victims, whether women or men, as inferior because they are "feminised" and subject to a violent physical onslaught. Conversely, the same embodiment guarantees the masculinisation of the perpetrators and the domination of the Pakistani army. Since the frontier is one of ethnicity as well as gender, the bodies involved are simultaneously racialised through the surveillance of the absent skin on the penis and the rape of many of those who are precisely identified as Muslim because they are deemed to be an impure or inferior variant. The feminisation and racialisation of the Bengali Muslims highlight the gendered performativity of rape during collective violence which ensures the gendering of men and women's bodies as female and constitutes them as political signs, territories on which political programmes get inscribed.

Yet there remains a major difference in the relationship of rape to normal sexual practices. Since homosexual acts are thought to be reproved by "Asian cultures" generally, and perhaps especially by the military culture of the "warrior hill tribes" which informs the ethos of the West Pakistan army, rape of males was a taboo subject for perpetrators. As a calculated attack on Bengali Muslim masculinity, male rapes equally constituted a taboo subject for the Bangladeshi government after independence. It was not possible to declare victims the male equivalent of the *birangonas*, the women rape victims who were designated war heroines, without calling into question the gendered order of the new postwar state.

Conclusion

This chapter has attempted to address the racialised and gendered discourses inscribed on the bodies of men and women through sexual violence during the Bangladesh war. Feminist theorisation of sexual violence rightfully analyses the role of power, domination and subordination in these violent encounters. It is important not only to explore the experiences of these violations among men and women but also to understand their broader symbolic significance. Incidents of sexual violence have often been used by governments and states in order to further national interests. During the partition of India in 1947, the "abduction" and "recovery" of women across Hindu and Muslim communities pertained to more than just family and community. These events marked the formation of the new nations of India and Pakistan, where the kinship norms of purity and honour were articulated in a public discourse. In Bangladesh, the Pakistan Army's discourse of genetic inscription in the act of sexual violence against women seems to suggest an attempt to transform the very substance and personhood of Bengali Muslims into pure Muslims. It was also an attempt to leave behind a trace of the Pakistani soldier in the womb of Bengali women with the hope that the children born would reflect the characteristics of their biological father and thus of the nation of Pakistan. Once independence had been achieved, the eulogisation of raped women as "war heroines", and their rehabilitation, was also rooted in a modernist agenda that symbolised the dynamism of the new nation that arose out of the "traditions and taboos of Muslim society".

However, the rape of men constituted a hidden register of subordination during the war by which Bengali Muslims, while not killed as their Hindu fellow countrymen were likely to be, were "feminised" by means of violation and also ethnically stereotyped as inferior and only imperfectly Muslim. With independence, the consequences of the Pakistani practice of feminisation and racialisation, dealt with by open recognition and public repudiation in the case of women rape victims, were consigned to oblivion in the case of sexually violated Bengali men. To extend the same public recognition to male victims would be to undermine the re-gendering of the new nation in terms of the masculinity of its Muslim majority.

Notes

1. This essay was made possible by the Wenner Gren Foundation for Anthropological Research (New York).
2. F. Ahmed, "The Structural Matrix of the Struggle in Bangladesh", in K. Gough and H. P. Sharma, eds, *Imperialism and Revolution in South Asia*, London, Monthly Review Press, pp. 419–48 (422). See R. Sobhan, "Politics of Food and Famine in Bangladesh", *Economic and Political Weekly*, Bombay, 1 December 1979, for an account of these economic disparities.

3. The figure of three million dead is an upper limit (see Leo Kuper, *Genocide: Its Political Use in the Twentieth Century*, New Haven, Yale University Press, 1983), with Frank Chalk and Kurth Jonassohn putting the figure between one and three million (*The History and Sociology of Genocide: Analyses and Case Studies*, New Haven, Yale University Press, 1990).
4. Although 200,000 is the official number of women raped (see Susan Brownmiller, "Bangladesh" in her *Against Our Will. Men, Women and Rape*, in various government reports and press articles the number: London, Secker and Warburg, 1975, pp. 76–86; the higher figure of 300,000 was cited soon after the war; 400,000 was the number stated by an Australian doctor, Geoffrey Davis (*Banglar Bani*, Genocide Issue, December 1972). This figure has been used in recent books (M. A. Hasan, *Juddho O Nari* [*War and Women*], Dhaka: War Crimes Facts Finding Committee [Trust] and Genocide Archive & Human Studies Centre, 2002).
5. N. Mookherjee, *The Spectral Wound: Sexual Violence, Public Memories and the Bangladesh War of 1971*, Durham, NC, Duke University Press, forthcoming; idem, "'Remembering to Forget': Public Secrecy and Memory of Sexual Violence in Bangladesh", *Journal of Royal Anthropological Institute* (*JRAI*) 12:2 (June 2006), pp. 433–50; idem, "'My Man (Honour) is Lost but I still have my Iman (Principle)': Sexual Violence and Articulations of Masculinity", in R. Chopra, C. Osella and F. Osella, eds, *South Asian Masculinities*, New Delhi, Kali for Women, 2004, pp. 131–59. The research was originally undertaken in 1997–98.
6. S. Akhtar, S. Begum, H. Hossein, S. Kamal and M. Guhathakurta, eds, *Narir Ekattor O Juddhoporoborti Koththo Kahini* (*Oral History Accounts of Women's Experiences during 1971 and after the War*), Dhaka, Ain-O-Shalish-Kendro (ASK), 2001; N. Ibrahim, *Ami Birangona Bolchi* (*This Is the "War Heroine" Speaking*), Dhaka, Jagriti, 1994–95 (2 vols).
7. T. Ali, *Can Pakistan Survive? The Death of a State*, London, Penguin, 1983, p. 91; S. Brownmiller, "Bangladesh", in idem, *Against Our Will*, pp. 78–86; M. Guhathakurta, "Dhorshon Ekti Juddhaporadh" ("Rape Is a War Crime"), *Bulletin of Ain-O-Shalish Kendra* (ASK) (February 1996), pp. 6–8.
8. M. Cooke and R. Rustomji-Kerns, eds, *Blood into Ink: South Asian and Middle Eastern Women on War*, Colorado, Westview Press, 1994; C. Enloe, "When Soldiers Rape", in idem, *Manoeuvres: The International Politics of Militarizing Women's Lives*, Berkeley, University of California Press, 2000, pp. 108–52; J. S. Goldstein, *War and Gender: How Gender Shapes the War System and Vice Versa*, Cambridge University Press, 2001.
9. For varied analysis of sexual violence and conflict see V. Das, "National Honour and Practical Kinship: Of Unwanted Women and Children", in idem, *Critical Events*, New Delhi, Oxford University Press, 1995, pp. 55–83; U. Butalia, *The Other Side of Silence: Voices from the Partition of India*, New Delhi, Viking Penguin India, 1998; R. Menon and K. Bhasin, *Borders and Boundaries: Women in India's Partition*, New Delhi, Kali for Women, 1998; C. Enloe, "When Soldiers Rape"; R. Littlewood, "Military Rape", *Anthropology Today* 13:2 (1997), pp. 7–16; A. Stiglmayer, "The Rapes in Bosnia-Herzegovina", in idem, *Mass Rape: The War against Women in Bosnia*, trans. Marion Faber, Lincoln, University of Nebraska Press, 1994, pp. 82–169; D. Zarkov, "The Body of the Other Man: Sexual Violence and the Construction of

Masculinity, Sexuality and Ethnicity in the Croatian Media", in C. Moser and F. Clark, eds, *Victims, Perpetrators or Actors? Gender, Armed Conflict and Political Violence*, New Delhi, Kali for Women, 2001, pp. 69–82.

10. C. Levi-Strauss, *Elementary Structures of Kinship*, rev. edn, trans. J. H. Bill, J. R. Sturmore and Rodney Needham, London, George Allen and Unwin, 1969.
11. Stiglmayer, "The Rapes in Bosnia-Herzogovina".
12. See the reading of Toni Morrison's *Beloved* where she briefly alludes to the violation of male slaves, by R. Fields, "Tracing Rape: The Trauma of Slavery in Toni Morrison's *Beloved*", Women Writing Rape: Web Based Papers, University of Warwick, English and Comparative Literary Studies, www2.warwick.ac.uk.
13. J. K. Puar, "Abu Ghraib: Arguing against Exceptionalism", *Feminist Studies* 30:2 (2004), pp. 522–34.
14. J. Butler, *Gender Trouble*, London, Routledge, 1990; M. Strathern, *Gender of the Gift*, Berkeley, University of California Press, 1988.
15. Butler, *Gender Trouble*, p. 140.
16. Strathern, *Gender of the Gift*, p. ix.
17. N. Lindisfarne, "Starting from Below: Fieldwork, Gender and Imperialism Now", *Critique of Anthropology* 22:4 (2002), pp. 403–23; C. A. MacKinnon, "A Rally against Rape: Sex and Violence", in idem, *Feminism Unmodified: Discourses on Life and Law*, Cambridge, MA, Harvard University Press, 1987, pp. 81–92; Littlewood, "Military Rape".
18. Mookherjee, "My Man (Honour) Is Lost".
19. See Ali, *Can Pakistan Survive?*; R. Ahmed, ed., *Understanding the Bengali Muslims: Interpretative Essays*, Dhaka, University Press, 2001; A. Roy, *Islam in South Asia: A Regional Perspective*, New Delhi, South Asian Publishers, 1996, pp. 131–8, for an account of the various practices of claiming an Islamic identity based on Arabic origins.
20. N. Kabeer, "The Quest for National Identity: Women, Islam and the State in Bangladesh", discussion paper 268, Institute of Development Studies, 1989.
21. Guhathakurta, "Rape Is a War Crime".
22. *Kafer* is "used to designate non-Muslims, castigate Muslims of different opinion or to draw boundaries when alternative values and practices are explicitly rejected" (see K. Ewing, ed., *Shariat and Ambiguity in South Asian Islam*, Berkeley, University of California Press, 1988, p. 2).
23. For the colonial origins of a racial and gendered discourse concerning Bengali men, see M. Sinha, *Colonial Masculinity: "The Manly Englishman" and the "Effeminate Bengali" in the Late Nineteenth Century*, Manchester University Press, 1995, and M. Sinha, "Giving Masculinity a History: Some Contributions from the Historiography of Colonial India", *Gender and History* 11:3 (1999), pp. 445–60.
24. H. H. Rahmana, ed., *Bangladesher Svadhinota Yuddha Dolilpotro* (*Documents of the Bangladesh Independence War*), Dhaka, Gonoprojatantri Bangladesh Sarkar, Tathya Mantralaya (People's Republic of Bangladesh, Information Ministry), 1982–85, 16 vols.
25. See Zarkov, "The Body of the Other Man", for an analysis of a similar invisibility and absence of the reporting of male rapes in the Croatian media.
26. C. Taylor, *Sacrifice as Terror: The Rwandan Genocide of 1994*, Oxford, Berg, 1999.

5

Rape, Blaming the Victim and Social Control in Paramilitary Enclaves: An Approach to the Case of Colombia

Natalia Suarez Bonilla
Translated by Helen McPhail

For several decades Colombia has been a theatre of civil war. Since the mid-1960s, armed guerrilla movements began to challenge a power seen as iniquitous, and from the early 1980s they in turn have been violently opposed by paramilitary groups which are largely tolerated by the state. The highest price for the ferocious confrontations is paid by non-combatants: with the opposing forces calculating their strength on the scale of the suffering inflicted on law-abiding civilians, the latter have become the main target for violence aimed at harming the enemy. One of the particularities of this violence is, frequently, its gendered nature. In the enclaves controlled by armed activists, soldiers, paramilitaries and guerrilla troops it is normal practice to use violence, including rape, to instil discipline over the women's bodies and behaviour.

Such practices are exacerbated by the context of civil war but have earlier roots in discriminatory cultural beliefs and attitudes which perpetuate the helplessness of women and young girls.[1] In provoking the dislocation of family, social and community structures, such crisis situations correspondingly undermine mechanisms of protection and reparation.[2] This is seen in forced population displacement which, scattering families and communities, frequently exposes women and young girls to the violence of armed activists.[3] The pattern is aggravated by the collapse of the rule of law and the virtual impunity enjoyed by those responsible for such actions.

How significant are rapes committed in this context of civil war? How do they display territorial control and assert paramilitary power? Despite being victims within their own community, women who suffer sexual violence find that they are blamed by their own people. Can it be argued that acts of paramilitary violence are in effect legitimised by the population, because they reassert the traditional patriarchal order?

This article is the result of a long ethnographic study of different enclaves controlled by paramilitary groups. The data comes from interviews with local people about everyday life situations that are not necessarily related to the subject under study. In a context of heightened surveillance, where the control by armed men is so powerful as to be invisible, gendered violence can only emerge in stories of everyday life. Politically motivated conflicts, conflicts arising from security concerns, or those resulting from small scams, accusations of theft or jealousy, reveal the gendered forms of violence committed by paramilitary soldiers. For fear of reprisals, these events are narrated as rumour. The anonymous nature of rumour allows the speaker to remain outside of the story recounted. Therefore, stories of such gendered violence were reported as a set of rumours related in the course of everyday situations such as sharing a meal, listening to music or watching the sunset.

The place of sexual violence in the war

The armed struggle in Colombia brings together two forms of armed confrontation which complicate understanding of the conflict. One can be described generically as guerrilla warfare which was instigated by clandestine minority groups in the mid-1960s. Mostly hidden away in the countryside, these groups set themselves up in opposition to the central power. From the 1980s until the present day, these confrontations increasingly acquired the form of a full-scale civil war. In effect, minor currents which are close to the state structure have formed paramilitary groups to combat the guerrillas.

The violent clashes between these two groups of activists are particularly evident in the different territorial dynamics of the confrontations.[4] On the side of the paramilitaries can be seen a shared national desire for the control of corridors that are strategically essential for access to economic resources and the formation of enclaves in the zone of conflict, but under their exclusive control.[5] The guerrillas are more thoroughly established in a regional dynamic. It is a matter of ensuring control over the interior of the regions, notably in peripheral zones where the lesser presence of national institutions leaves the field open to the misappropriation of state resources and consequent clientelistic practices.[6] Finally, the conflict acquires a local dynamic which can be seen as a struggle within urban regions or even small hamlets. This encourages barriers between urban centres of administration, more easily controlled by paramilitaries or the national army, and a rural periphery in which guerrilla forces can operate more freely.

Whatever the intention and direction of such confrontations, they operate through the intermediary of the non-combatant population,[7] as the two warring sides use civilians to measure their capacity for territorial capture and control. It is against them that reprisals are directed; it is civilians who are massacred, displaced or "made to disappear" if they are seen as the enemy. In this sense, the term "combatant" or "belligerent" initially used with reference to those who fight, gradually comes to include the ensemble of the populations affected; the figure of "the enemy" becomes irreparably extended to include everyone, armed or unarmed, who can be defined as belonging to the other side.

The violence perpetrated against non-combatants takes various forms, including assassination, torture, forced disappearance and involuntary displacement. Gender-related violence – particularly the rape of women – is an essential element in the pattern.[8] The pattern varies with the different stages of the war.

During the phase of incursion into a territory, raping the women is a form of violence inflicted on civilian populations, while those close to the enemy are tortured to death – part of a strategy to destabilise the enemy. It is not possible for the actors to achieve the total submission or eradication of their enemies; but they can strike at the enemy persistently, hoping to provoke it into a state of political destabilisation which they hope will favour their cause. This effect sought by rape, among other factors, is based on an understanding of gendered relations in which women are the depositories of the community's honour.[9] Sexual violence fosters a climate of terror and humiliation in the enemy which is capable of driving all members of the targeted groups to flee the territory.

Rape is also practiced during the phase of settling in and consolidation of territorial control by armed groups. It is in particular a matter of dissuading the female civilian population, who may be suspected of emotional attachment to members of the enemy, from provoking the arrest, imprisonment or death of members of the armed groups.[10] Sanctions "for the sake of example", such as rape, are used by each side to hinder the enemy's objectives by making any form of rapprochement with the other side impossible.

This use of rape amongst the non-combatant population is not exclusive to zones of armed confrontation or the peripheral areas under the military control of an armed operator. Women and young girls who have left their own territory to escape the consequences of war are also exposed to sexual violence in their places of refuge.[11] This situation is widespread throughout the country and acts of violence against women, whether sexual, physical or psychological, reach alarming levels in Colombia.[12]

Despite the scale of the phenomenon, sexual violence as an element of armed conflict remains under-documented. In the protocols used in forensic medicine to carry out autopsies in the conflict zones, there is nothing to indicate to the official whether or not the victim has been raped. These crimes are generally not granted the same level of serious consideration as forced disappearance, assassination or torture. Obvious cases of rape are relegated to the domestic sphere, without any attempt to establish whether the act was committed by a paramilitary or guerrilla fighter. This relates particularly to the data collected each year by forensic medicine among victims of sexual violence: of the 53,800 sexological examinations undertaken between 1999 and 2002, one of the bloodiest periods of the civil war, no one considered the armed operators as potential perpetrators.[13]

The same failure emerges in the figures from governmental institutions charged with gathering and analysing national data on the situation of the female population.[14] It is accentuated by the absence of denunciation of rape by victims: silence is preferable to the fear of stigma and, indeed, to losing their lives.[15] The situation is by no means helped by official attitudes – those charged with receiving complaints never attempt to find out if complainants have been raped.[16] The absence of data on sexual violence in war also emerges in the reports prepared by Colombian NGOs concerned with human rights.[17] Despite their concern to gather as much information as possible on socio-political violence since the 1980s, very little material touches on acts of sexual violence.

The absence of precise data on the number of victims of sexual violence is also explained by the difficulty of recognising and identifying those responsible for such practices. The only known data come from 193 statements in a survey carried out in 2009 by the Colombian Constitutional Court.[18] Despite the modest size of the sample, the results of this work attributed 58 per cent of rapes to paramilitaries, 23 per cent to forces of order and only 8 per cent to guerrilla movements, with 9 per cent of the aggressors remaining unidentified. Despite these data, the true respective levels of responsibility on each side remain under-recognised.

Sexual violence as a method of social control

Although sexual violence against women is perpetrated by the various armed activists throughout Colombian territory, the practice takes a particular form in certain zones of the country under the exclusive control of paramilitary forces. Indeed, even without taking account of the revolutionary enemy, sexual violence against women persists across time as a perennial form of action aimed at maintaining paramilitary order.

This phenomenon is linked to the nature of the territorial control established by the paramilitaries. Although violence has been used to repel guerrilla warfare in some zones which have come under this paramilitary control, the risk of recapture remains. In consequence, a continued presence and sustained surveillance is indispensable in the liberated territory to prevent the development of new revolutionary centres. Apart from the establishment of a complex security system designed to reveal any internal enemy, territorial control also operates through military discipline over individual and collective behaviour. What the paramilitaries call putting in order or making people go straight means operating so that their word has the value of law and is universally accepted.

This system of territorial control by establishing paramilitary order in fact installs a permanent state of war. Order is established not with a genuine and identified enemy in view, such as revolutionary groups, but against a hypothetical internal enemy. The latter does not need to be under objective suspicion because of his past or his attitudes, it suffices for him to be "a carrier of opinion" to be seen as putting paramilitary order in danger.[19] The paramilitary forces thus pursue not merely hostile acts but any form of behaviour – whatever its purpose – which would defy their control.

Designating the enemy by its opinions can only operate when the paramilitaries impose their norms – the product of their view of the world – on local society. In proclaiming themselves the defenders of morals, the paramilitaries take charge of regulating social order. In the end they dictate the most intimate behaviour of each person: the paramilitary order can thus ordain the pattern of sexual behaviour, acceptable styles of clothing or hair, or forbid over-individualistic features such as tattoos or piercings.

It is characteristic of this regulation of behaviour that it cannot be questioned by the local population. Any form of resistance is taken as a manifestation of hostility towards the paramilitary authority: paramilitary power is not open to discussion. Because it compels cooperation, the possibility of criticism is simply excluded, as is any possibility of challenging the situation. With criticism and questioning removed, justification is no longer necessary. The paramilitary power has no need to explain its laws, but can designate its enemies, controlling them with fear of the force which may descend on them.

This is the context in which sexual violence can occur. Unfaithful women, or those whose clothing allows certain parts of their bodies to be glimpsed, as well as those who squabble over a man, risk humiliating sanctions that are frequently organised around public display of the female body undergoing punishment. Punishment thus contributes to an economy of the visible: rather than reprimanding the individual for acts committed, it is a matter of showing the punishment.[20] The manner in which those sanctioned are exposed to the view of others illustrates this wish to make a public display. As a witness recounted, who was later removed from this enclave,

> As for girls' clothing, particularly very low-cut dresses or mini-skirts, the paramilitaries took the megaphone and publicly told them to stop dressing like that if they did not wish something to happen to them. It might happen that, as punishment, the girls would be set to stitching up the offending part of their clothing which allowed the body to be seen in full public view in the middle of the central square. But one day a girl who reoffended had her shirt torn off with the comment: "You want to walk about naked? Well go on then, walk round the village completely naked!"[21]

The paramilitaries' use of such forms of public humiliation is the clear expression of the force of their moral injunctions and the need to obey them. But their power over the population was equally visible in the right that they granted themselves to dispose of women living in those areas. This happened in the hamlet of La Soledad in northern Colombia where the paramilitaries had turned rape of local women into normal behaviour. For more than four years they organised beauty contests for the village girls in order to assess and mark out their future victims. Many of the women, married or single, were to remain available for the paramilitary chief and his men. A young girl in the hamlet stated that the only way she could avoid rape was to flee:

> There was a paramilitary incursion into the village [...]. The paramilitary chief wanted me to go with him. But my father did not want

> this, nor did I. So he wanted to take me by force, he said that he would keep me alone, he even tried to rape me. One day he came to my house, although I didn't want to open the door to him because I was afraid, but in the end he managed to convince me because I was young and inexperienced. Then he came into the living room, he tried to touch me. But then my father came in and they began to fight. I went in between them to protect my father. In the end they told me that he must leave the village because they would kill him any time they felt like it.[22]

The opportunity to inflict sexual violence on women with total impunity shows the intrinsically gendered nature of paramilitary power, relating to the means and values socially attached to concepts of masculine and feminine.[23] This power exists on a wholly asymmetric basis by which force gave the right to appropriate women and to assume the privilege of sanctioning their sexuality. The paramilitaries use violence to regulate the unequal relations between men and women; the gendered control that they exercise is guaranteed by the use of violence and the effective death threat which weighs on the civilians. No resistance appears possible except flight.

Blaming the victim of sexual violence

In the spaces where authority is de facto represented by paramilitaries, no possibility whatever exists to denounce the aggressor to national institutions. Outside these territories, and despite the presence of official authority outside paramilitary control, women keep silent for fear of reprisals against either themselves or those close to them.

This silence over sexual violence cannot, however, be attributed exclusively to the daily climate of fear in these paramilitary enclaves. Sanctions against women, particularly those who transgress against the order by their conduct, gradually gain a certain collective approval. The persistence of a concept linking honour with women's sexuality contributes considerably to this attitude, and such ideas deny the women any autonomy over their own sexuality and reproduction. Although elsewhere in Colombia control over women is still limited to the private family space, in the armed enclaves it becomes guaranteed through recourse to armed men.

Although it is only the paramilitaries who punish guilty women, they depend on statements and denunciations from those who, preferring to be close to them, are quick to designate transgressors against the instituted order. In this sense, respect for order comes to lie not only with the armed operator but also with all those who identify themselves with the new authority to the extent of becoming its representatives within the community.

This situation is known to all, and particularly to women. All learn to live under this surveillance which extends throughout the population. As a result of this network the paramilitaries gain the advantage of being effectively omnipresent. In certain cases, women describe how they distrust even their own husbands – and, indeed, the paramilitary presence may be used to threaten wives with denunciation if they reject their husband's wishes or refuse to change their attitudes towards them. Husbands can threaten denunciation to the paramilitaries in order to exercise direct control over their wives, and particularly in respect of the conjugal duties which every wife should traditionally undertake: her husband's sexual fulfilment and running the household.[24]

In such ways surveillance of women's sexuality is undertaken, indirectly, by the community as a whole. This can be seen in reactions to acts of sexual violence inflicted on women reputedly of light morals. Thus, in a community on the Pacific coast of Colombia, young girls without a fixed partner find themselves exposed to group rape. Paramilitaries in their territory identify women whose conduct does not conform to the stipulated norms and appoint one of their number to seduce the girl. He takes her to a designated isolated spot: once there, she will be gang raped by the group.

In the daily climate of fear afflicting the local population in paramilitary enclaves, the recurrent attitude towards the violence of the order is to regard victims as the authors of their own fate. Inhabitants no longer seek to understand the motives for a rape or other forms of violence which may be applied to certain women in their community; they consider instead that if a women is the object of such acts of violence it is because she had something to answer for. Without being direct or uttered in public, most comments – discreetly and a posteriori – justify the paramilitary activities as part of "maintaining order".

This attitude of stigmatising the victim is not restricted to zones of conflict. In the country as a whole, women who are victims of aggression do not denounce such actions, despite the existence of a legal framework for this purpose.[25] Yet gendered social representations have greater force than legislation: instead of protecting the victim, society as a whole as well as the officials charged with gathering denunciations restore these acts of violence to the private domain, either seeing them as a problem for the couple concerned or linking them to a psychological problem for one of the couple, or as retribution against the victim for not having fulfilled her marital duties.

In the paramilitary enclaves this phenomenon takes on a new form: the exercise of patriarchal authority escapes from the personal and private domain and the armed operator assumes the right to discipline women in their bodies and their behaviour.[26] In the community as a whole, by administering acts of punitive aggression through diffuse sanctions such as community blame and reproof, it guarantees the reproduction of gendered social order. By applying blame, individuals confirm the existence of a group which respects and takes responsibility for assignations of gender. Transgression can lead only to stigmatisation of the wrong-doer. This attitude implicitly traces the frontier clearly established between those who adhere to the social order imposed by the armed agency and those who transgress against it, at the risk of violence and the application of social exclusion for transgressors. In this sense, the paramilitary actor, having imposed a state of order, can rely on the civilians who themselves have become watchful supervisors.

In the light of the situation in Colombia, we see how in a civil war acts of violence against women, and particularly rape, can be defined in large measure as the continuation of practices already established before the war. Gender stereotypes – but also other forms of socio-economic, racial and ethnic discrimination which exist in times of peace – remain intact or even intensified in critical times. They explain the particularity of acts of violence committed against women in times of war. In effect, those who make war apply the range of inequalities which propose violence against women as part of a patriarchal order. This is evident in the many obstacles encountered by efforts to denounce rape in this country.[27] The various reports on the subject all emphasise the fact that sexual violence is largely absent from public narratives. This is particularly true of those who rely on the current policy of reparation for victims of armed conflict to seek justice from national authorities. Many women may now denounce the disappearance or assassination of those close to them but sexual violence is never mentioned in their statements. For them, as for the many officials charged with gathering their statements, rape is still not seen as a criminal act.

In this sense, a time of war confirms the subordinate status of women in both public and private life.[28] The latter exists as the moment when the power of domination emerges in its most radical form, thus reaffirming the representations of a traditional feminine figure and her unalterable place in Colombian society.

Notes

1. Laura L. O'Toole and Jessica R. Schiffman, eds, *Gender Violence: Interdisciplinary Perspectives*, New York University Press, 1997.
2. Krishna Kumar, ed., *Rebuilding Societies after Civil War*, Boulder, CO, Lynne Rienner, 1997.
3. Susan R. Sanday, "The Socio-Cultural Context of Rape: A Cross-Cultural Study", in O'Toole and Schiffman, eds, *Gender Violence*, pp. 52–66.
4. Carlos Miguel Ortiz, "Actores armados, territorios y poblaciones", *In Análisis politico* 42 (2001), pp. 67–75.
5. Fernan. E. González, Ingrid J. Bolívar and Teófilo Vásquez, *Violencia politica en Colombia. De la nación fragmentada a la construcción del Estado*, Bogotá, CINEP, 2003.
6. Maria Victoria Llorente and Malcom Deas, eds, *Reconocer la Guerra para construir la Paz*, Bogotá, CEREC, UNIANDES, Editorial Norma, 1997; Y. Arauca, "Politics and Oil in a Colombian Province", PhD dissertation, Oxford University, 1991.
7. François Jean and Jean-Christophe Rufin, eds, *Economie des guerres civiles*, Paris, Hachette, 1996.
8. Oxfam International, "La violencia sexual en Colombia. Un arma de guerra", 2009, at www.oxfam.org/sites/www.oxfam.org.
9. Nancy Farwell, "War Rape: New Conceptualizations and Responses", *Affilia* 19:4 (2004), pp. 389–403.
10. Natalia Suarez, "Le travail de résistance des femmes persécutées dans les situations de guerre: le cas de la Colombie", in J. Freedman and J. Vally, eds, *Persécutions des femmes, savoir, mobilisations et protections*, Paris, Edition de Croquant, 2007, pp. 273–86.
11. In 2008, 70 per cent of displaced persons were women. Of this number, 15 per cent had been victims of rape, of which 52.9 per cent occurred before they were displaced. See Registro Unico de Accion Social (RUPB), 2008, pp. 165–8.
12. Fondo de desarrollo de las Naciones Unidas para la Mujer (UNIFEM), "Situación de la mujeres en Colombia", 2007, at www.acnur.org/biblioteca/pdf/3809.pdf.
13. Luz Piedad Caicedo, "Acceso de las mujeres a la justicia en el marco de la Ley 975 de 2005", in *VII Informe sobre violencia sociopolitica contra mujeres, jóvenes y niñas en Colombia, 2006–2007*, Bogota, 2008.
14. Luz Piedad Caicedo, "Gravedad penal de la violencia sexual cometida en el marco del conflicto armado colombiano", at www.humanas.org.co/html/doc/ponencias.
15. Amnesty International, "Cuerpos marcados, crimines silenciados" 2004, at http://www.amnesty.org/es/library/info/AMR23.
16. Luz Piedad Caicedo, "Acceso de las mujeres".
17. Oxfam International, "La violencia sexual".
18. "Auto 092 por la dignidad de las mujeres victimas des desplazamiento", 9 March 2009, at http://inforiente.info/index2.
19. Hannah Arendt, *Les origines du totalitarisme. Le système totalitaire*, Paris, Seuil, 1972, p. 154.

20. Michel Foucault, *Surveiller et punir. Naissance de la prison*, Paris, Gallimard, 1975, p. 69.
21. Interview with Carlos, displaced from the region of Santander, Cucuta, April 2007.
22. Interview with Jimena, a young displaced girl from the Atlantico region, Cucuta, 2007.
23. Françoise Héritier, *Masculin/féminin la pensée de la différence*, Paris, O. Jacob, 1996.
24. Elisabeth Brusco, *The Reformation of Machismo. Evangelical Conversion and Gender in Colombia*, Austin, University of Texas, 1995.
25. In Colombia, among the various laws which sanction violence towards women, we find law 1257 of 2008 which recognises violence against women as a violation of human rights. Similarly, national legislation includes different international instruments relating to the human rights of women, such as the United Nations declaration on the elimination of violence towards women, and the Belem do Pará Convention.
26. Christine Delphy, *L'Ennemi principal*, vol. I, *Economie politique du patriarcat*, Paris, Syllepse coll. Nouvelles questions féministes, 1998.
27. Farwell, "War Rape".
28. Nasreen Mahmud, "Crimes against Honour: Women in International Refugee Law", *Journal of Refugee Studies* 9:4 (1996), pp. 367–82.

6

After "Teutonic Fury", "Belgian Fury"? Fact and Fiction in the Revenge of Belgian Soldiers in the Rhineland in 1923

Anne Godfroid

Translated by Helen McPhail

On 19 November 1940, King Leopold III travelled to Berchtesgaden to meet Chancellor Hitler at the Berghof. The king expected assurances over his own future fate and that of his nation but the conversation took an unexpected turn. As he sought to explain the development of national public opinion in Belgium, Leopold III referred to the behaviour of German soldiers during the First World War – Hitler himself had of course been one such soldier. The Führer reacted promptly to the reference: he spoke of the allied forces of occupation in the Rhineland, the Saarland and the Palatinate and their behaviour which, he asserted, had been much worse than that of the German troops in occupied Belgium. According to him, some 17,000 rapes had been committed in the Rhineland alone; this had not happened in Belgium, where such crimes would immediately have incurred the death penalty.[1] This view clearly bears the stamp of propaganda – the 17,000 rapes supposedly perpetrated by the occupying forces bear some relation to the figures put forward in relation to the campaign against colonial troops, or the *Schwarze Schmach* (black shame), stationed in the Rhineland.[2] At its peak, in the spring of 1921, coloured soldiers were accused of committing more than a hundred rapes every day. The campaign attacked France but spared Belgium, whose *Force publique* (colonial troops from the Belgian Congo) was not present in the Rhineland. While for psychological and practical reasons France used colonial troops in its contingent posted to the left bank of the Rhine, Belgium preferred to send troops from its own homeland. In November a ministerial circular gave explicit instructions "not to accept the engagement of colonial natives" and to demobilise young coloured conscripts who would previously have joined the corps of Congolese volunteers established in August 1914.[3] More than 15,000 men were sent to the fourth occupation zone, close to the Belgian frontier around Aachen. From December 1920 veterans, war-hardened by a static war of nearly four years, were gradually relieved on the field by young conscripts, the *miliciens*. These men who had experienced the war in very different ways – in the trenches for the former, living under invasion and occupation for the latter – now took on the role of occupying force. How did the climate of cohabitation between yesterday's occupied inhabitants and occupying forces develop, once they had reversed their roles in this way? What was the weight of revenge in relationships between the two communities?

German troops committed rape during the Great War. During the invasion, from August to October 1914, sexual assaults were listed among the acts of violence recognised under the heading of "German atrocities". These did not form part of a systematic policy of terror but, to borrow the expression of John Horne and Alan Kramer, figured at "the individualist extremity of the spectrum of war crimes";[4] in other words, these attacks constituted an extension of other forms of current violence such as mass executions, arson or looting. For Stéphane Audoin-Rouzeau such patterns of behaviour constituted a brutal but localised response by soldiers to the trauma of modern war, facilitated by the absence of the norms and constraints of peacetime.[5] The frequently laconic or fantastical accounts of sexual attack and mutilation gathered by the various commissions of enquiry set up to investigate enemy crimes played a crucial role in the images that developed of "German atrocities".[6] For the Allies, these rapes, whatever the frequency or their cause, became virtually the symbol of the atrocities.

After the invasion, other forms of sexual aggression were committed throughout the hostilities by soldiers from fighting and support units in the occupied territories. Mainly occurring under the excuse of "flirting", they bear witness here more to the quest for sexual pleasure by young men deprived of women and keen to avoid the circuit of official prostitution and its constraints, notably condoms.

Beyond the River Yser, in the small part of Belgium not occupied by the German army, accounts of atrocities abounded, narrated by refugee witnesses and sustained by rumour. Many references can be found in the personal writings of soldiers, even if they veer away from explicit accounts as soon as any sexual reference is approached.[7] By fostering hatred of the enemy among the combatants, accounts of atrocities contributed greatly to their consent to a long war. Thus an infantry soldier described how one day in September 1914, when volunteers were lacking for a dangerous mission, his company commander "stepped out in front of us, saying that the Germans were in the course of raping our wives and killing our children, therefore they must be chased out of the country but we were too cowardly and selfish because no one wanted to take part in this dangerous mission".[8] The persistence of hatred of the *Boche*, already deeply rooted in combatant imaginations, was exacerbated further by the frequent harangues from leaders, who deliberately sustained the memory of German cruelty.

As the end of the war approached, "hatred of the *Boche* was expressed more vigorously than ever", coloured with a wish for revenge that was sharpened by their crossing of a landscape scarred by occupation and the enemy's retreat.[9] It was in this state of mind that Belgian troops prepared to move into German territory in accordance with the Armistice agreement. In their ranks, the future Abbé Froidure, who was then a war volunteer barely 20 years old, took part in the relief of troops stationed in occupied territory.[10] From 22 March 1919 he was stationed at Neuss in the Rhineland and his memoirs recall his state of mind in the spring of 1919, on the march into Germany: "Ah! We didn't exactly feel like men of peace as we headed there ... We were being sent 'over there'? Excellent, excellent!" Now "they would see what their victors could get up to! We had taken part in two great offensives and we still remembered clearly the indescribable horrors of war and of massacres."[11] In these circumstances, entering enemy territory was in part linked to an imagined idea of punishment, in particular that of the fantasised conquest of the body of German women.

Fulgence Masson, who became the Minister for War on his return from captivity, addressed the army, anxious to defuse any inclination towards reprisals:

> The population of the occupied territories owes respect and obedience to our officers and our soldiers; they in turn must exercise the authority invested in them without empty pride; they must take care not to harass or cause conflict, but they must never forget that they have before them our nation's most implacable and most pernicious enemy.[12]

In reminding everyone of all the rights and duties which fell on them as part of this conventional wartime occupation, the minister hoped to limit arbitrary acts.

On the German side, the imminent arrival of Belgian troops stirred the worst fears. At Trier the Rhinelanders showed their relief seeing

American troops, whose arrival dissipated their greatest fear: that of having to live side by side with Belgian or French soldiers.[13]

Yet in the zone of Belgian occupation, from January 1919 the monthly reports on German morale (*Rapports mensuels sur l'état d'esprit des populations allemandes*) mentioned the surprise at the behaviour of an occupying force that was so deeply feared. The Minister for War's exhortations appear to have been heard. Thus we learn that "Certain letters praise the conduct of our officers and soldiers. Some even express surprise at the leniency of our troops. It is clear that German officers and soldiers who committed or witnessed enemy cruelty in Belgium expected reprisals"[14] and in the following month that "The fear of reprisals, which at the beginning of the occupation was characteristic of the German population in respect of the Belgians, has given way to a certain esteem, even a certain sympathy."[15] This tendency continued through the following months even if "The population has had certain fears on the subject of the relief of our troops, and feared that the relieving troops would be thinking of reprisals. These fears have already vanished."[16] It was at this precise moment that Abbé Froidure arrived in the Rhineland, in the state of mind described above.

Despite this the attitude of the Belgian troops on the field did nothing to arouse strong criticism during the first months of their presence in Germany. At most there were complaints at their lack of flexibility in comparison with the other occupying powers, in the application of inter-allied instructions. The climate began to deteriorate after the signing of the Treaty of Versailles – a tendency which subsequently only grew worse with the arrival in the Rhineland of soldiery from the class of 1919 and later years, who were gradually incorporated from December 1920. This situation was considered alarming by the Minister for Foreign Affairs in Brussels, who favoured the political dimension of the Belgian presence on the left bank of the Rhine: "The Rhinelanders judge us almost exclusively on the actions of our army of occupation (AO). This decision should be less often forgotten by the AO High Command",[17] recalled the foreign affairs representative on the spot. In March 1922, Brussels explicitly linked the increase in the number of deplorable incidents registered during recent months with the arrival of new troops, who as it happened came from the military class of 1920.[18] This observation fits in with the comment by Bruno Cabanes, who sees the presence of young people who had lived through the occupation but not the trenches as the main reason behind the clashes between civilians and soldiers of the French Army of the Rhine by young people who had lived through the occupation but not the trenches: "the lack of respect [...] towards the civilian population is connected both to the phenomenon of youngsters outbidding one another in hatred of the enemy and to the bravado proper to young generations, fed at times by a feeling of guilt at not having been able to contribute to the war effort".[19] To restrict such outbursts the French General Degoutte, Commander in Chief of the occupying forces, strongly advised holding seminars for young soldiers designed to raise their sensitivities to the duties of their task: "We are not required to Frenchify the left bank of the Rhine", he stated,

> This population is German and France is not in the habit of annexing people against their will [...] we must try to dissipate the prejudices which a century of Prussian domination has fixed in their minds [...] All this was understood almost instinctively by the troops who entered the Rhineland at the beginning of the occupation. Remarkably, it has been understood all the better because of the sufferings of those troops in the war: the infantry more than other branches of the army, the regiments from the North more than those from other regions. Their attitude of calm, dignity and reserve made a great impression on the population. It matters that among our young troops who now hold the place of honour on the Rhine, without having endured the ordeal of the trenches, these traditions are respected more than ever.[20]

The tendency which General Degoutte deplored in the French ranks emerges equally on the Belgian side from examination of the archives of the field courts martial,[21] established in June 1919 on the left bank of the Rhine. Charged principally with repressing infractions of the military penal code – desertion, insubordination, abandonment of post and so forth, representing almost half of the files opened between September 1919 and September 1920[22] – they passed judgement on a steadily growing number of German citizens accused to various degrees of attacks on the security of the occupying troops. The publicity that surrounded these charges, of which the proportion grew from 20 to 33 per cent in twelve months, "effectively helped the organisation of billeting and the maintenance of order when troops were on the march in the Belgian zone of occupation".[23] These two axes of activity – infractions of the military penal code on one side and assaults, real or supposed, on the occupying troops on the other – appeared to be the priority concern for the occupying authority in matters of repression.

Among cases implicating the inhabitants of the occupied Rhineland, attacks on individuals (blows and wounds, rape and indecent attacks, murder and assassination) rose to 5.5 per cent, heavily outnumbered by attacks on goods (with theft and stealing food in the lead). This legal state of affairs relates to the situation recorded in the *Statistique judiciaire de la Belgique* for 1919: more suspects were charged and convicted for thieving than for personal assault. Yet this reduction in the absolute number of people convicted for acts of physical violence corresponds less to a development in behaviour than to a shift in the authorities' preoccupations over public order. "Faced with the volatile social climate and the perception of a revolutionary threat [...] the repression of theft as a priority could be interpreted as illustrative of the State's determination to protect rights of property, the corner stone *par excellence* of this bourgeois economic order."[24] In this climate, charges of sexual assault also diminished in number. Although during the entire nineteenth century they reached the level of 1 per cent, in 1915 they represented only 0.6 per cent of crimes and misdemeanours leading to conviction.[25] The tendency began to reverse from 1920: the number of convictions by the local Belgian courts for rape, attempted rape and indecent assault is twice as large in 1921 as in 1915. Was the situation the same on the left bank of the Rhine?

The records of hearings and registers of verdicts of courts martial in Aachen, systematically analysed for the periods of September 1919 to November 1920 and from January to December 1923, make it possible to calculate the activity of Belgian military jurisdiction in the occupied territories.

During the first period, before the massive incorporation of the military class of 1919, some 15 cases of sex-related charges were prosecuted by one of the three courts martial sitting in the Belgian zone of occupation, or 1.5 per cent of the thousand convictions recorded. Nine cases implicating Belgian soldiers, as authors or co-authors of the acts concerned, took place in the Aachen jurisdiction where they were heard. Two of them incriminated war volunteers who had been enrolled since 1916. The first complaint related to acts that occurred on 28 June 1919, the date of the signing of the Treaty of Versailles. On that day in Brandt Krauthausen, private soldier Marcel Sody attacked Anna Beuel, a minor aged 16 years.[26] The exact circumstances of the attack remain unknown: perhaps the events taking place that day in the Galerie des Glaces at Versailles, and the conflicting feelings that they aroused, may have been the catalyst. Whatever the truth, the case did not pass unnoticed: the Judge Advocate General (*Auditor General*), on the request of the cabinet of the Minister for War, enquired with Judge Advocate (*auditeur militaire*) as to the outcome of this case. Having proceeded to confrontations, taken various courses of enquiry and ordered a medical report several months after the event, the latter concluded that guilt was not established. Yet the superior officers of the accused saw it as their duty to send the case to the court martial, considering no doubt that the evidence was convincing and deeming the acts too serious to give rise to a simple disciplinary sanction. However, the accused was acquitted by the court martial, which made much of his "general good conduct" and his "courage during the campaign of the autumn of 1918" which had indeed earned him a "mention in dispatches" in March 1919. Circumstances spoke in his favour: in 1916, aged barely 17, he had left Belgium secretly and reached the recruitment office in Folkestone (Great Britain), where he joined the Belgian army. The victim was ushered out without any further hearing. Two months after the verdict, Marcel Sody was demobilised and returned home. The case left no trace in his military file and did not hinder his moves to obtain pensions and decorations. René Scohy, on the other hand, another war volunteer who also joined the army in 1916, suffered a different fate after he and Gustave Verschaffel were charged with the rape of Bertha Lampman. His denial of the events, which took place on 13 August 1919 in Heinsberg, was disproved by the victim's statement and above all by the confessions of his accomplice. Both were condemned conditionally, in November 1919, to three months in prison. The judge justified the apparently mild sentence through the attenuating circumstances which he took into account on behalf of those charged, in their case their prolonged presence at the front (although marred by incidents), their drunken state at the time of the events and above all "the low morality of the victim".[27] After more than two months in preventive detention, the accused were finally demobilised even before the verdict was announced. Their personal files still show the guilty verdict, despite an amnesty in 1921.[28]

Seven other cases of immoral behaviour were tried during this period by the Aachen court martial. All concerned volunteer recruits who joined the army at the end of 1918 and early 1919. Not a single charge of rape was recognised and sanctioned by the court.

The second period, from January to December 1923, was marked by strong political tensions: evidence of passive resistance increased among the Rhineland population following the Franco-Belgian occupation of the Ruhr basin, which began in January of that year. Reinforcements were sent by the two governments and measures of repression against German civilians became more frequent, hence the considerable increase in the number of verdicts pronounced by the three courts martial located in the Belgian Zone – from one thousand in 1920 and 1921 to 2058 in 1923.[29] Still within the jurisdiction of Aachen, 14 cases of sex-related charges implicating Belgian soldiers as authors or co-authors were heard. All involved new recruits, mainly from the military classes of 1921 and 1922. They formed what Nicolas Mignon called the "generation of the Ruhr",[30] the last one to reach "the age of reason" in 1914 and thus to have retained very vivid memories of the war and the occupation. Among the often multiple charges against them (public drunkenness, theft, abuse of authority etc.) figure also indecent assault or moral turpitude for actions which would otherwise clearly have been qualified as rape. For example, three soldiers from the 1st Regiment of Mounted Chasseurs, Raymond Luycks, Pierre Dehombreux and Georges Duffos, were accused of rape; they attempted to exonerate themselves from this accusation by arguing the consent of the plaintiff, which the enquiry was quick to disprove. One of the accused had in fact held his scabbard in front of the young girl's eyes throughout the rape, removing all possibility of resistance on her part and enabling the three men to achieve their purpose. Despite the results of the enquiry, the accused men were finally found guilty only of indecent assault and escaped with a prison sentence of eight days. This tendency to re-designate the crime during the case with the aim of minimising it was almost systematic. Stanislas Jeannesson has noted a similar phenomenon in the functioning of French courts martial in the Ruhr: rapes became attempts, the victims consented and so forth.[31] But this factor was not, according to him, the only one to explain the marked differences between French and German statistics in relation to attacks. After a summary enquiry, certain cases turned out to be pure inventions of German propaganda and left no trace in the files of military justice.

In Belgium, this belief was so widespread that certain accusations were immediately regarded with suspicion. The comments of the Belgian Ministry of National Defence are eloquent in this respect: to his colleague in Foreign Affairs, who sought details on a specific file, Devèze replied that "the precedents in general show the extent to which the complaints of the *Reich* are vexatious and devoid of foundation. It is extremely unfair to give them greater credence than they deserve."[32] For his part, although he conceded that in effect "certain misdeeds imputed to the Belgian occupying forces were without doubt invented or at least strongly exaggerated by the Germans", Rolin Jacquemyns, Belgian High Commissioner in the Rhineland territories, equally deplored the attitude of some of our soldiers who "frequently behave as if the occupation was the continuation of the war and their revenge for the German occupation of Belgium [...] with conduct more appropriate to times of war than peacetime". Jacquemyns added that "this state of mind explains both the exaggeration of sentences applied to Germans and the great indulgence showed in the repression of the many misdemeanours committed by the Belgian soldiers".[33] And in fact the German population was convinced that they were suffering from a denial of justice. Their local press was full of articles vilifying the Belgian military justice and its total lack of fairness. Because the ordinary man appeared not to expect anything from the iniquitous Belgian military justice, he turned to the German authorities (notably to the *Reichskommissar*). The latter in effect encouraged victims to denounce sex crimes in which they were said to be the victim by establishing lists which they then circulated widely. Under the title of *Denkschrift über die Ausschreitungen der Besatzungstruppen im besetzen rheinischen Gebiet* are listed the assaults committed by the occupier. The edition of January 1923 recorded 300 such cases, including 170 indecent assaults. The periodic updates show figures rising on each occasion.[34]

The local press did not restrain its eagerness and was quick to note incorrect behaviour by members of the occupying army. Thus in August 1921 the *Deutsche Allgemeine Zeitung*, under the provocative headline "Promotion of Belgian Culture?", related the attack suffered by the young Maria Steffens some months earlier. The young girl and her friend, another girl, were accosted by a Belgian soldier who demanded to see their identity cards. Because they were unable to show them the soldier ordered the older girl to follow him to the patrol which was waiting not far off, forbidding the younger girl to go with them under threat from a weapon. The solder seized the arm of the older girl and forced her to follow him. When they reached a small copse, he raped her. Unfortunately the young girl, after several confrontations, was unable to identify her attacker. From that moment, despite witness statements and a medical report, the case was dismissed. The official steps having remained fruitless, the case appeared in the press and ended up on the desk of the Minister for Foreign Affairs in Brussels, who could only deplore the negative publicity which once again besmirched Belgian military justice in occupied territories.

To avoid further similar cases, the main representatives of Belgian justice and foreign affairs *en poste* in Germany, the Judge Advocate General and the High Commissioner, pleaded together for a reform of military justice in the occupied territories, to improve transparency. Too many complaints, although apparently well founded, were in effect dismissed either because the author of the facts remained unknown, as in the Steffens affair, or for no reason at all. Impunity, already frequent in cases of sexual attack,[35] is multiplied here by the implication of the military element in the different phases of a legal procedure inherited from the nineteenth century.[36] It was in fact a matter for the suspect's superior officer to decide, on the basis of a rapid enquiry, if the file should be passed to the Judge Advocate, if he should sanction it through disciplinary measures or if he should dismiss the case. If the case was handed over to military justice, it was then examined by a commission in which the public prosecutor was the only civilian. His report of enquiry and his conclusions were then submitted again for the approval by the accused's superior officers before being officially recorded. Finally, the application of the verdict depended on the Divisonal General who could decide to suspend its execution. Further, the military status of the accused and his behaviour in the military sphere influenced the severity of the sentence, which was automatically duplicated in this kind of affair by a moral evaluation of the victim.

In conclusion, if the sources examined to date have not made it possible to define precisely the circumstances of the rape, nor even to hear the victim, they have the merit of throwing light on the existence of a two-speed military justice, showing, whatever the charge, systematic indulgence for Belgian soldiers, "members of the corps", and severity towards German civilians. In this respect, sexual attacks were only one example among many others. Yet contrary to the fears of the inhabitants of the Rhineland anticipating occupation and what the future Belgian occupants might have announced, the reprisals so much feared by the one side and so fantasised by the others occurred only marginally and unsystematically. They were almost exclusively the actions of new recruits from the liberated territories in the aftermath of the Armistice, resisting cultural demobilisation. As deplored by General Degoutte, Commander in Chief of the occupying troops, the soldiers of the young classes did not adopt "the spirit of moderation and correction for which their seniors were honoured in the aftermath of the victory".[37] In this particular context, branded more than ever by the seal of the war culture, rape appeared to these young men as a means of acquiring the "privilege of masculinity" sometimes seen as a rite of initiation, sometimes as a manifestation of group solidarity, sometimes as the satisfaction of an impulse.

Notes

1. Jan Velaers and Herman Van Goethem, *Leopold III. De koning, het Land, de Oorlog*, Tielt, Lannoo, 1994, pp. 587–8.
2. On this point the following can be consulted: Estelle Fohr-Prigent, "La 'Honte noire': Racisme et propagande allemande après la Première Guerre mondiale", *Relations internationales* 106 (2001), pp. 165–77; Jean-Yves Le

Naour, *La honte noire. L'Allemagne et les troupes coloniales française 1914–1945*, Paris, Hachette, 2003; Sally Marks, "Black Watch on the Rhine: a Study in Propaganda, Prejudice and Prurience", *European Studies Review* 13:3 (1983), pp. 297–334; Keith Nelson, "The 'Black Horror on the Rhine': Race as Factor in Post-World War I Diplomacy", *Journal of Modern History* 42:4 (1970), pp. 606–7; Dick Van Galen Last, "De zwarte schande", in Patrick Nefors and Pierre-Alain Tallier, eds, *When the Guns Fall Silent*, Brussels, pp. 107–26.

3. *Journal militaire officiel*, 1914 and 1919; Willy Wilmotte, "Le corps des volontaires congolais", *Militaria Belgica*, Brussels (2008), pp. 93–104; "Une armée noire pour la Belgique", *Belgique militaire*, Brussels, 2296 (1920), pp. 683–4.
4. John Horne and Alan Kramer, *German Atrocities 1914, A History of Denial*, New Haeven, Yale University Press, 2001.
5. Stéphane Audoin-Rouzeau, *L'Enfant de l'ennemi (1914–1918). Viol, avortement, infanticide pendant la Grande Guerre*, Paris, Aubier, 1995, p. 77.
6. Between August 1914 and October 1915 the Commission d'enquête sur la violations des règles du droit des gens, des lois et des coutumes de la guerre, created on 7 August 1914, published 22 *Rapports sur la violation du droit des gens en Belgique*. A second Commission, established in February 1919, published four volumes of *Rapports et documents d'enquête*. Finally, the Bryce Commission, instituted in December 1914, completes the group.
7. On this point, the following are useful: Benoît Amez, "La guerre 1914–1918 des soldats belges à travers leurs écrits non publiés. Analyse de leur expérience de guerre et des facteurs de résistance", dissertation, UCL, 2003; Bruno Benvindo, *Des hommes en guerre. Les soldats belges entre ténacité et désillusion 1914–1918*, Brussels, Archives générales du Royaume, Etudes sur la Première Guerre mondiale, no. 12, 2005, pp. 117–21; Ria Christens and Koen De Clercq, *Frontleven 14/18. Het dagelijks leven van de Belgische soldaat aan de Ijzer*, Tiel, Lannoo, 1987; Marc Maloir, "Les récits de guerre belges: analyse d'une forme d'expression d'un vécu de souffrance", dissertation, UCL, 2002.
8. Diary of an anonymous soldier, 04.09.1914, Musée royal de l'Armée et d'Histoire militaire (MRA), Personalia 14–18, no. 2, cited by Bruno Benvindo, *Des hommes*, p. 122.
9. Report on troop morale, 09/10/1918, MRA. General HQ, IIe section, no.10, postal service and censorship, cited by Bruno Benvindo, *Des hommes*, p. 119.
10. Paul Guerin, "Edouard Froidure. Un ecclésiastique dans son temps", *Feuillet de la cathédrale de Liège* 42–45 (1999), pp. 3–30.
11. Edouard Froidure (Abbé), *Coup d'oeil sur le passé*, vol. I, *Un gamin en guerre*, Brussels, Stations de Plein Air, 1967, p. 187.
12. "Ordre du ministre à l'armée et au peuple, Bruxelles, 9 janvier 1919", *Journal militaire officiel* (1919), p. 20.
13. *Rheinische-Westfälische Zeitung*, 11/12/1918, quoted by Erika Kuhlman, "American Doughboys and German Fraüleins: Sexuality, Patriarchy and Privilege in the American-Occupied Rhineland, 1918–1923", *Journal of Military History* 71:4 (2007), pp. 1077–1107.
14. Ier Rapport mensuel sur l'état d'esprit des populations allemandes, 05/01/1919, MRA, Fonds Moscou, 185-14-6924: Armée d'occupation, IIe bureau.
15. IIe Rapport mensuel sur l'état d'esprit des populations allemandes, 07/02/1919, MRA, Fonds Moscou, 185-14-6924: Armée d'occupation, IIe bureau.

16. IVe Rapport mensuel sur l'état d'esprit des populations allemandes, 07/04/1919, MRA, Fonds Moscou, 186-14-6924: Armée d'occupation, IIe bureau.
17. Divergences de vue entre autorités civiles et militaires en territoires occupés. Griefs contre armée d'occupation et sûreté militaire en territoires occupés; Note from Capelle to the Minister for Foreign Affairs, 04/09/1922, Ministère des Affaires étrangères (MAE), Brussels. Political dossier 10.448.
18. Divergences de vue entre autorités civiles et militaires en territoires occupés. Griefs contre armée d'occupation et sûreté militaire en territoires occupés; Agissement des troupes d'occupation 03/1922 MAE, Brussels. Political dossier 10.448.
19. Bruno Cabanes, *La victoire endeuillée. La sortie de guerre des soldats français (1918–1920)*, Paris, Seuil, 2004, p. 248; and idem, "La 'guerre après la guerre': détestation de l'ennemi et violences antiallemandes chez les soldats français (1918–1920)", in Stéphanie Claisse and Thierry Lemoine, eds, *Comment (se) sortir de la Grande Guerre*, Paris, L'Harmattan, 2005, pp. 99–100.
20. Note by General Degoutte, Commander in Chief of the occupying troops, 24/07/2930, Service Historique de l'Armée, Armée Française du Rhin, carton 90, dossier 3.
21. Rolande Depoortere, *La juridiction militare en Belgique 1796–1989. Compétences et organisation. Production et conservation des archives*, Brussels, Archives générales du Royaume, Miscellanea Archivistica Studia, no. 15, 1999, pp. 184–6; John Gilissen, "La juridiction militaire belge de 1830 à nos jours", in *Actes du colloque d'histoire militaire belge (1830–1980)*, Brussels, 1981, pp. 477–8.
22. Between 1914 and 1919, while the Belgian army was on a war footing, military misdemeanours and crimes constituted 80.5 per cent of the total of cases dealt with by courts martial, against 19.5 per cent of misdemeanours and crimes in common law. Stanislas Horvat, *De vervolging van militairegerechtelijke delicten tijdens wereldoorlog I. De werking van het Belgisch Krijgsgerecht*, Brussels, VUB Press, 2009, p. 123.
23. "Nos soldats se font respecter", *Belgique militaire*, Brussels, 2230 (1919), pp. 18–19.
24. Xavier Rousseaux and Antoon Vrints, "La répression étatique d'un phénomène de crise social. Le banditisme pendant et après la Première Guerre mondiale en Belgique", in Nefors and Tallier, eds, *Quand les canons*.
25. Axel Tixhon, "La poursuite et la répression de la 'violence' en Belgique (1820–1900). Le discours de la statistique cirminelle", in Ginette Kurgan-van Hentenryk, ed., *Un pays si tranquille. La violence en Belgique au XIXe siècle*, Brussels, ULB, 1999, p. 68.
26. Report of hearing. Affaire Sody Marcel, October 1919, Archives Générales du Royaume AGR), Anderlecht, Auditorat militaire (Moscou), 1722-1-190 and personal dossier Sody Marcel, Office central de la Matricule (OCM) Evere, 101717.
27. Account of hearing. Case of Scohy, René/Verschaffel, Gustave, November 1920, AGR, Anderlecht, Auditorat Militaire (Moscou), 1722-1-189 and Register of verdicts. Affaire Scohy, René/Verschaffel, Gustave, November 1920, AGR, Anderlecht, Auditorat Militaire, 81.1.
28. Law of 28 June 1921, modifiying and extending the amnesty law of 31 October 1919. Moniteur belge, 7 July 1921, p. 5042.

29. Gilissen, "La juridiction", p. 477.
30. Nicolas Mignon, "La Belgique francophone et l'occupation de la Ruhr (1923–1925). Occupation et représentations", dissertation, UCL, 2005, p. 156.
31. Stanislas Jeannesson, "Ubergriffe der französischen Besatzungsmacht und deutsche Beschwerden", in Gerd Krumeich and Joachim Schröder, eds, *Der Schatten des Weltkriegs die Ruhrbesetzun 1923*, Essen, Klartext, 2004, p. 214.
32. Letter from Devèze to Jaspar, 14/08/1922, MAE. Political dossier, 10.448, *Actes de violence à charge des troupes belges de l'AO*, 1918–23.
33. Rolin report, 09/10/1922, MAE, political file. 10.448. *Divergences de vue entre autorités civiles et militaires en territoires occupés. Griefs contre armées d'occupation et sûreté militaire en territoires occupés.*
34. Georg Reismüller and Josef Hofmann, *Zehn Jahre Rheinlandbesetzung. Beschreibendes Verzeichnis des Schrifttums über die Westfragen mit Einschlusz des Saargebietes und Eupen-Malmedys.* Breslau, 1929, pp. 144–5.
35. According to the *Statistique judiciaire de la Belgique* established in 1915, one crime in two against persons where the perpetrator remains unknown or where the charges are revealed to be insufficient is of a sexual nature. *Statistique judiciaire de la Belgique. Statistique pénale 1915*, Brussels, 1920, p. 12.
36. Stanislas Horvat, *De vervolging*, pp. 189–260.
37. Note from General Degoutte, Commander in Chief of the occupying troops, 24/07/1920, SHAT, AFR, carton 90, dossier 3.

7

The Practices of War, Terror and Imagination: Moor Troops and Rapes during the Spanish Civil War

Maud Joly
Translated by Helen McPhail

In 1947, the programme for the first Congress of the Unión de Mujeres Antifascistas Españolas (Spanish Women's Anti-Fascist Union) reproduced members' speeches from various occasions. Their subject was Republican women's experience of the violence of the Spanish Civil War and the early years of the Franco regime. Paintings, engravings and photographs recalled the martyred heroines, the shelling, the shaving, the prison atmosphere, as well as the rapes. A drawing – unsigned, undated – shows a rape scene. The man is hanging, the woman lies on the ground with her breasts and sexual parts naked. Her face shows only terror and pain.

The scene immediately raises comment: it emphasises the dual formula of sexualised penalties in representations of the Spanish Civil War: man killed/woman raped. In other respects it clearly represents a violent assault committed at the rear, on civilians in their homes, at the heart of a destroyed village. The overturned chair indicates the looting of the household which has accompanied the devastation of bodies. The location of the violence is thus indicated clearly. A second observation concerns the identity of the executioners: two Moor soldiers are shown in the background as they move away with a final look at their supposed victims. On the walls of the ruined village the insignia of the Spanish Phalange and the crooked cross, or swastika, designate – from a post-war Republican point of view – their allegiance to the camp of those known as nationalists. In addition, these two men are carrying, respectively, a rifle and a blood-stained knife. Attributes and instruments of violence among the Moor troops, these weapons refer to their part in the summary executions and mutilation of bodies.

This deliberately frightening image is a brutal evocation of rape by Moors which contributes as much to the exposure of violence in war

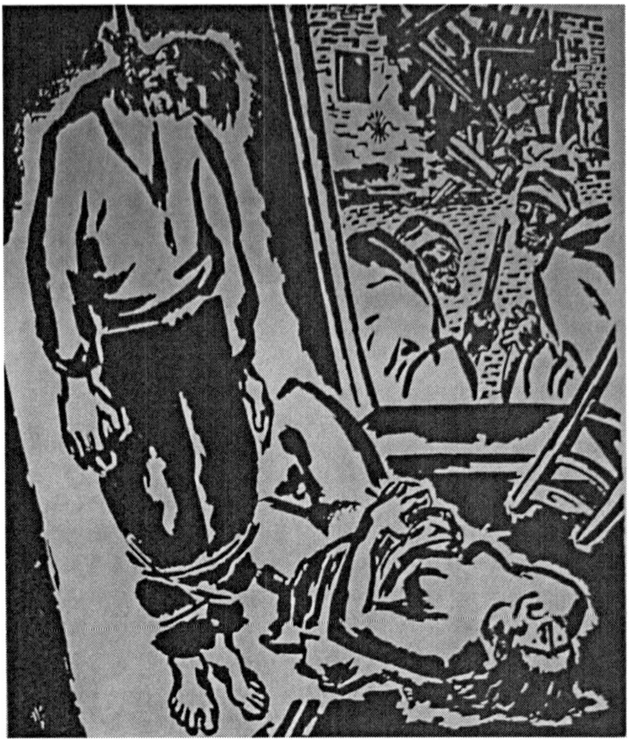

Figure 7.1 Untitled. Unión de Mujeres Antifascistas Españolas, Consejo Nacional, 1947 (Fundación Pablo Iglesias, Biblioteca/Archivo: b 4013).

as to the creation of "the brutal enemy". We note that the very nature of this document poses the essential question of sources which depict these events – traces relating to these rapes are rare and fragmentary. The historian relies almost exclusively on various accounts and images, sources of immediacy, created by men and women who have not raped or suffered rape but who have witnessed these acts; these rapes have left no traces of legal, police or medical proceedings. Some military documents testify to the application of punitive sanctions against the rapists, but they remain marginal to the extent that the majority of rapes were perpetrated in a broad context of impunity – notably in the early months of the war, characterised by the brutal advance of the Nationalist front and the need to overcome the enemy rapidly. This is why oral history constitutes a precious source to throw light on certain shadowy areas – yet the essentially intimate nature of the violence neutralises the words of victims, then and now. The identity of the rapists intensifies the taboo aspect of the outrage, insofar as they are associated with savage African barbarity.

There is no reason for these circumstances to remain as an obstacle to consideration of this subject. Indeed, we must try to use the sources available to grasp both the meaning of these rapes as a symbolic authentication of the time of war and the scope of the "real", in other words, the reality of the practice of rape by this identified and designated group.

Creating the fear of rape, creating the enemy rapist: instruments of conquest and submission

Republican literature transferred a crystallisation of fears of rape on to a generic enemy: the "savage Moor". Multiple rumours circulated around this Other, reflecting simultaneously reality experienced, reality feared and reality reconstructed from experiences or accounts of the past. The Moor embodied barbarity in the service of the Nationalist project, part of an "imagining of horror" from the first weeks of the reconquest of national territory. This imagining of horror was awakened by and through the Civil War, but its foundations took root in the Moroccan colonial war, the final wartime cultural reference for Spanish society.[1] The first marker of the transfer of violence, the repression of revolutionary movements in October 1934, was characterised by a "re-run" of acts of colonial violence, including sexual assault.[2] In fact the "Africanists", officers leading the operations in Morocco, mobilised Moor troops in the Asturias who served as shock troops in the application of terror. In accounts of these events, rape – simultaneously real and phantasmagoric – holds a significant place. The martyr figure of the miner's wife, often the young, innocent and virgin woman, assaulted and sexually tortured, functions as the symbol of a barbarity imported from Africa which transgresses rules of behaviour towards enemy bodies, male or female. The immediate reawakening of this memory of 1934 explains the circulation during the Civil War, from July 1936, of rumours of rapes committed by the Moors. Such rumours formed part both of the process of the creation of the enemy and of expressing the violence of war. The Moor, the brute imported by the Nationalist Spanish enemy, is simultaneously the rapist, the foreigner, the Black and the wicked libidinous savage. These representations are saturated with racial prejudice, and sexual and scatological fables.

Raid/rape: the Republican accounts of violence and looting premises go along with looting/violating the body. The female body is related to the warrior's reward. A warrior who is foreign to the national political stakes of the conflict, including military mobilisation, should receive a material reward. This view of a potential sexual aggressiveness, exacerbated by the stakes of the outbreak of the war, feeds the fear of the acting out itself. Announcement of the arrival of African soldiers in a locality thus creates gusts of panic among the civilian population. The troops' advance is accompanied by the advance of rumour (this uncontrollable and proliferating branch of speech) about rapes, and provokes disturbance and flight. Submission and domination of the territory to be conquered is achieved simultaneously by applying violence and implementing terror by exacerbating collective fears. At the heart of the accounts of fear of the brutal and rapist Moor, a key point contributes to description of his savagery and animality, and to illustrate the climate produced by his passage through a district: an animal-warrior giving a terrifying cry. And this cry functions as "the announcement of rape", the sad divertissement of horror, between alcohol, excess and fury.

In the Spanish Civil War the word of the authorities – political and intellectual – held pride of place. It expressed the war and gave it meaning. It constructed the registers of Good and Evil, defined the contours of the opposition between "Them" and "Us", between barbarity and humanity. It transmitted the projects of a group by its sufferings as well. The utterances became part of an ensemble "of ideas, deeds, values and myths" which made group cohesion and the pursuit of the war effort possible and which formed the foundation of propaganda at the time of the Civil War.[3] Thus discourse developed in the two camps on the Moorish soldier, developed by recognised writers: they spoke of the sexual violence which men embody and commit in times of war. Depending on the speaker, the conclusion differed: instilling terror in the enemy camp or denouncing enemy barbarity, dwelling on courses of action deemed paradigms of the enemy's cruelty. In both cases the discourse on violence is part of the creation of fear or of the creation of the enemy: two processes eminently political and ideological, constituents of the economy of speech in war time.

In the early days of the war a veritable instrumentalisation of the power of imagination, and of fears linked to the figure of the "Moor-rapist", was established on the Nationalist side, to announce rape through verbal means. A tool for the mobilisation of one's own camp and a weapon of war to frighten the enemy, the radio supplied an extremely suitable means of diffusing and instrumentalising rumours about the brutality of the Moor troops. By announcing military actions with Moor troop participation, it was part of the creation of terror.

The famous speeches of General Queipo de Llano are enough on their own to illustrate how fear of the rapist-Moor was exploited by the military authorities of the Nationalist camp. Two extracts, from 23 July 1936 and 29 August 1936 respectively, offer examples:

> Our brave Legionnaires and Regular troops have taught the Reds what it is to be a man. At the same time, they taught their women too who, now, have finally known real men and not castrated militia men. Kicking and shouting will not save them. (1936)[4]

> Up until the present day, I know that many munitions and other equipment have fallen into our hands, as well as numerous male and female prisoners. The Regulars are immensely pleased! (1936)[5]

Phrases of rare violence, these two extracts exemplify the thought-provoking intensity of the violence of this war – as much in the choice of words as in the acts described. The Nationalist general makes skilful use of the threat of rape by the Moors as a psychological weapon designed to terrorise the enemy and also to humiliate him by proclaiming the outrage to his women. To "enable rape" of the enemy by a foreigner – seen as nearer to a savage beast than to a civilised human – intensifies his degradation, ridicules his honour and symbolically makes the military leadership more powerful. The women's body is represented as a front, and looting it advances elimination of the male enemy and the whole group. In presenting rape by the Moor troops as the expression of primitive impulse, the general clearly shows such violence as natural. The use of possessive pronouns shows the extent to which these violent men "belong" to the commander who skilfully uses their sexual aggression to "tame" the enemy. Rape is here imagined as a genuine weapon of war: by excluding the domain of masculinity from Republican men, mastery of this weapon helps to affirm the exclusive possession of masculine values[6] by Nationalist men. This virile power is evoked by showing power over bodies which are described in a state of total subjection. Bodies are seen unambiguously as objects. This type of discourse illustrates the application of a "didacticism through terror"[7] characteristic of the first period of the Civil War. The Moor troops are imagined, represented and proclaimed as punitive expeditionary forces. The impact of these words is considerable, particularly because the "narrative of cruelty is in itself a form of cruelty inflicted on the hearer".[8] On the subject of these addresses, Yannick Ripa speaks of the "constant appeal to violence, the abusive, commonplace and pornographic denigration of the enemy".[9]

On the Republican side, identification of the figure of the violent Moor joins the discourse that functions by testifying to violence suffered, part of the identification of war "atrocities". The words of politicians or intellectuals represent – in their reappropriation – the intimate experiences, individual and collective, of rapes in times of war. It thus constructs identifying narratives through the application of the "transmutation of trauma by 'Ourselves', the 'Us'"[10] and develops documentation designed to alert international opinion. It mobilises the emotional springs relating to diffusion of the rumour of the brutal Moor. A further degree of instrumentalisation of the imagining was constructed around these troops from North Africa: in focusing on a sensitive element in the repertoire of forms of violence in war – true and/or false – it summarises eloquently the cruelty of an enemy who employs brutal foreign soldiers to undermine resistance. This contributes to the construction of Woman as victim-figure, symbol of the civilian population overtaken by war. The rape of their women by foreign invading soldiers is compared to the rape and looting of national integrity, both physical and symbolic – a nation in which the two sides dispute exclusive and legitimate membership.[11] To offer this nation to looting in its incarnation as Woman is close to high treason, to symbolic soiling of the nation.

The theatre of war constitutes one of many aids to the diffusion of these forms of discourse. Germán Bleiberg's play *Sombras de héroes*,[12] produced in 1937, evokes the rape of a Republican woman by a Moor soldier in the Basque country. An assault which precedes the victim's summary execution, the rape is the consequence of the Spanish commanding officer's gift of the bodies of Red women to the sexual appetites of the Moors. At the heart of the plot, this gift operates in an ambiance of laughter, scorn and sadistic play. The rape is perpetrated with the complicity of the military hierarchy, in a secluded place. The victim then becomes a ghost haunting the survivors, and linked to the ruined landscape of the town of Guernica: martyrdom of towns and martyrdom of bodies are one. The theatre is a mirror sensitive to the challenges of war, so that singular writing, the setting of genuine experience, for and by the group, transmits the collective experience. It is a gift, a precious substance for the study of the word which constructs the representation of the war. It illustrates the impressive mobilisation of pen and ink in this struggle to utter the truth of the war, at the very moment of its events.

What about the correspondence between the word and the reality of the acts exposed? How, through the feelings expressed in the chaos of war, is it possible to identify the forms of violent actions? A challenge which is all the more delicate in that "the gap between sources and realities, impossible to bridge in any case, is never so great as when it is a matter of sexuality".[13] None the less, it is necessary, even if only in fragmentary and partial ways, to attempt a re-creation of such practices of acts of sexual aggression.

The difficulty of writing the "real": witnesses' word

Reconstructing the facts of rape is an arduous task because of the very nature of the sources, which are in addition brief and fragmentary. Accounts of war, iconography, direct or indirect evidence, information recorded by the Republican army, most are produced by the Republican side and are full of a complex blend of descriptions of violence, imaginings projected on to these men arriving from elsewhere, interpretations of the acting out. Further, there is also the realist exposé of violence and intense empathy for the victims. However, critical reading and confrontation of this material makes it possible to suggest ways in which the rapes can be analysed by disconnecting the various registers of utterance from the violent event.

> The Moors raped the women whom they encountered along their route, before killing them. It happened very frequently that the authorities, generally the mayor, told me of atrocities committed by the Moors and the Tercios as they entered villages. I have myself met those who were close to victims of the Moor troops. (1938)[14]

This rare and precious evidence from a high official of the Nationalist side active in Andalusia, published during the war in 1938, refers clearly to rapes committed by the Moor troops. In his *Memorias de un Nacionalista*, the rapes appear as a time of violence: that of territorial conquest and submission. He describes them as an unforeseeable and incidental phenomenon, affecting women blindly, indeterminately, and repeated on the regional or even national scale; a time of violence which, further, preceded the death of the female enemy victim. Proposing himself as a privileged eyewitness (since he was part of the group administering violence), he judges acts of sexual violence as extreme. Because they are synonymous with behaviour exceeding acceptable war violence? Because they affected a vulnerable civilian population? Because they were committed by foreign mercenaries in order to inflict pain? He stresses the fact that these actions were known to the authorities. He thus introduces the link between rape and consent, denunciation and permissiveness by members of the agents of power.

The commanding officers of the Nationalist army had prepared for the confrontation between these men and the women of the aforesaid Republican camp through deliberate denigration of the women. Objectified, demonised, the Reds (*Rojas*) were the incarnation of perversity, depravation, atheism, communism, untamed sexuality. It is, however, difficult to assess the degree of assimilation and acceptance of these assertions by men who, in many cases, had enlisted under threat or because they hoped to escape a wretched future. These Spanish women, white women, could – representing strangeness – signify simultaneously repulsion or desire, forbidden territory, or simply the gendered and sexual female body (in the war setting, denoted in terms of prey). Can this configuration be seen as the inversion of the "erotic colonial imagination"?[15] These interstices in moving towards the act[16] are impossible to decode because this is a real silent story, in that we have no statements whatever from these men on this topic. The women had been presented explicitly as part of the spoils of war (the expression recurs frequently in the original material), thus as objects made available, free from any prohibitions. It was without doubt through these elements in the construction of the rewards of war that the soldiers were most thoroughly conditioned. Such considerations bring with them questions of the responsibility of the authorities. François Godicheau speaks of "permission given"[17] to these troops to carry out the rapes that they had been promised. For this purpose they were allowed some hours of freedom in places they had conquered, as compensation for their war effort. However, this in no way means that all the men were routinely given to these practices.

It seems that the paroxysmal point of these rapes corresponds to the earliest period of the war, from the uprising of July 1936 to the arrival of the Nationalist troops in Madrid in the autumn of 1936, passing through Merida, Badajoz, Talavera de la Reina and Toledo. They thus touched Andalusia and Estremadura most strongly: regions crossed by military columns on their way to the capital. In other regions, however (Asturias, the Basque Country, Catalonia etc.), the Moor soldiers were (re)mobilised, each time as shock troops, to consolidate specific and brutal operations of submission and to establish crucial fronts. Thus the situation of invasion and occupation of territories went hand in hand with this range of acts of violence. Arriving at a quantitative total of such rapes remains impossible, because of both the particular pattern of troops available at the time and the distorting prism of the sources of rumour.

The rapes committed by the Moor soldiers were revealed – indirectly – through the "evidence of shame", of children born of the outrage. Rare, they can none the less be seen as a twist in a war story. The colour of the child's skin visibly perpetuated the violence and humiliation by identifying those responsible for the sexual degradation:

> Today, these infamous actions begin to bear their fruit. In the maternity clinic in Vittoria, twenty women raped with the sick complicity of the Phalangists have given birth to black children, irrefutable evidence of the authors of the rape ... More than fifty women will give birth at any time now, and all of them know that what is stirring in their bellies is the blood of dishonour. (1937)[18]

The question of "the child of war rape" is a fundamental element in this sexual violence. In effect, the rape of women of "the other side" as political punishment puts into logical perspective, "by omission", the question of parentage.[19] This child is the sign (visible here through the stigma of skin colour) of violence committed – by identifying its perpetrator – and of violence suffered in the impossibility for the victim to hide the wrong. His or her existence perpetuates the victim's suffering through the continual reminder of ill-treatment and shame – a shame which may lead to suicide. This death provoked recalls the reality of the physical and psychological suffering inflicted by enemy rape: the body of the woman (her "belly"/womb) is irreversibly marked with the stamp of cruelty. In a war which questioned the concept of race from both sides[20] and in a society which, ever since the Reconquest, had held purity of descent as traditional, the possible birth of these "black" children is like a shame of identity added to the wounding of body and defining matrix.

In the accounts we note rapes which correspond to a true sexual criminality, part of a warrior practice and instigated as part of a deliberate operation to inflict terror. The most generally described pattern is that soldiers enter the houses, and loot and rape the women who are present: mothers and daughters. The desecration of sex and body goes with desecration of the setting, the intimacy of the household. It is paralleled, in the sources, with the practice of *razzia*, pillage, a practice associated routinely – as part of war culture – with these contingents. Several witness statements recount cases of rape which the son and husband have been forced to watch; during the Civil War, in fact, we see in the execution of violence at the rear a combination of "terror and spectacle".[21] The drawing at the beginning of this essay would suggest this characteristic of the assault, in presuming the presence of the husband at the rape of his wife.

John Horne and Alan Kramer have shown that "rape before a captive audience indicates that the invasion as a gendered process was not a two- but a three-way relationship – between perpetrator, victim and the victim's male compatriots".[22] And this spectacle of humiliation affected more than the intimate family sphere. Cases attest to rapes in the presence of Phalangists, of civil guards, of Spanish men from the opposite camp who watch the humiliation of the female enemy: "María Gonzáles, del Serallo, as recalled by a witness, married and mother of several children, was raped and murdered in her own house by the Moors, in the presence of several Phalangists who applauded the savage scene with great bursts of laughter."[23]

In these cases, the rapes are seen as a political form of violence: the Nationalist purpose consisted of the visible physical and symbolic submission of places and bodies. Véronique Nahoum-Grappe considers that "suffering inflicted offers a prime spectacle for politics: it produces an effective bodily change in the enemy. "The enemy finds himself vilified, stripped bare, bloody, disfigured."[24] Thus the rapes committed by these foreign soldiers are re-used to serve the project to destroy the Reds. Further, the mention of the "married woman" and of the "mother" shows the extent to which it was also a humiliation for the male – and the group – which was intended in the offence against the woman's body.

A further question arises, that of the future of these raped women. The rape may be a moment preceding the death of the victim, selected sometimes because of her political identity (individual or familial). And the bodies of these women were made available to the Moor soldiers as an object for the relief of inhibition by the Spanish authorities before the summary execution of the victims.[25]

An historic act of violence

The rapes committed by the Moorish soldiers served the purpose of eliminating the Republican enemy established by the "Rebels". Simultaneously psychological weapon and physical weapon of destruction, they were part of the swift and brutal submission of bodies and territories during the first months of the war. The terrifying figure of the "African rapist" was associated with the spectre of death, symbolic of and, in certain cases, leading to actual death.

Traces of the event, even partial, remain significant in the literature of the violence of war. In this way they show, with dazzling effect, that these violent events did indeed make history during the Spanish War. And for this reason their history fully deserves to be written.

Notes

1. Eduardo Gónzalez Calleja, "La cultura de guerra como propuesta historiográfica: une reflexión general desde el contemporaneísmo español", *Historia Social* 61 (2008), p. 83.
2. Eduardo Gónzalez Calleja, "Experiencia en combate. Continuidad y cambios en la violencia represiva (1931–1939)", *Ayer* 76:4 (2009), pp. 37–64.
3. Eduardo Gónzalez Calleja and Fredes Limón Nevado, *La Hispanidad como instrumento de combate. Raza e imperio en la Prense franquista durante la Guerra Civil Española*, Madrid, Consejo superior de Investigaciones Cientificas, Centro de Estudios Históricos, 1988, p. 7.
4. Ian Gibson and Queipo de Llano, *Sevilla verano de 1936 (Con las charlas radiofónicas completas)*, Barcelona, Grijalbo, 1986, p. 84.
5. Gibson and Llano, *Sevilla*, p. 85.
6. Yannick Ripa, "Feminin/masculin: les enjeux du genre dans l'Espagne de la Second République au franquisme", *Le Mouvement Social*, "Féminin et masculin", 198 (January–March 2002), pp. 111–27.
7. Paul Preston, "Los esclavos, las alcantarillas y el capitán Aguilera. Racismo, colonialismo y machismo en la mentalidad del cuerpo de oficiales nacionales", in Javier Muñoz, José Luis Ledesma and Javier Rodrigo, eds, *Culturas y politcas de la violencia España siglo XX*, Madrid, Siete Mares, 2005, p. 197.
8. Véronique Nahoum-Grappe, "Anthropologie de la cruauté. Quelques pistes au sujet de la guerre en ex-Yougoslavie", in Marie-Rose Moro and Serge Lebovici, eds, *Psychiatrie humanitaire en ex-Yougoslavie et en Arménie*, Paris, Presses Universitaires de France, 1995, p. 27.
9. Yannick Ripa, "Armes d'hommes contre femmes désarmées: de la dimension sexuée de la violence dans la Guerre civile espagnole", in Cécile Dauphin and Arlette Farge, eds, *De la violence et des femmes*, Paris, Albin Michel, 1997, pp. 135–6.
10. Jacques Sémelin, *Purifier et détruire. Usages politiques des massacres et génocides*, Paris, Seuil, 2005, pp. 41–2.
11. Xosé Manoel Núñez Seixas, *¡Fuera el invasor! Nacionalismo y movilización bélica durante la Guerra Civil Española (1936–1939)*, Madrid, Marcial Pons, 2006.
12. Germán Bleiberg, *"Sombras de héroes" Teatro de agitación politica, 1933–1939*, Madrid, Cuadernos para el Diálogo, 1976, pp. 133–64.
13. Stéphane Audoin-Rouzeau, *L'Enfant de l'ennemi (1914–1918). Viol, avortement, infanticide pendant la Grande Guerre*, Paris, Aubier, 1995, pp. 53–4.
14. Antonio Bahamonde Y Sánchez de Castro, *Un año con Queipo de Llano (memorias de un nacionalista)*, Buenos Aires, Ediciones Republicanas, 1938, p. 108.
15. Alain Corbin, "L'imaginaire érotique colonial", in Alain Corbin, Jean-Jacques Courtine and Georges Vigarello, eds, *Histoire du corps*, vol. 2, Paris, Seuil, 2006, pp. 193–8.
16. Dagmar Herzog, ed., *Brutality and Desire. War and Sexuality in Europe's Twentieth Century*, Basingstoke, Palgrave MacMillan, 2009.
17. François Godicheau, *Les mots de la guerre d'Espagne*, Toulouse, Presses Universitaires du Mirail, 2003, p. 123; Yannick Ripa, "La violence nationaliste contre les femmes pendant la guerre civile espagnole: un enjeu politique", in *La place des femmes. Les enjeux de l'identité et de l'égalité au regard*

des sciences sociales (international research conference, Paris, 1995), Paris, La Découverte, 1995, p. 483.

18. Ceide de Negri, *Tragedias de la retaguardia: estampas vivas del dolor de España*, Madrid, Nuestro Pueblo, 1937, pp. 17–19.
19. Véronique Nahoum-Grappe, "L'usage politique de la cruauté: l'épuration ethnique (ex-Yougoslavie, 1991–1995)", in Françoise Héritier, *De la violence [II]*, Paris, Odile Jacob, 2005, p. 283; Fabrice Virgili, "L'Ennemie dans l'Europe en guerre au XXe siècle", *L'Autre. Cliniques, cultures et sociétés. Revue transculturelle, "La pensée sauvage"* 3:1 (2002), p. 45.
20. Santos Juliá, "De 'guerra contra el invasor' a 'guerra fratricida'", in Santos Juliá, ed., *Victimas de la Guerra Civil. Una aportación imprescindible a un debate que sigue abierto*, Madrid, Ediciones Temas de hoy, 2004, pp. 11–54.
21. Angela Cenarro Lagunas, *El fin de la esperanza. Fascismo y guerra civil en la provincia de Teruel (1936–1939)*, Teruel, Instituto de Estudios Turolenses, 1996, p. 67.
22. John Horne and Alan Kramer, *German Atrocities, 1914. A History of Denial*, New Haven and London, Yale University Press, 2001, p. 199.
23. Ramón García Piñeiro, *Los mineros asturianos bajo el franquismo (1937–1962)*, Madrid, Fundación 10 de Mayo, Área de Historia, 1990, p. 183.
24. Nahoum-Grappe, "L'usage politique", p. 282.
25. Ronald Fraser, *Recuérdalo tú y recuérdalo a otros. Historia oral de la Guerra Civil Española*, Barcelona, Critica, 2007, pp. 205–6; John T. Whitaker, *We Cannot Escape History*, New York, MacMillan, 1943.

8

Promising Rape: Private Militias against Maoist Guerrillas in the State of Bihar (India)

Alexandre Soucaille

Translated by Helen McPhail

Rape is indifferent to war or peace times. But it was a fundamental fact in the creation of two separate Indian and Pakistani nations at the partition of 1947. Rape, abduction followed by forced marriage, carving the war cries of opposing camps (*Allah Akbar, Jai India*) on women's bodies, amputation of breasts as a physical attack on the symbols of womanly nourishment and thus of social reproduction, all are acts of extreme violence open to interpretation as the transformation and reduction of woman to a *sign*, a means of expression between men in conflict.[1] Not simply confined to Indian space, this dialogue between men over the violated female body shows the essentially masculine order of the nation.[2] In the ordinary course of daily life in times of peace, the presence of rape maintains this order, by ambiguous laws condemning the action and its author but also, frequently, the victim.

This particular economy of rape – linking the meaning and the role of womanhood to war violence and the legal and social order of the nation – is what enables us to see how rape is used in the armed conflict in the state of Bihar, which has set private militias of the higher castes, the Sena, against the various groups of Maoist guerrillas, the Naxalites.

By an ethnographic and interpretative approach of social observances and discourses in Bihar,[3] the focus on rape's ideologies aims to explore both the local arguments defending violence and the deep links between these arguments and the normative thinking about rape in Indian society. More particularly, in considering this conflict I will seek to show how the language of rape used by the Senas has deep foundations in the ordinary registers of caste domination in Indian society and in national representations of women. But we will also see how engagement in the armed Maoist struggle, by displacing caste membership through the established regime of war, eventually reconfigures the social consequences of rape. This article would like to show the performative power of words as an important part of rape's violence and as the space both of social suffering and of reproduction of social domination in time of conflict.

Swearing extermination

Extremes have two faces: one is certainly related to this idea of excess and its gratuitousness elucidated by Bataille, the other is anchored in the reasoning which defines its possibility. We find these two principles in the oath of Ramadhar Singh, founder in December 1990 of the Savarna Liberation Front, widely disseminated in the press, some tracts and also in the thinking of certain low Bihari castes: "*Mara ixias mastodon kid chital par likha jayega*", "My name will be written on the pyres of labourers".

This private militia, consisting of Bhumihars (high-caste Brahmin landowners), was created to protect their caste interests, which were challenged by national policies of land reform and the Naxalite groups operating in Bihar.[4] There is nothing new about the emergence of such a militia in Bihar. The first, the Kuer Sena, a militia of Rajputs (castes belonging of the second *varna* of Kshatriya, the class of power and warriors), had appeared 11 years earlier in this same central belt of Bihar which includes the districts of Palamau (from 2000 a district in the new state of Jharkhand), Aurangabag, Gaya, Jehanabad and Bhojpur.

The Savarna Liberation Front is partly an offshoot of the Bramharshi Sena, the first Bhumihar militia, created in 1984. A glance at the members of these militias shows certain fusions and affiliations among the Sena which mainly follow a caste- or faith-based logic, such as the Ali Sena, a militia of Moslem landowners. After the arrest of its leader in 1994, the Savarna Liberation Front was to be founded in its turn on the most recent and famous of these militias, the Ranvir Sena.

In the Sena world, Ramadhar Singh's militia stands out to some extent. On one hand, this former teacher at Kirani College in the town of Gaya developed a pattern of conflict theory based, as we shall see, on the mythology of the origin of caste. On the other hand, a new use of language and communication is clearly visible, as in the widespread publicity which followed this oath by the leader of the Savarna Liberation Front.

The gesture of the oath, as opposed to a new act, really belongs to a conservative register, as shown by Glorgio Agamben.[5] For this militia, the matter to be preserved is the legacy of a social nature on the foundation of the caste system, a hierarchical pattern of agency based on the four classes, or *varna*: Brahmin, Kshatriya, Vaysha and Shudra. According to Vedic hymns, the order came from the sacrificial dismembering of primordial Man, the Purusha.[6] The conservationist purpose of a system in which the Bhumihars find themselves at the tip of the hierarchy takes strength from constant reference in the militia's communications to the original founding hero of their caste, the sixth avatar of the god Vishnu, Parashurama ("Ram with the axe"). Their struggle draws its justifying logic from the myth of Parashurama and becomes the continuation of a warrior lineage.

To understand the actions of Ramadhar Singh, a short detour is needed through the mythological corpus which directs the Brahmin universe. The stakes of power and hierarchy in the Hindu world are in fact at the heart of the story of Parashurama. With all the complexity which is part of Hinduism in matters of status and fundamentals, and which is already visible in relation to the term *jati* ("caste"), signifying "species" and its articulation in the Varna system, the figure of Parashurama is built on the hierarchical opposition of Brahmin/Kshatriya. Born of the union of Jamadagni, a Brahmin of great ascetic rigour, and Renuka, daughter of King Prasenjit, Parashurama thus reflects the hybrid nature of status. This does not in itself establish an equality arising from the alliance, still less does it create an intermediary category between the Brahmins and the Kshatriya – quite the reverse: the violent part of Parashurama, his Kshatriya part, will be of service in establishing Brahmin domination, and the subordination of Kshatriyas to Brahmins. After the conflict in which he opposed King Kartavirya Arjuna and his sons, and which brought about the death of his father, Parashurama threw himself into limitless vengeance which ended with the extermination of 21 generations of Kshatriyas. Halted by the gods, the work of Parashurama none the less, according to myth, established definitive Brahmin domination over the caste world.

The tales of Hindu mythology and their violence[7] provide the Sena of Ramadhar Singh with the ideological foundation of duty and confer on the foretold extermination the natural resolution of a line of descent. Located as part of an ancestral martial legacy, the Sena thus became determined to protect an order under threat; in the Bihari context, with its long history of violence to confirm hierarchical relationships between castes,[8] this signifies keeping the lower castes in their place by the use of murderous violence. A famous former soldier and criminal, Bindu Singh, was a significant contributor to this enterprise: his task was to train members of the Sena and organise them into a true paramilitary group. A caste war developed in the name of the Bhumihars, its legitimacy founded on the myth-creating story of Parashurama, an exact precursor of the contemporary situation in which the Naxalite guerrillas contest the social order of castes. It is not a matter of restoring an epic era but of sustaining its consequences, recognising and sustaining its primacy by the logic of first principles as an inevitable part of cosmic order, the Dharma, supposedly protected by universal respect by everyone in his own place, his *svadharma*. But this struggle in the name of natural order also has the effect of normalising acts and actors while driving away some normality. It is a feature of war that it redefines relationships with others in terms of nature, just as with caste relationships – established as so fundamental – introducing to them in reverse the problem of change. We will return to the ontological shifts which result from conflict, but we should observe at this point that in the conflict which sets landowner militias against Naxalite groups in this way, we are dealing with a caste war on one hand and a class war on the other, two concepts of engagement which merge together and which can be distinguished in their relationship from rape.

The promise of rape as routine

In 1992, shortly before his arrest, Ramadhar Singh launched a campaign of systematic rape in the districts of Gaya and Jehanabad. Rape is by no means a new weapon in the repressive arsenal of dominant groups in Bihar. Often the act of subordinates from an organised criminal world, the Lathaith or Pahalvan, it has also been part of operations undertaken by the Sena ever since their creation. These operations consist principally of attacks directed against hamlets of low-caste people suspected of helping the Naxalites; any men present are usually assassinated, the women always molested, sometimes mutilated, in some cases raped and killed, and the houses systematically destroyed.

What Ramadhar Singh introduced is not therefore this use of rape but an effect of proclamation. Why bother to announce that there will be rape when it is already widely practised? First, because rape is no longer contingent, because it is no longer a chance part of reprisals. In announcing the "*balalkar* campaign", this systematisation of rape, Ramadhar Singh's intention was to turn it into an entirely separate method of repression. This also responds to the Naxalite group of the

MCC (Maoist Coordination Committee) which had limited the practice of rape by the Sena by promising the death of any rapist.

Although very different, the particular interest in rape among the Naxalites and the Sena shows shared knowledge of its social relevance. And if the former try to block its effects, the latter in contrast use it to further their own interests. The social effects of rape in India are clearly set out in the proposals of Nursul Islam, one of the legislators who worked for the reform of penal laws on rape in the early 1980s: "Ours is a country of Sita and Savitri and traditionally we regard our women as such and to our women chastity is everything. If it is lost, everything is lost; not only lost, socially she becomes dead."[9] Here we can see mythology in operation, calling on the female figures in the Ramayana and Mahabharata epics which established once and for all a certain value of Woman; a woman is above all a mother and a faithful wife, to the point of self-sacrifice. Faced with these representations, the raped woman undergoes a profound disruption in her bodily and social status. Suffering rape, she suffers exclusion by society because she is no longer *a woman*. Raped, she is no longer the bearer of the values of the Sanskriti, the "Indo-Hindu culture" which substantiates "Woman" through the categories of mother or of wife. Further, in the eyes of the figure of Sita, she is guilty of not having killed herself either before the rape, to avoid shame, or after it, to relieve her fellow women of her burden (cf. the following section, Ontological Shifts Specific to the War Regime).

And yet the legislator's recourse to the epic does not represent an ideological intention to define a certain image of woman in society. Rather, India's legislative reforms show a certain degree of social reproduction, linked to the judge's power in legal decision-making: the execution of justice is very often the fruit of the judge's interpretation of how his verdict will be accepted in society, and is also based on public opinions of the day, at the same time reifying them through judicial decision. In fact, Nursul Islam does no more than reproduce current values largely shared by the ensemble of castes in defining the place and role of women, and assert social attitudes in the case of rape.

From the castes to the state, this solid anchoring of values relating to women and rape forms the background to the campaign of rape announced by the Sena. Pre-existing knowledge of the consequences of rape is in effect exploited by the militia for its implications: the power of submission to rape is no longer based only in the brutal violence of the deed but, through this knowledge of its social consequences, can be applied independently of the actual perpetration of the act, through the imposition of styles of behaviour which correspond to a regime of fear.

None the less, in announcing this campaign, the leader of the Sena is not so much playing on the actual fear of rape, already established in the attitudes and daily actions of women of low status in the region, as on the performative aspect of the announcement which would introduce doubt as to the "morality" of women of low status in a hamlet, village or caste in the region. This intention to cast suspicion is supported by the phenomenon of rumour, a particularly important method of communication in India.[10] The militia therefore aims to isolate and destroy social relations within these families of low status, in other words it targets their social death by the very announcement of rape.

Among responses to this mechanism of exclusion by rape, silence or denial are attempts to establish a counterbalance which frequently offers greater advantages to society than to the raped women – as seen in the management of acts of rape at the time of partition in 1947. Those rapes often ended with the marriage of the woman to her rapist,[11] thereby denying the act of rape since at that time marital rape was not recognised by the legal systems of India or Pakistan.

In the Bihari context of recent decades, rape seeks effacement or denial through the silence that surrounds it, an attempt which opposes the effect of the Sena announcement and of the rumour which never fails to circulate about rape, whether actually perpetrated or not. Silence versus rumour: an inevitably unequal and perverse conflict. In effect, silence restores the power of the high castes which commit *these rapes which no longer appear as such* because they are never mentioned. Silence restores what certain high castes never stop proclaiming through the Sena: that they are the owners of all "things", which it can use and abuse.

In other words, this campaign of rape foretold has brought rape out of the restricted setting of operations to the murder of low-caste people. Set out as an entirely separate routine practice, it has left only two alternatives for the low castes: either the implosion of their family in its heart and daily social relations by denouncing the rape, or submission to the regime of domination by the higher castes by keeping silent.

Reinforcing this process of silence, the real execution of this campaign rests on many enigmatic points. Beyond the announcement and hearsay of rumour, only the very well informed can testify to its scope. According to some of them, this campaign will have affected more than 150 women. Venkitesh Ramakrishnan, journalist on the magazine *Frontline*, gives larger figures – stating that 200 women between the ages of 6 and 70 were raped by the Savarna Liberation Front between March and July 1992.

Figures for the murders and rapes committed by this militia remain difficult to establish. In two years of activity, nearly 50 murders of low-caste peasants or members of Naxalite factions were attributed to the Savarna Liberation Front. In his book on the socio-economic situation in Bihar, Jose J. Nedumpara mentions that during an interview that he had with Ramadhar Singh, the latter claimed to have committed a hundred murders himself.[12]

The imprisonment of Ramadhar Singh led to the reorganisation of his militia in the Ranvir Sena, which was to dominate the Bihari scene even after the arrest of its leader, Brahmeshwar Singh, in 2002. The latter, also Bhumihar, was to turn the Ranvir Sena into by far the most murderous militia. Taking up the ideology of the Savarna Liberation Front, the Ranvir Sena concentrated on very large-scale violence and extended its geographical area. If rape was no longer the object of an appeal, it was there, present, alongside torture and murder, culminating in 1997 with the massacre in the village of Laxmanpur-Bath which resulted in 57 deaths. By chance, it left four survivors – three children and a woman. Of the 27 women assassinated, the rape of at least ten was witnessed, of which three were found with their breasts cut off. Between its creation in 1994 and the arrest of Brahmeshwar Singh on 29 August 2002, more than 400 official murders were registered as the work of the Ranvir Sena.

Ontological shifts specific to the war regime

The values considered to be incarnated by Woman, far from protecting her, lead via the burden of rape to an expanded categorisation of "feminine". The construction of the figure of "Woman" in effect corresponds to the construction of "deviant woman", involving a radical redistribution of patterns of behaviour towards her. In war, it is less the prescribed attitudes, observed or not, which predominate, than the fact that the quality of "Woman" is no longer attributed to the womenfolk of the Other. This was again revealed by acts of rape during the partition of the Indian subcontinent, with men of each side condemning the Other as rapists at the same time as they raped the Other's women in reprisal. There, too, the rumour of rapes played a part, resulting in numerous collective suicides of women, particularly among Sikhs, to avoid the shame of having been raped falling on the community as a whole. Such a deed inevitably evokes the epic era once again, notably the repudiation of Sita in the Ramayana after Ram had rescued her,[13] followed by her immolation to prove her purity.[14] Also evoked in this way was the medieval history of India and the famous collective suicides, the Jauhar, in the face of the victory of the Shah's armies in Rajasthan, all contemporary referents for conservative ideologies.

In the context of the Sena, the relevance of these epic stories and these historic events feed the constitutional forms of enemy "Otherness", coinciding with the divisive *jati* or species of the caste system. On one side they have their own women bearing the values of society, on the other, women of low castes and Naxalite militant women, of no consequence. The former are to be protected, the second can be raped.

This separation is seen also in the militia-related representations of the practice of rape among the Naxalites. In the case of the Savarna Liberation Front and the Ranvir Sena, the women are trained to handle weapons. But since this training is acknowledged above all as defensive, it is not so much learning to kill as being able to kill oneself if necessary.

Such conditioning to suicide upholds the values towards women that are defended on the basis of honour to be guaranteed, and remains within the ideological structuring of the struggle of the Sena. Even the latter recognise that, for the Naxalites, rape cannot be an act of reprisal. This does not mean that there is no case of rape committed by individuals of these groups – the anti-Naxalite blog *Naxal Terror Watch* (naxal-watch-blogspot.com) recounts a certain number – nor that they spare women or children. But what the militia members prefer to denounce as rape among the Naxalites relates to an internal phenomenon: women raped by their companions in arms.

The phenomenon of rumour appears here more easily open to exploitation than the reality. Although little information filters out over the reality of these rapes, it is none the less convenient to consider the possibility, as much practical as ideological, among the Naxalites.

The Naxalite engagement calls for a break with the conditions of a life linked at birth to caste relationships. Guerrilla warfare calls not only for a different distribution of power, above all it implies a radical and immediate change of status for the Dalit (Untouchables), the Adivasi (an expression used in India for indigenous peoples) and the low castes which join them. The break relating to the engagement has a real impact not only from the point of view of the high Bihari castes, which perceive it as an overturning of the very order of the world – their world – but also for the combatants who are in fact abandoning their old pattern of social patterning linked to their caste membership.

This break is visible in the introspective examination undertaken by some Naxalites of the circumstances of their journeying. One of these combatants described himself as an Adivasi, a Ho constrained to submit to the surrounding society, and that to relieve himself of this origin he must in some way un-make himself by changing his everyday life. This would be achieved through specific acts such as the armed struggle, recourse to violence, acts of a nature that would make others forget some part of his origin, his status or at least the relations which this status implied hitherto in the dominant society. In other words, to be a Naxalite combatant, Adivasi, Dalit, of low or even high caste, was different from being an Adivasi, a Dalit, a member of a low caste or a Brahmin.

Such a change which conditions the most ordinary deeds just as much as murderous military acts against the state and the high castes leaves no ideological place for rape. Rape is seen as a means for the dominators to enforce the submission which is proper to them, relating to a relationship with women which in practice is challenged by the mixed nature itself of the combatants. There is a real work of adequation between ideology and practice among the Naxalite combatants: each deed should be ideologically justifiable, each pronouncement should have its place in the practices. The relationship between acts and ideologies is therefore important because they determine the individual sense of the change in condition, and they are also the object of continual polemic, at times bloody, between the different Naxalite factions. In these conditions, if rapes occur, it is because the relationships of dominance between men and women have not been redefined, or at least that they have not been redefined in such a way that rape can no longer take place within these new relationships.

If there is then a point on which Naxalites and militias may agree, it is indeed on the change inherent in the former group's armed struggle. It is moreover such a change that the militias condemn through the denunciation of internal rape. From their point of view, it is because individuals, men as well as women, no longer obey their predetermined origin in society – specifically because of the mixed nature of the armed struggle which blurs the difference between the sexes – that the possibility exists of turning against their *own* women: it is a much greater shame for these militia members of high caste to denounce their womenfolk than the very practice of rape to which they turn.

The presence of rape in the Naxalite sphere is, rather, the fact of accepting raped women. It is not unusual for women to join the Naxalite ranks in the aftermath of a rape. Part of their engagement consists of this redefinition of relational frameworks arising from the struggle, which thus makes it possible to escape from the social consequences of rape. The singularity of the experience undergone in effect comes up against epistemological frameworks of the condition of rape, the reasoned space which did not prevent it and which remains unchanged after the event, despite the event. In establishing their history, their rape, in a war regime, the women now become activists, the war declaring a regime of disjunction which thereby expects to counter the social consequences of rape; it is to be re-established in other modes of understanding which would reverse some of the violence and domination which is expressed in it, perhaps with the engagement of these women in guerrilla warfare, or of Drapaudi, the Naxalite heroine of a novella by Mahasweta Devi.[15] Drapaudi, refusing to put her clothes on again, faces the instigator of her rape entirely naked – in that instant she overcomes the act of domination that she had suffered, enjoying and playing on the values of the woman who in India cannot be naked in the presence of a man, through this very nakedness which becomes the negation of the masculinity that has raped her: "What's the use of clothes? You can strip me, but how can you clothe me again? Are you a man? [...] There isn't a man here that I should be ashamed."

Further, the raped women are in themselves the bearers of a social critique which already takes account of the ordinary experience of a war, permanent and ignored, concerning women. This has been suggested, following others, by Virginie Despentes.[16]

The domination of rape between war and peace

What appears to emerge from this conflict is the porosity of rape as it is expressed in the practices of militias and more generally in Indian society. The social manifestation of rape appears as a condition of its use and extends, beyond its perpetration, to the exercise of a local domination. At the same time, and even while distinguishing between them, the Sena commit atrocities against the low castes on one hand and against their elements who hope to escape this condition on the other. The distinction takes account of a double domination: that of the daily violence with its rapes and murders testifying to the very exercise of the domination which is part of caste relationships and respect for the existing hierarchies, and the demonstrative domination which turns to massacres and the rape of those who are trying to get away from this established order, or would like to do so. As we have seen, domination exploits the regime of silence, a relative form of protection in the face of the social consequences of rape, and correlates to the effect of the proclamation of rape.

But the language of rape in the conflict, coinciding with the language of caste domination, does not develop a pattern of expression which would be exclusive to rape. It relies on the expression of a daily domination which does not exist, or no longer exists, in contemporary India by the sole fact of high castes over others, but is evident in the hierarchies of lesser differences of rank, as in the modest gaps between low castes. It is this which is evidenced by, among others, the sadly famous case of the village of Khairlanji in Maharashtra where, in 2006, Surekha Bhotmange and his daughter Priyanka, who belonged to a neo-Buddhist Dalit caste,[17] were raped, tortured, mutilated and killed by other members of low castes in the village, although of a higher status. For Anand Teltumbde, an activist in human rights in India,

> Khairlanji represents the quintessence of caste India – that people have to observe their ascriptive statuses; stay put in their place [...] Kharilanji lays bare the self-righteous arrogance of the caste Hindus and their assumptions about and demands from the subordinated castes. Paradoxically, Khairlanji also represents their vulnerability. It represents resistance, defiance and struggle – howsoever feeble – of the subaltern castes. While caste oppression can be said to be embedded in the system, a caste atrocity is invariably the result of a defiant response from the victims. Khairlanji demonstrates that the caste system, howsoever oppressive, is essentially a self-regulative system that expects people to conduct themselves according to its code.[18]

What matters in this link of rape to war and peace is perhaps the deconstruction which stands out between the conservative regime on one hand based on the social regulation of rape and the systems of present domination which pursue the masculine order of the nation, and, on the other hand, potentially, a regime of rupture which, *via* war, overturns the conditions for rape. In establishing an entirely different relationship to the ideological regimes which they oppose, the "entering war" redefines the epistemological regimes face to face, because the war is above all a regime of *a different life* – and because, here, it is the very fact of the exercise of this other life, after rape, after tortures, at the risk of death. The Naxalite engagement of raped women thus attempts to exhaust the common springs of rape like those of the regime of domination which expresses itself in, by and beyond rape; an engagement which by disconnecting the different registers of belonging can at a given moment make domination totter. The violence of rape is still there, but once domination is denied, violence is perhaps then, and only then, without foundation, unjustifiable.

Notes

1. Veena Das, *Critical events. An Anthropological Perspective on Contemporary India*, New Delhi, Oxford University Press, 1996; idem, *Life and Words. Violence and the Descent into the Ordinary*, Berkley, University of California Press, 2007.
2. Rada Ivekovic, *Dame nation: nation et différence des sexes*, Ravenna, Longo, 2003, and *Le sexe de la nation*, Paris, L. Scheer, 2003.
3. I have been confronted by the presence of rape during research for my thesis on the relations between the Adivasi (the generic expression designating the indigenous peoples of India) and people of caste in Bihar. It was within this framework in the region that between 1995 and 2002 I met women who had been victims of rape both "ordinary" and relating to the conflict between the Sena and the Naxalites, as well as Naxalite combatants or some of their sympathisers. This intermittent presence over these seven years also enabled me to grasp the context of this conflict, both from the side of the Adivasi and the lower castes and that of the lower and middle urban bourgeoisie consisting mainly of the middle and higher castes.
4. Louis Prakash, *People Power: The Naxalite Movement in Central Bihar*, Delhi, Wordsmiths, 2002.
5. Glorgio Agamben, *Le sacrement du langage. Archéologie du serment*, Paris, Vrin, 2009.
6. On the sacrifice, see Charles Malamoud, *Cuire le monde*, Paris, La Découverte, 1989, and concerning the hierarchical consequences according to the Untouchable leader Bhimrao Ramji Ambedkar, "father" of the Indian constitution, see Olivier Herrenschmidt "'L'inégalité graduée' ou la pire des inégalités. L'analyse de la société hindoue par Ambedkar", *Archives européennes de sociologie* 37 (1996), pp. 3–22.
7. Das Veena and Nandy Ashish, "Violence, Victimhood, and the Langage of Silence", *Contribution to Indian Sociology* 19:1 (1985), pp. 177–95.
8. See in particular Babri Narayan, "Honor, Violence and Conflicting Narratives: A Study of Myth and Reality", *New Zealand Journal of Asian Studies* 5:1 (June 2003), pp. 5–23. The origin of caste and the determinations which it is supposed to imply are still present among the Bhumihars and of course among the extremists of this caste; see for example the contribution of Vivek Sinha on the blog "Bhumihars and the legend of Parashuram" at http://prafulkr.wordpress.com.
9. Pratiksha Baxi, "Rape, Retribution, State: On Whose Bodies?", *Economic and Political Weekly* 35:14 (April 2000), pp. 1196–1200.
10. Ranajit Guha, *Elementary Aspects of Peasant Insurgency in Colonial India*, New Delhi, Oxford University Press, 1983.
11. Urvashi Buthalia, "A Question of Silence: Partition, Women and State", in Ronit Lentin, ed., *Gender and Catastrophe*, London and New York, Zed Books, 1997, pp. 92–109.
12. Jose Nedumpara, *Political Economy and Class Contradictions*, New Delhi, Anmol Publications, 2004.
13. Valmiki, *Ramayana*, 6:115, trans. A. Roussel, Paris, Adrien Maisonneuve, 1903.
14. Valmiki, *Ramayana*, 6:118.

15. Mahasweta Devi, "Draupadi", in *Breast Stories*, trans. G. C. Spivak, Calcutta, Seagull Books, 1997, pp. 19–38.
16. Virginie Despentes, *King Kong théorie*, Paris, Grasset, 2006.
17. The neo-Buddhists designate in India the castes of Dalits who followed B. R. Ambedkar in his conversion to Buddhism, not having been able to eliminate the Hindu caste system.
18. Teltumbde Anand, *Khairlanji. A Strange and Bitter Crop*, New Delhi, Navayana Publishing, 2008, p. 14.

9

The Weight of Imagination: Rapes and the Legend of Women Snipers in Chechnya

Amandine Régamey[1]
Translated by Helen McPhail

> From overhead, our helicopters sprayed the area with anti-tank missiles, down below we were firing all our mortars, and then all at once, this tousled bitch shot out into the street, stinking of cellars and burning. So we caught her round her thighs: "So who are you?" Any fool would have known that this was a sniper. As for her, she began to scream: according to her, her twelve-year-old daughter was supposed to be in the cellar and her legs, that's what she said, were torn off [...] So this kid of 12, she was a sniper too! All these people, all of them, they are all savages. With them, soon as they can walk, everyone shoots [...] Well let her die! That's what I thought. She carried bandages to these wretched *boeviki* and she was telling us rubbish: "Seda" she shouted, "Seda! My little girl!" and we led her up to the sixth floor, we satisfied her female lust, for the last time .. what a joke .. and then we strapped F-1 grenades round her and threw her out of the window. She didn't even have time to cry out: level with the second floor, all the grenades exploded. She was torn apart. Not a bit reached the ground.[2]

This account from an alcoholic veteran describing the capture of Grozny in 2000 is fiction: very little testimony exists on the rapes committed by Russian troops since 1999 in Chechnya. If sexual violence occurred in the "filtration camps", at control posts, in military barracks and during village raids, their scale is difficult to assess, if only because of the victims' silence. The lack of evidence makes it even more striking that several sources of different types (testimony from victims and soldiers, literary texts, press articles) trace a link between rapes and the legend of women snipers in Chechnya.

The legend in which women sharpshooters were fighting in the enemy camp was in fact very widespread among the Russian troops in Chechnya, which raises questions as to the relation between imagination and the perpetration of acts of violence. In allowing suspicion to hover over all women encountered, could this legend justify the acts of violence that were committed? Could the legend itself push the soldiers to perpetrate the violence, to "neutralise" or take revenge on women seen as a threat? And how to explain the place that this legend holds in the imagination of soldiers who saw service in Chechnya?

Enemy women ...

When the war in Chechnya broke out again in the autumn of 1992,[3] the Russian authorities shelled the towns and villages with extreme violence, and then over a few months deployed an army of over 80,000 men.[4] However, despite the disproportionate forces and the brutality of the methods used, Moscow never managed to achieve total control over Chechen territory. Opposing forces, calculated at several thousand fighting troops, set up multiple ambushes and attacks. The soldiers and police, established in military bases or mounting guard at checkpoints, were faced with a population which they distrusted.

The term sniper, like that of *franctireur*, or sharpshooters in other cases of military occupation, offers "a portmanteau image that could account for any unexplained firing and convert harmless civilians into an embodiment of [...] fear".[5] In Chechnya, this fear crystallised around women: as soon as a sniper is part of a narrative, women's features appear, and when the presence of women is evoked among the Chechen troops, they are systematically designated as snipers. Moving beyond the role of rumour, the legend develops round two types of narrative: "In Chechnya, soldiers were in contact with a woman, supposedly a civilian – she turned out to be a sniper", and/or "In Chechnya soldiers were threatened by a sniper – this marksman turned out to be a woman."

In the wars of Transnistria (1992) and Abkhazia (1992–93), the Russian troops were already talking about the "white tights". They were said to be élite shots from Baltic countries, former biathlon champions, and are immortalised in *Chistilishe* (*Purgatory*, Nevzorov, 1998), a film on the 1995 battle of Grozny. A year later the tragi-comedy *Blokpost* (*Command Post*, Rogozhkin, 1999) introduced the figure of the young Chechen sniper.

The media, particularly the large circulation press, seized on the legend with headings such as "The White Tights fought in Dagestan" (*Nezavisimaia Gazeta*, 2 October 1999), "Masha the sniper promised to shoot only at the knees" (*Nezavismaia Gazeta*, 28 January 2000), or "The wild geese with white tights" (*Trud*, 1 April 2000). In circular style, rumours on the ground, the media and mass culture were feeding off each other.

Yet the existence of these snipers has never been proved. Very few women held an active military role in the Chechen army groups, and the journalist V. Voronov, who investigated the existence of the "white tights" recognised that he had "not succeeded in meeting a single living witness: no one had seen them, even if everyone had heard of them".[6] None the less the rumour remains the object of widespread beliefs in the army as in Russian society, no doubt because it is "born of collective representations which exceed its own birth" and it moves "in the direction where everyone's thoughts were already moving".[7] In fact, it enabled the soldiers to give meaning to their experience and to give them back a coherent image of themselves, of their enemies and of the civilian population.

The legend of women snipers is a way of showing a Russian army under attack on all sides by hostile nations, Balts, Chechens or Ukrainians. Thus it is possible to imagine blond and cruel Baltic snipers, impelled by the "hatred of Russians that they drank in with their mother's milk", the memory of an SS grandfather, vengeance for an aunt who died on deportation to Siberia, and "of course, money!"[8] Invoking the presence of many experienced mercenaries (Baltic and Ukrainian snipers, Afghan mujahidin, Arab and African Islamists) enabled the justification of military setbacks and the inversion of the image of their aggression. Russia was shown in the defensive position, when in reality she had twice launched her troops against a Chechnya whose independence she did not recognise.

On the other hand, the image of the female Chechen sniper further strengthens the distrust of civilians. Since the nineteenth century the Chechens have been portrayed as a warrior people by nature, hostile and cunning – representations which are regularly reactivated within the army, in political statements or in popular spectacular films.[9] Thus the heroine of *Blokpost*, who prostitutes her sister and demands payment in bullets, is "barely 14 years old" but already sees her rifle "as a friend, a faithful friend, who never lets her down". The woman symbolises all the ambiguity of the soldiers' relations with the civilian population: she should not be taken as a target but at the same time the soldiers should beware of her if they wish to survive.

This defiance was moreover fed by the military command itself. General Trochev, Commander in Chief of the military district of the

Northern Caucasus, asserts that he was confronted in Chechnya with women combatants and that "the majority of them were snipers".[10] Similarly General Chamanov, former commander on the western front of the army of the Northern Caucasus, considers that if they did not want to be treated as "bandits" the combatants' wives would merely have to leave their husbands, and wondered publicly "how to distinguish the wife of a combatant from a sniper".[11]

This suspicion had its effects on the ground, as can be seen in the testimony of Zulikhan, a Chechen encountered by the journalist Anna Nivat on the road out of Grozny, in January 2000:

> I would never have thought that it would be so difficult to get out of this hell. For several days they have engaged a woman from the Ministry of the Interior who searches you from head to foot, and does not hesitate to humiliate you. She turned my tights inside out, and my socks, telling me all the time that I had sniper's eyes, that I must certainly be a combatant.[12]

The danger to which the women were exposed was all the greater because the "proofs" held against them by the Russian troops were as arbitrary as they were fantasy. As with the men, the slightest detail could be declared suspect, and a woman could be arrested if she did not live at the address shown in her passport, if her identity photo was badly stuck down, if she showed bruises or wounds and so forth. Any sign, any document could be interpreted to justify the accusation. The journalist who claimed to tell "the true story" of the sniper known as "Lolita" offered as her only proof of her activity a little red notebook which bore the signature of the war leader Bassaev.[13] In another article, an officer who had arrested a women carrying a precision rifle emphasised that "when we got near her, we noticed that she had only one earring". The paper specifies that "wearing a single ear-ring, for women, is considered by investigators as an indirect sign that this is a sniper. The second sign is the bruise on the shoulder caused by the rifle butt."[14] It is difficult not to see in this missing earring, taken off supposedly to make firing easier, a reminder of the Amazons and the legend that they cut off a breast in order to pull their bow better.

Legitimising sexual violence

Drawing on "all the themes that the human imagination [...] has been dwelling on since the dawn of time",[15] the legend of the women snipers could be used to justify forms of violence committed against women. In March 2000 Colonel Budanov, based near the village of Tangi-Chu in Chechnya, seized, raped and killed a young Chechen girl. Coincidentally, the affair was denounced by the military high command. The Budanov trial opened in April 2001 and despite several attempts to exonerate him from responsibility, he was finally sentenced in July 2003 to ten years imprisonment.[16] In fact Budanov's entire defence was constructed on the fact that he took the young girl for a sniper and believed her responsible for the death of several of his men. According to him, he must have lost control of himself during the interrogation and strangled her in a moment of frenzy. Many witnesses proved, however, that on that evening the drunken colonel had shelled the village for his own amusement, and had then set off "to find a woman there". Yet Budanov's defence was effective: the conclusions of the enquiry found it credible that he had gone into the village with the aim of arresting a sniper. His interpretation of the facts seeped into public opinion: according to a survey in July 2002, 28 per cent of those interviewed explained the Budanov affair by the fact that "Budanov had strangled the young Chechen girl when he had learned that she was a sniper"; only 10 per cent replied that "Budanov had raped and killed a young Chechen girl".[17]

Above all, the rape had disappeared from the charges of the accusation: a second medico-legal expert claimed that the rape had taken place after death. One of the soldiers ordered by Budanov to bury the body "acknowledged" having abused it with the handle of a spade, and even though he later withdrew his declaration he was immediately convicted and pardoned. The disappearance of rape from the indictment thus made it possible to transform the nature of the crime. There was no further reference to acts of sexual violence, but rather of degradation committed by a soldier in the exercise of his functions. Public debate could thus concentrate on a single question: is it excusable, even legitimate, to kill an enemy without a legal verdict?

The Budanov affair thus shows how the legend of women snipers can operate to justify acts of violence by transforming the victim of a sex crime into a female enemy combatant who is a priori guilty. But if the role of the legend in the legitimation of acts of violence can be demonstrated, the relation between the legend and the perpetration of such acts is less easy to establish.

Undoubtedly, several statements collected for organisations for the defence of human rights show that women who had been raped or were the victims of sexual violence had been accused of being snipers by the

Russian soldiers or police who detained them. This happened to "Alisa Riskhanova" who was arrested at a checkpoint on the pretext that she did not look like her passport photograph:

> Four Russian soldiers accused Riskhanova of being a sniper, gave her a rifle and ordered her to dismantle it, to reassemble it and to fire. Riskhanova has declared to Human Rights Watch that she had never held a rifle and did not know how to manage it. One of the soldiers hit her, knocking her to the ground. Two others then set about kicking her. Riskhanova records that the soldiers said to her: "You'll never be able to have kids." Then the soldiers raped her.[18]

Similarly, "Fatimah Akhmedova", held at the Chernokozovo detention centre, told how the eight soldiers who were holding her had forced her to undress and had accused her of being a sniper.[19]

The consequences of suspicion of women are clearly visible here: the legend of the women snipers supports the non-existent "proofs" and the arrested woman thus finds herself held in the inexorable mechanism of assaults carried out within places of detention. It is known that torture was applied there routinely, and the acts of sexual violence committed against men and women were no doubt far more numerous than the testimonies which could be assembled.[20] Thus, out of 35 people of Chechen origin followed up by a British NGO because of the tortures they had suffered between 1999 and 2004, 16 women and one man had been victims of rape. The NGO report makes it possible to outline a typology of acts of sexual violence, noting that

> there were 16 cases of vaginal rape, 5 cases of anal rape and 2 cases of oral rape [...] The frequency of these rapes varies between one and several times (for example every day for a month). The number of men implicated as perpetrators runs from one to "more than 10".[21]

Tracing a direct link between the legend and actual assaults remains delicate, however, since even if the victims of sexual assaults had been accused of being snipers, nothing enables us to know whether the perpetrators consider their own accusations important. Some soldiers evoke the fear of women snipers to explain their behaviour, but there too nothing makes it possible to confirm that they did not find justifications for it after the event. Their testimonies, however, make it possible to grasp more firmly the beliefs which prevailed in the army and the link made between rapes and women snipers.

In a report of April 2000, the personal evidence collected by the Mothers of Saint Petersburg Soldiers organisation[22] shows how a generalised suspicion of women could stimulate acts of violence. Soldier Nikolai N., who served in Chechnya early in the war, admitted that he had himself shot 14 civilians, including a Russian woman who was eight months pregnant. It seemed to him that the woman was a sniper: "she was crying, she was down on her knees, she was screaming, she begged not to be killed. But how could I let her live if within an hour she took a rifle and began shooting."[23]

Some witness statements were more precise about rapes and sexual violence. Andrei, for example, a soldier who served in Chechnya in the autumn of 1999, describes how "in the Argoun valley we caught a sniper, then we stuck a grenade in her vagina, we pulled the pin out and ran away. She was shredded." He said he had seen how a female sniper had been attached to an armoured vehicle and dragged along the road until all her flesh was scraped off.

> In Grozny, two women snipers were arrested. One of them started screaming that she hated the Russians and she was shot immediately. The other asked to be set free. The soldiers took her up to the fifth floor, they had good fun with her, then they tied a grenade on her, pulled out the pin and tipped her out of the window.[24]

The striking resemblance between this testimony and the fiction extract quoted in the introduction is self-explanatory when one knows that the writer took his inspiration from statements collected among the Mothers of Saint Petersburg Soldiers. However, how can one explain the resemblances between this tale from 1999 and the one told as authentic by the Chechnya veteran Viacheslav Mironov? In his memoirs he relates that in Grozny, in 1995, some Russian soldiers had found the hiding place of a sniper, no doubt a woman:

> The men spent a day in ambush, without moving. No peeing, no smoking. It paid off in the end. No one knows what happened, but the Chechen girl flew off the roof of a nine-storey building. A real bird. And on the way she was scattered all over by a grenade explosion.[25]

Threats to virility and symbolic revenge

In fact there are very many variations on this story. On his website the nationalist singer Alexandre Krylov acknowledged that he had heard the tale "of the sniper-bitch, thrown of the roof of a building with a grenade stuffed between her legs" from veterans of almost all the conflicts of the former USSR, differing only in "the name of the countries and the towns where this happened, as well as the number of storeys in the building".[26]

The narrative of rapes and assaults on women snipers thus shows all the characteristics of a legend: "localised and individualised accounts", "objects of collective beliefs", and in which each one related to individuals and episodes "which revolved round a very small number of well-defined themes".[27] In referring to these narratives as legend, it is not a question of denying that such acts of violence took place. During the "cleansings" of the second Chechen war, civilians were indeed torn apart by grenades[28] and it is possible that grenades were used as part of sexual torture in the same way as other weapons (truncheons, rifles), the use of which is confirmed. But the statements of veterans, who only pass on what was said in the army, cannot be taken as evidence.

These declarations are, however, significant to the state of mind which dominated among the Russian troops, revealing the powerful feeling of impunity which held sway in the army, since the soldiers do not hesitate to boast about having committed crimes. They also enlighten us on the representations of Russian soldiers who regard rape and sexual violence as legitimate in a perspective of symbolic revenge and self-affirmation.

Encountered in 2001, Guerman, a young conscript back from Chechnya, explained that the *kontratniki*[29] "said that they if they caught a female sniper, they always raped her, without fail".[30] His evidence is an echo of the statements of Roman, recorded by the Mothers of Saint Petersburg Soldiers organisation in 2000 concerning Russian women operating as snipers on the side of the Chechens: "those women, the whole company looked after them, all of them who really wanted it".[31] From grenades in the vagina to being torn apart by armoured vehicles, the works of fiction add further imaginary punishments (death by explosive bullets fired between the legs in *Chistilishe*, rape with a Kalashnikov in the "Ballad of the White Tights" by Vs. Emelin, a poet close to the Nationalists-Bolshevists),[32] but the meaning remains the same: a routine rape is imagined which not only prevents the woman sniper from doing harm but reduces her to nothingness.

These accounts of rape offer a symbolic victory over the enemy, a compensation all the more valuable because the Russian army failed to achieve genuine control of the Chechen territory. Further, talk about the rapes also holds a central place in the symbolic restoration of the soldiers' virility, which is simultaneously built up and undermined by the war. Military service, like departing to go to war, in effect forms the moment when the boy reaches adulthood, becomes a man, like the *kontratniki* mentioned above by the young soldier Guerman. Faced with very young conscripts (championed by the associations of soldiers' mothers), these men are the incarnation of a virility that is symbolised by their physique (piratical knotted scarf, tattoos, bare torso).

At the same time, the war threatens men in their habitual role of husband, father and family supporter. To classic fears of adultery or distance from the family were added in Russia the colossal economic problems of the Russian army (regular pay not forthcoming, the difficulty for professional soldiers to get decent housing for their families) and the currency crisis linked to the collapse of the USSR in 1991.

Further, charged with policing and patrol operations, very rarely engaged in combat, Russian soldiers or policemen did not have genuine opportunities to demonstrate their virility and courage (two expressions translated in Russia by the same adjective, *muzhestvennyj*). "The enemy, if he is at a distance, does not enable the soldier to show his courage. So, under shelling or under sniper fire, it is not Men who die, but small boys."[33] The women snipers, the embodiment of a particular military situation, thus remind the soldiers of the image of this weakened virility, and are even the embodiment of much more direct threats.

In fact, the men were equally afraid of returning from the war impotent or mutilated: hence, in very many more or less fictional narratives, the presence of women snipers emasculating the soldiers. The military journalist S. Tiutiunik describes thus the "authentic" story of a woman sniper falling in love with a Russian soldier: as the latter did not respond to the advances that she made to him by radio, she shot at three of his soldiers: "All the shots hit them ... in the crotch."[34] In "The She-wolves in White Tights", sub-titled: "The women snipers fire between the legs", the journalist evoked a figure famous in the army, of the "mercenary biathlon [Milita Trankautene who] had achieved fame for the cynicism with which she castrated young Russian soldiers by accurate shooting." The journalist V. Voronov had also met in Abkhazia "witnesses" who described how the shots fired by the women snipers had "whistled between their legs".[35] Similarly, in Nevzorov's film *Chistilishe* it was explicitly in revenge against Baltic snipers "who hit our boys in the balls" that the young Russian soldier wounded them with a shot in the crotch, then left them dying.

The legend of the women snipers thus established a narrative of overturning the "natural" order of things (a woman giving death, men threatened in their role as males and as soldiers), and a symbolic re-establishment of this order which is embodied in an act of sexualised and sexual violence. This explains clearly that the individual of enemy sniper must be more or less exclusively female.

We should underline in conclusion that this legend makes it possible simultaneously to construct and to exorcise the fears of soldiers: fear of hostile civilians and of the enemy who strikes without being seen, fear of not behaving like a man, terror of being wounded or mutilated, haunted by a genuine or symbolic emasculation. The legend was thus the expression, in a particular context, of fears proper to all soldiers in a war situation – fears which are expressed in different styles according to the armies concerned, the situation on the ground and the nature of relationships with the resident population. Thus during the Vietnam war it was Vietnamese prostitutes, accused of hiding harmful objects in their vagina or of transmitting incurable sexual diseases, on whom these same terrors were focused.[36]

The dimension of the discourse is fundamental in the legend of women snipers and deserves study in itself: it expresses the experience of soldiers but also, by diffusing the legend throughout society, a certain vision of what the Russian army is doing in Chechnya and of the enemies against whom it is fighting. At the same time, the legend is not without connection to actions and exactions committed in Chechnya: if it has not driven soldiers to commit crimes, it has in any case been used to justify such crimes, feeding a climate of impunity which was able in its turn to aggravate acts of violence.

Notes

1. This article has been supported by the "Emergence" programme of the Mairie de Paris (project: "Une violence russe? Expériences de guerres, trajectoires sociales, pratiques institutionnelles", 2010–12).
2. Vladimir Kiveretski, "Il était une fois des gens", in Comité Tchétchénie, *Nouvelles de Tchétchénie*, Paris, Edn Paris-Mediterranée, 2005, trans. Daniel Mihalovic.
3. The first Chechen war, intended to bring the independent-leaning Republic back into the body of the Russian Federation, began in December 1994 and ended in a ceasefire in August 1996. The election of President Maskhadov in January 1997, under the auspices of the OSCE, has never been recognised by Russia, which used the pretext of an incursion of the war leader Bassaev into Dagestan as well as attacks attributed without proof to the Chechens to relaunch hostilities in September 1999.
4. It was not until after 2003 that the functions of the police were gradually transferred to the pro-Russian Chechen forces, although this did not prevent

the maintenance of very substantial contingents of the army, the Ministry of the Interior and special services (FSB).

5. John Horne and Alan Kramer, *German Atrocities 1914: A History of Denial*, New Haven and London, Yale University Press, 2001.
6. Voronov, "Russo-Chechen Myths", *Sluzhba* (*Service*), 2004, http://www.library-jes.ru/online.
7. Marc Bloch, *Réflexions d'un historien sur les fausses nouvelles de la guerre*, 1921, Paris, Allia, 1999, pp. 48–9.
8. This is how Sherbakov imagines Ute/Fatima, an Estonian sniper, on the website www.artofwar.ru, devoted to the prose of Russian veterans of local wars. Apart from *Chistilishe*, this image reappears in films on the Chechen war such as *Proryv* (*The Breakthrough*, Vitali Lukin, 2004, or *Muzhskaya rabota* [*A Man's Work*], Tigran Keoasian, 2001).
9. Numerous articles have been devoted to representations of the Chechens in Russian society, for example: Galina Zvereva, *Chechenskaia voina v diskursah massovoi kul'tury Rossii: formy reprezentacii vraga* (*The Chechen War in Russian Mass Culture: Forms of Representation of the Enemy*), 2002, www.polit.cu; Amandine Régamey, Silvia Serrano, "Le sauvage et le barbare: le corps de l'Autre dans les représentations croisée russo-tchétchènes", *Textuel* 48 (2004), pp. 191–212; John Russell, "Terrorists, Bandits, Spooks and Thieves: Russian Demonisation of the Chechens before and since 9/11", *Third World Quarterly* 26:1 (2005), pp. 101–16; Anne Le Huérou and Amandine Régamey, "Russia's War in Chechnya: The Discourse of Counterterrorism and the Legitimation of Violence", in Samy Cohen, ed., *Democracies at War against Terrorism*, Basingstoke, Palgrave, 2008.
10. *Rossiskaia Gazeta*, 28 March 2001, http://www.rg.ru (last accessed 2007).
11. "La Shamanov" ("I am Shamanov"), interview with A. Politkovskaia, *Novaia Gazeta*, 19 June 2000, http://novayagazeta.ru.
12. Anne Nivat, *Chienne de guerre*, Paris, Fayard, 2000, p. 242.
13. Elizaveta Maetnaia, "The She-Wolves in White Tights", sub-titled: "The women snipers fire between the legs", *Moskovskiy komsomolets*, 6 April 2001.
14. Z. Lobanova, "Sniper Ana. How a young girl from Moscow learned to kill Russian soldiers in Khattab camps", *Komsomolskaia pravda*, 9 August 2001.
15. Bloch, *Réflexions*, p. 40.
16. For the Budanov affair, see Amandine Régamey, "L'opinion publique russe et l'affaire Boudanov", Pipss.org issue 8, 2008, www.pipss.org.
17. Survey carried out by VtsIOM (Russian Study Centre on Public Opinion) in July 2002 in a sample of 1600 individuals throughout Russian territory, www.levada.ru/press.
18. Human Rights Watch, "Serious Violations of Women's Human Rights in Chechnya", Report to CEDAW, January 2002.
19. Human Rights Watch, "Serious Violations".
20. See for example: "No Happiness Remains: Civilian Killings, Pillage and Rape in Alkhan-Yurt, Chechnya", Human Rights Watch Report 12:5, April 2000; Mémorial/FIDH, "Tchétchénie, crimes contre l'humanité, un an de crimes impunis", October 2000, pp. 30–31; Amnesty International, "Russian Federation (Chechnya): Rape and Torture of Children in Chernokozovo 'Filtration Camp'", 23 March 2000; Amnesty International, "Russian Federation: Continuing Torture and Rape in Chechnya", 8 June 2000; Yakin

Ertürk, *Report of the Special Rapporteur on Violence against Women*, "Mission to the Russian Federation", January 2006, doc. E/CN4.2006/61/Add.2.

21. Doctor Charlotte Granville-Chapman, "Rape and Other Torture in the Chechnya Conflict: Documented Evidence from Asylum Seekers Arriving in the United Kingdom", Medical Foundation for the Care of Victims of Torture, London, April 2004, www.torturecare.org.uk.
22. Founded in 1991 to protect the rights of conscripts and to work for reform in the army, the Association of Mothers of Soldiers of Saint Petersburg gave its support to deserters or to soldiers wounded during the Chechen war, while also working to bring the war to an end (see the website www.soldiers.mothers/ru/).
23. "Violation of Human Rights during the Chechen Conflict between September 1999 and February 2000", report in Russian, English and French presented by the Organisation of Mothers of Soldiers of Saint Petersburg at the session of April 2000 of the Parliamentary Assembly of the Council of Europe (sl, sd) undated, personal archives.
24. Ibid.
25. Viacheslav Mironov, "Ia byl na etoj voine" ("I took part in this war"), in *My byli na etikh voinakh, Svidetelstva uchastnikov sobytij 1989–2000 godov* (*We Took Part in These Wars, Testimony of Events in the Years 1989–2000*), Saint Petersburg, Zvezda, 2003, p. 127.
26. Alexandre Krylov, *Suchka* (*The Slut*), http://alexanderterski.narod.ru.
27. Fernand Van Langenhove, *Comment nait un cycle de légendes, francs-tireurs et atrocités en Belgique*, Lausanne, Payot, 1916, pp. 236–7.
28. During the cleansing operations in the village of Mesker-Iourt, in May–June 2002, several bodies were blown up with grenades (see the document from the Memorial Human Rights Centre on www.memo.ru/hr/hotpoints/N-Caucas/).
29. The *kontraktniki* are experienced soldiers and officers serving on the basis of short contracts agreed with the army or the Minister for the Interior.
30. Guerman, a Russian originally from Bachkiria who had served in Chechnya, left the army and was then discharged. Interview undertaken in the premises of the Association of Mothers of Soldiers of Saint Petersburg in March 2001.
31. "Violation of Human Rights".
32. http://curtain.ng-ru/poems.
33. Cf. D. Mikhel, "Muzhciny, malchiki, pole boja" ("Men, Little Boys, Battlefields"), *Gendernye Issledovania*, June 2001.
34. Sergej Tutunik, *12 pul' iz chechenskoj obojmy* (*12 Bullets from a Chechen Barrel*), Moscow, Vremia, 2005, p. 118.
35. Voronov, *Sluzhba*, www.library.cjes/ru/online/.
36. Monte Gulzow and Carol Mitchell, "Vagina Dentata and Incurable Venereal Diseases. Legends from the Vietnam War", *Western Folklore* 39:4 (October 1980).

10

Breaking the Silence: New Approaches to the Consequences of Rape in Some African Conflicts, 1994–2008

Nadine Puechguirbal
Translated by Helen McPhail

The transition from war to peace cannot be achieved without reconciliation between the various groups within society who have been fighting each other – a reconciliation that also takes place through the acknowledgement of sexual assaults on women. Too often the law of silence condemns these women to remain on the periphery of their society, withdrawn inside their own suffering, unable to grieve for a violent past. In March 2009 the international community hailed the peace agreement between the government of the Democratic Republic of the Congo (DRC) and the rebellion of the National Congress for the Defence of the People (CNDP). This agreement provided for Kinshasa's promulgation of a law of amnesty for former rebels. The part played in acts of sexual assaults on women by rebels of the CNDP has been very fully documented in various reports by organisations for the defence of human rights. Despite the advances in international human law which recognise sexual assault as a serious crime of violence, it is clear that impunity continues to prevail for violators of the rights of women.

In South Africa, the women questioned by the Commission for Truth and Reconciliation tended to minimise the ordeals which they had endured in the days of apartheid. Seeing themselves primarily as mothers, wives, sisters and daughters of combatants, they kept silent over their own suffering in order not to cast a shadow over the courage of male heroes (this is essentially true for the sexual violence which is profoundly taboo in most societies). Citing the proposals of activists working with women victims of rape during the confrontations in KwaZulul/Natal[1] in South Africa in the 1980s, Ashnie Padarath has written, "These women would talk about what had happened to their sons, brothers and husbands. When we would ask them about what they had gone through, they would say: 'Yes, I was tortured in prison, but that's not important.'"[2] Such women had interiorised their own pain to give the men in their family full scope to express their sufferings.

Beyond the efforts at reconciliation, we must consider the responsibility for dealing with post-conflict trauma – above all for women who have been raped, in order to enable them to be reintegrated into society by lifting guilt and acknowledging the social and political dimension of the assaults that they have suffered. In Somalia, sexual assaults on women have repercussions which are simultaneously political, legal and social in a country where the culture of impunity reigns. In Eritrea, little attention has been paid to the psychological well-being of demobilised women combatants or women who suffered violence within the civilian population during the war years.

In Rwanda today, women are at the heart of political life and work to change the discriminatory laws which have for so long operated to restrain them to a status of second-class citizen. Yet for many years they bore collective responsibility for the genocide and served as an outlet for the anger of their community. They felt guilty at having survived as sexual objects instead of joining their husbands and families in death. The survivors' guilt can be summed up in the phrase, "I have survived because I abandoned my children."[3] Ultimately, the men die as heroes, the women survive as guilty.[4]

A question arises at the outset: what space can be created for women who have been raped in wartime to enable them to take an active part in the reconstruction of their society?

The Listening Houses in the Democratic Republic of the Congo

When his father died in 2001, Joseph Kabila replaced him at the head of the DRC. He took the lead in a transitional government and, seeking to pacify the country, he tried to blend the different rebel movements together within the army. Certain rebel chiefs, including Laurent Nkunda, from the Congo Democratic Assembly (RCD), refused to accept the rank of general, disbelieving the will of Kinshasa to reform the country and bring an end to ethnic discrimination. In 2006, posing as defender of the Tutsi minority in the Congo, he created the CNDP. In January 2007 Nkunda agreed to take his troops into a new process of integration into the national army; in exchange, this enabled him to take legal control of the territories that he coveted. The new process failed. Fighting began again between the CNDP and the Congolese army, with the former reproaching the army with forming an alliance with the Rwanda Hutu genocidal killers of the Democratic Forces for the Liberation of Rwanda (DFLR). For its part, Kinshasa accused Kigali of supporting Laurent Nkunda.

There was fighting against the Congolese army, which was routed in December 2007. The Goma Conference ended with all belligerents signing a ceasefire agreement in January 2008. Agreements have been regularly violated since then, just like the peace programme which has still not been established. This long period of instability led to the resumption of violent fighting in August 2008. It is estimated that northern Kivu, with a population of five million, has more than a million displaced people. According to the latest report from Human Rights Watch, the United Nations Population Fund (UNFPA) has indicated the registration throughout the territory of 15,996 new cases of sexual violence in 2008. In the province of North Kivu alone, to the east, 4820 new cases have been registered.[5]

Of course we must be vigilant with figures which are no more than an estimate of a dramatic reality on the ground. None the less, these figures give a sufficiently precise view of the scale of the problem which calls for multiple responses in such areas as health, economic security, legal help and psychosocial support.

In the DRC, the experience of the International Committee of the Red Cross (ICRC) programme of aid for victims of sexual violence shows the importance of the psychosocial approach to relieve women affected by this scourge.

Although it is contrary to the concept – which is widespread in certain humanitarian circles – that mental health is not a priority matter of urgency, the experience of the ICRC in Kivu shows that psychosocial support for victims should be offered as fast as possible in order to relieve them of the burden of the violence endured. At the same time, community networks should be used to defuse stigmatising reactions towards them and thereby encourage their social reintegration. The victims testify to the importance, in their own words, of "restoring memory" and of "gathering scattered ideas". They insist on the relief felt at being able to speak to a Psychosocial Assistant, male or female, about the rapes they suffered and to emerge from their isolation, from the inward-looking disposition which cut them off from their community. Before the introduction of the Listening Houses (*Maisons d'écoute*), the victims explained that they came together in groups to talk or pray to give themselves strength and to escape the ostracism that afflicted them. This was the only "coping mechanism" that they could find. The availability of Listening Houses provides a therapeutic aspect which was missing from unstructured conversation groups. Questioned between October and December 2008 on the problems which handicapped them most severely, 35 per cent of victims mentioned physical pain and changes, 30 per cent spoke of changes in psychological factors, 26 per cent of economic problems and 10 per cent of social changes.[6]

A Listening House is a place where vulnerable individuals (victims of sexual violence and of other traumatic situations) can meet a Psychosocial Assistant who listens to them, helps them to identify their needs and to find solutions or alternatives to improve their current situation, directs them towards services according to the needs defined (medical or legal services etc.). The Listening House also offers temporary accommodation for people who cannot return home for reasons of protection.

As the neuropsychiatrist Boris Cyrulnik has written,

> When the surroundings are destroyed or when the cultural myth encourages withdrawing solidarity from the wounded, abandonment hinders the work of recovery. The affective negligence of a distorted family ... the cultural negligence of a society which "casts off" its incapacitated members because they have lost all value – all these ways of distancing paralyse the recovery of resilience and enclose part of the population in a kind of psychic camp for refugees who can no longer participate in the social venture.[7]

The psychosocial approach should be understood as a mechanism of protection which helps victims to reconstruct themselves and to return to their daily lives as soon as possible, thus favouring their social reintegration. This approach does not replace the need for justice, which is essential for the repair of the social fabric, of course, but it enables victims to "get back on their feet" after a trauma. The combination of several forms of action, both the urgent (free care) and the developmental (support for local organisations), and at the same time involving activities linked to prevention and reintegration (communal sensitisation), reflects a global pattern of thinking which responds to the physical, psychological and social needs of members of the community.

The elements of community protection should be privileged (victims frequently feel alone in facing their suffering). Psychosocial protection can be defined through several aspects. "Facing up and reconstructing oneself": each person, according to his or her psychological make-up, surroundings and the circumstances of events experienced, has a different reaction to violence and to suffering as well as to loss and a capacity to face up to these and to self-healing (resilience). "Self-esteem and the indispensability of each one in his or her own community": the solitude of victims leaves them helpless in the face of a failure of self-esteem. This solitude can then lead the individual, as in a spiral, to a breakdown of communication and social relations.

The men should be involved in the strategies to reintegrate the victims in their society. The influential men at the core of a community (traditional chiefs, community leaders etc.) can be active in instigating a change of behaviour, notably the importance of working on the prejudices and beliefs which legitimise sexual violence and affect the reintegration of women victims who have been rendered responsible for the stained honour of the husband, the family and the community. In certain situations, as in the DRC, the engagement of groups of men against sexual assaults has made good results possible. These groups can reinforce the understanding that sexual violence is not only a "woman's affair"; the credibility that they confer on this question can convince other members of the community to join with them, for credibility evolves in relation to the masculine norm of reference; moreover, it is possible that the community has only begun to take sexual violence seriously since men have become its victims. In the DRC it is observed that the number of men who approach the Listening Houses is growing; interestingly, more than any other trauma their chief problem concerns the sexual impotence which has affected them – men are more touched in their symbolic role of protector at the level of the family, the community and head of the household.

Psycho-counsellors in Rwanda

The genocide that afflicted Rwanda in April 1994 was one of the bloodiest of the twentieth century, with nearly one million deaths. This genocide had its roots in the complex history of the country in which the Tutsi minority opposed the Hutu. The Belgian colonial authorities who supported the Tutsi when they were in power changed their attitude sharply at the time of independence, in 1959. As a result, the Tutsi were kept out of government and suffered discrimination until the genocide of 1994. On 6 April 1994 the President of Rwanda, Juvenal Habyarimana, was assassinated – his aircraft was fired on and crashed as he was preparing to land at Kigali. This night attack triggered the genocide which was launched by Hutu Power.[8] The massacres were to reach heights of horror in the scale of cruelty inflicted on civilians (pregnant women were ripped open to kill the foetus, sexual assaults were frequent, killings took place within mixed families etc.) and the number of activists. From 10 April and starting in the north of Rwanda – a zone on the Uganda border retaken between 1990 and 1993 from the Rwanda armed forces, in other words the Rwanda regular army – the rebels of Paul Kagame's Patriotic Rwandan Front (PRF) occupied the lands of their origin to take power.

A report from the United Nations Development Fund for Women (UNIFEM) draws up the balance sheet for the situation of acts of sexual violence against women in today's Rwanda.[9] This report investigates acts of violence suffered by women in private and in public, and the type of help available to them. It also summarises the laws and texts which the Rwanda government has adopted since the genocide to make a stand against violent attacks on women. It is interesting to note that, according to UNIFEM, some 37 per cent of surviving women stated that in the wake of acts of sexual violence they had suffered problems requiring psychological treatment.

The organisation *Médecins sans frontières* (MSF) was one of the first to take part in training female psychological counsellors to help women who were victims of sexual assault at the time of the genocide; these counsellors would in turn train psychosocial operators in the rural zones, with the aim of decentralising so as to reach women in the most remote locations. The approach was one of community adoption of responsibility, with counsellors of the same nationality who organised conversation groups in full confidentiality. MSF developed this programme at the end of 2000, following an analysis of demands from Rwandese aid associations for refugees; these bodies reported that many women were suffering from post-traumatic stress which was often discovered during a routine medical consultation when the patients complained of psychosomatic problems. Elsewhere widows suffering from AIDS, now incapable of working their fields, came to take part in these discussion groups in order to find some support from other women. None the less, at the time, MSF recognised that beyond the action of these groups no centres existed that were suitable to treat cases of trauma in Rwanda, no listening centres where victims could talk about their sufferings in confidence. A vast amount of work thus remained to be done in order for the suffering of the surviving women to be heard and fully recognised, and treated on a national scale, with the necessary financial means and human resources.

In the early 2000s, therefore, the Rwandan Association of Counsellors in Traumatism (RUHUKA), in partnership with MSF, the Ministry of Health and the National Association for the Aid of Survivors of the Genocide and Massacre in Rwanda (FARG), worked to train counsellors, men and women, in matters of trauma. The women who had survived the genocide were the target group for this programme, which also cared for men seeking this support. Thus the generalist doctors who discovered post-traumatic signs among their patients referred them to RUHUKA counsellors for psychological follow-up.

Victims were very active after the genocide in finding shelter, food and water in order to meet the immediate needs for survival. After this stage, traumas emerged when the victims began to think back over events and to lose their taste for life. According to the coordinator of RUHUKA, such women came to a session of psychological support when they had lost all hope, had given up taking care of their children or their household and had isolated themselves from the community. They were driven to seek consultation by other women who took part in the groups and who were conscious of improvement of their own mental health. Several years after the genocide, defence mechanisms were beginning to break down; these women had wanted to show that they were strong, that they could resume activities and continue to live – and then one day everything collapsed and they became vulnerable, without any form of help. RUHUKA was set up in 1998, but took time to develop because psychological counselling was a new activity for Rwanda. At first it was said that those who sought counselling were mad; in Rwandan culture it was better to keep silent to avoid being ostracised. An analysis of reports from trauma counsellors undertaken by the FARG on a national scale between January and August 2003 had revealed that rape came only third in the scale of motives for visits for psychological counselling, far behind grief and more general post-traumatic stress; it is clear that most of the women interviewed in this survey did not always tell the truth because Rwandans do not talk openly of rape. The scale of this problem therefore remained under-estimated for a long time. Further, certain counsellors, themselves victims of the genocide, had to undergo a therapeutic programme for their own state of mind before being able to look after their patients. All this took time. As a Rwandan psychiatrist explains, the survivors need people who can help them and listen to them just as, in the countryside, a chance encounter while carrying a heavy basket on the head might be someone who can relieve you of the burden on your head so that you can catch your breath a little. Talking would help to lift the trauma from the heads of the survivors.[10]

Silence for Somali women

Somalia has had no central government since 1991, when factions overthrew President Siad Barre and then began fighting between themselves for military and political supremacy. Since then Somalia has experienced 27 years of periodic conflicts between rival factions, leading to massive displacement of people and serious economic disturbance. The irruption of Islamist militias was a brutal revival of tensions in the region. In a few weeks, the Union of Islamist Tribunals (UIT) managed to take control of the Somali capital, Mogadishu, and then to unify nearly one-third of the country under its control. Ethiopia, against which the Islamist Tribunals had launched a jihad, provided military support for the federal government of transition, and on 24 December 2006 launched a major offensive against them. The forces of the Islamist Tribunals suffered heavy losses in a murderous battle after which they evacuated Mogadishu; on Thursday 28 December, governmental and Ethiopian forces entered the city unhindered. The Islamist forces retreated to the south-east, near the Kenyan frontier where they suffered a defeat at Kismayo on 1 January 2007. Combatants of the Union of Islamist Tribunals, in alliance with tribal militias, continued to sustain insurrection in Mogadishu.

Today, the escalation of violence in the country is part of the increased number of sexual assaults on women and girls and the spread of AIDS, according to various humanitarian sources. Very little information filters out of Somalia and it is consequently difficult to give an accurate idea of the situation of women and girls.

Nonetheless it emerges that the UNFPA has trained community health agents across the country in order to be in a position to offer medical and psychosocial help to survivors, both men and women, of sexual violence. Somalia has no system to enable victims of rape to receive the Post-Exposure Prophylaxis (PEP) kit;[11] victims frequently receive antibiotics and analgesics but no AIDS treatment. In 2007 the UNFPA decided to introduce PEP kits in programmes of support for victims of sexual violence and supported a doctor specialising in gynaecology and obstetrics at Baidoa hospital, in the south of the country.

In past years, Somali women survivors of rape in the refugee camps did not speak of these ordeals through fear of suffering victimisation within their own group, and also because the psychological impact was colossal. In relating their experiences, the women interviewed spoke of "women and girls who were raped", using this expression to avoid speaking personally. Rape victims in Somalia continue to suffer in silence,[12] a law of silence which has serious consequences for Somali society since it prevents the detection of sexually transmitted disease, including AIDS. Further, since a woman's virginity is given up only at the moment of marriage, it is clear that a young woman who has been raped sees her chances of finding a husband reduced. In the refugee camps it has been reported that families had even asked the United Nations High Commissioner for Refugees (UNHCR) to relocate their raped daughters to other camps because of the shame that dishonours the whole family.

Somali women are forced to face a constant threat of rape in the refugee camps, in addition to the psychological distress which is part of their loneliness and isolation. Outside the camps, the women have been psychologically disempowered by the presence of armed men and youths maintaining a permanent climate of fear. We lack information on the existing structures in the country concerned with women's psychological well-being, as well as of the number of professionals and health centres capable of dealing with transmissible sexual disease.[13] If the women manage to overcome their traumas, this would be due to local systems of informal support, less visible, which need to be identified. How to speak of psychosocial reintegration of the victims of sexual violence in a dysfunctional country where a civil war is raging, with regional impact? In Somalia it is necessary above all to protect women and girls against the consequences of the conflict, every day, to give them access to humanitarian support – which is in itself a daunting task.

The demobilisation of women fighters in Eritrea

The war between Eritrea and Ethiopia ran from May 1998 to June 2000.[14] The two nations, among the poorest in the world, had to suffer the loss of tens of thousands of people killed or wounded in the conflict, which ended with minor frontier changes. In a decision handed down by an international commission at The Hague, Eritrea was found guilty of violating international law and of launching the war by invading Ethiopia. On 25 May 2000, having regained most of the contested territory and having heard that the Eritrean government would withdraw from all the other territories that they had occupied at the outbreak of the fighting, in accordance with the demand of the Organisation of African Unity (OAU), Ethiopia declared the war over. At the end of May 2000, Ethiopia occupied nearly a quarter of Eritrean territory, involving the exodus of 650,000 people and the destruction of key elements of Eritrean infrastructure. On 18 June 2000 the parties concluded an initial accord of overall peace, providing in addition for obligatory arbitration on their points of difference within the framework of the Algerian agreements. A "zone of temporary security", 25 km wide, was created within Eritrea, controlled by United Nations Mission in Ethiopia and Eritrea (UNMEE). A peace agreement between the two nations was signed on 12 December 2000, but the tensions remain strong.

In 2005, the NGO HealthNet TPO set up a programme of mental health for the Eritrean people who had suffered more than thirty years of conflict with Ethiopia. The aim of the programme was to reinforce the capacities of local community, as well as of the government and NGOs, to intervene effectively on questions of mental and psychosocial health by training health staff at different levels of expertise. Veterans were particularly targeted. None the less, there is no indication whether ex-combatant women, who represented nearly 30 per cent of the Eritrean People's Liberation Front (EPLF), have had access to this programme and, if so, whether it has helped them to reintegrate into a conservative society in which they were not necessarily welcomed with open arms at the end of the war.[15]

A survey undertaken by the ACORD NGO at the time of demobilisation has shown that a significant number of former female combatants spent almost their entire demobilisation grant on rent and daily expenses to feed their children, and that these women risked being marginalised for lack of potential work. They lived on the edge of towns in precarious and unsanitary conditions. The hard reality for some of them was shown to be far from their expectations of being able to live a dignified and independent life following their years of commitment to the "war of liberation".[16]

Programmes of Disarmament, Demobilisation and Reintegration (DDR) provided economic projects for the ex-combatants, for example, but without any psychosocial contributions. A sample of 3000 soldiers was selected from more than 200,000 veterans registered for DDR (those who were sick or disabled, and women soldiers, were recommended for priority demobilisation). Out of this sample, therefore, some 13 per cent of veterans were suffering from psychological problems.[17] Initiatives were taken by the international community to train psychosocial counsellors, men and women – but in inadequate numbers, which made it impossible to deal with the accumulation of psychological problems, high rates of disorientation, suicide and alcoholism among ex-combatants.

During the war which set Eritrea in opposition to the Ethiopian regime, women were victims of violation of their rights and forced to suffer torture, above all when they were suspected of sympathising with the EPLF. In lands occupied by Ethiopia, Eritrean girls worked as cooks, cleaners and prostitutes. The writer Amrit Wilson reported that

> no woman was safe. We lived in fear of rape. It was very common and many of us have been forced to bear the children of Ethiopian soldiers. They used all kinds of pretexts to attack us sexually. They would ask us to go to meetings or classes and try to abuse us there and, in the [military] base, they had women servants whom they used as prostitutes.[18]

The problem of reconciliation and the silence which surrounds acts of sexual violence is linked to the place which the women occupy at the heart of patriarchal societies: a woman is seen as a symbol of purity. The family operate around this symbol. Then came the brutal attack against this symbol which stigmatised every member of the family. This stigma perpetuated the humiliation which had repercussions on the survivors and their entire families. In this sense, rape was worse than death.[19]

It is fundamental that the women who were victims of sexual violence during the armed conflicts must be consulted so as to determine the best response to their physical and psychological ills: to remove from them this means of intervention in relation to their own suffering is to take from them a bit more of the power of decision concerning their own sufferings (women are the activists within their communities and not merely helpless victims). Thus the psychosocial approach should be privileged in the phase of transition between war and peace to give these women the tools for their own inner reconstruction. This aspect of reconstruction has often been neglected, with the process limited to the rehabilitation of infrastructures, the rebuilding of institutions within society – justice, the police, the military and local authority – without integrating a gender perspective into each stage of the process of national recovery.

Post-conflict traumas are experienced in different ways by men and women. Studies carried out in Mozambique and Zambia notably have shown that women are more concerned over their families, their relations with their husband and children, while the men think of access to resources outside the household. These studies show also that the women feel the strongest feelings of impotence in the face of events because of weak social capital limited to their extended family; if the women heads of families are particularly isolated, it also seems that marriage may, for many women, be a source more of stress than of support, above all when the husband is violent and abuses his wife.[20]

Yet there is little literature illustrating the impact of the conflicts on women's psychological well-being and the forms of help available in the face of these traumatic experiences, while numerous studies have been devoted to the psychiatric treatment of victims of torture, based almost exclusively on male cases. The report of the Independent Experts of the UNIFEM cites a study carried out on trauma in situations outside conflict zones which shows how the responses to trauma vary according to sex: "Although the lifetime prevalence of traumatic events is slightly higher for men, women run twice the risk of developing post-traumatic stress disorders, suggesting that certain types of trauma may have a deeper and longer term psychological impact on women."[21]

The impact of sexual violence on the social reintegration of women is great and requires an appropriate response, at the risk of excluding the victims from the process of post-conflict reconstruction. The following question then arises: "Is it possible to reconstruct a post-war society when those who are relied on to weave the social and moral fabric of a society, namely women, are themselves maimed?"[22]

Notes

1. KwaZulu was an autonomous "homeland" created in 1977 and dominated by the Inkatha Freedom party. From the 1980s, the Inkatha party undertook a struggle for influence against Nelson Mandela's African National Congress (ANC). Today, the former KwaZulu homeland has been integrated into the province of Kwazulu/Natal.
2. Ashnie Padarath, "Les femmes et la violence au Kwazulu-Natal", in M. Turshen and T. C. Twagiramariya, eds, *Ce que font les femmes en temps de guerre: Genre et conflit en Afrique*, Paris, L'Harmattan, 2001, p. 90. Ashnie Paradath is the Regional Director of Pietermaritzburg Black Sash, a women's defence organisation in South Africa.
3. Radio programme, *France Culture*, "Rwanda, le génocide oublié?", 5 August 2003.
4. As for the men who survive the wars, they can also feel guilty at not having been able to protect "their" women from sexual abuse, which may lead to even more violence towards women when the frustrations of these men are unable to find an outlet.
5. Human Rights Watch, *Les soldats violent, les commandants ferment les yeux: violences sexuelles et réforme militaire en RD Congo*, 16 July 2009.
6. ICRC, *Quarterly Report of the Activities of the Integrated Programme for the Support of Victims of Sexual Violence/Other Vulnerable Populations in the Two Kivu Regions* (October–December 2008), p. 2.

7. Boris Cyrulnik, *Autobiographie d'un épouvantail*, Paris, Odile Jacob, 2008, p. 50.
8. Hutu Power was an extremist Hutu movement whose core, *Akuzu*, constituted those near to the families of President Juvenal Habyarimana and his wife.
9. UNIFEM (UNDFW), *Enquêtes de Référence sur les violences sexuelles basées sur le genre au Rwanda*, June 2008.
10. Naasson Munuyandmutsa, in "Rwanda, le génocide oublié?"
11. Post-exposure prophylaxis: the PEP Kit generally consists of anti-retrovirals, antibiotics, pregnancy tests and the "morning after" pill.
12. ACORD, "Gender-Sensitive Programme Design and Planning in Conflict-Affected Situations", *Research Report and Case Studies*, Somalia, Rwanda, Eritrea, 2002, pp. 17–40.
13. Tania Power-Stevens, "Somalia Case Study", in B. Bridget, ed., *Gender, Conflict and Development*, BRIDGE-Development-Gender, Report 35, vol. II, 1996, p. 102.
14. Between 1961 and 1991, Eritrea waged a civil war against Ethiopia. It ended with a territorial separation in 1993.
15. It would be interesting to consider whether the presence of a high percentage of women combatants in the EPLF has affected the incidence of rape in the civilian population. Elsewhere, no information is available on attacks that women combatants may have suffered within their own ranks.
16. Hasebenebi Kaffel, "Reintegration Programme for Demobilised Fighters, a Gender Prospect", Conference on Gender, Armed Conflict and Political Violence, 10–11 June 1999, World Bank, Washington, DC, p. 7.
17. Amanuel Mehreteab, "Border Conflict 1998–2000 and Its Psychological Impact on the Youth", in Sally Healy, "Eritrea Economic Survival", summary record of a conference held on 20 April 2007, Africa Programme, Chatham House, the Royal Institute of International Affairs, 2007, p. 46.
18. Amrit Wilson, *The Challenge Road: Women and the Eritrean Revolution*, London, Earth Scan, 1991, p. 108.
19. Robert Jay Lifton, psychologist in genocide in Rwanda, cited by P. Landesman, "A Woman's Work", *The New York Times*, 15 September 2002.
20. Bridget, ed., *Gender, Conflict and Development*, vol. II, p. 45.
21. Report of Independent Experts, *The Independent Experts' Assessment on the Impact of Armed Conflict on Women and Women's Role in Peace-Building*, UNIFEM, October 2002, p. 42.
22. A. Krog, "Locked into Loss and Silence: Testimonies of Gender and Violence at the South African Truth Commission", in C. O. N. Moser and F. Clark, *Victims, Perpetrators or Actors? Gender, Armed Conflict and Political Violence*, New York, Zed Books, 2001, p. 212.

11

The Body That Writes: Reflections on the Process of Writing about Wartime Rape Avoidance in the Israeli–Palestinian Conflict

Tal Nitsán

In the past few decades, the study of rape has focused on a variety of topics, such as the physical, psychological and cultural effects of different kinds of rape upon individuals and communities. Less attention has been given to the effects upon scholars themselves of studying rape. In this essay I would like to shift the focus from the studied phenomenon to the scholar who studies it, by focusing on my own work and its public response.

My Master's thesis, which examined the rarity of rape in the Israeli–Palestinian conflict,[1] is an example of "anthropology at home", meaning studying one's own society as opposed to anthropology's traditional endeavour to study other cultures.[2] Accordingly, my position within my research was very different from that of the traditional external viewer/participant. Moreover, I did not study a minor, "exotic" sect within my society, but mainstream society, to which I belong and with which I share many of its cultural views. Studying the reactions to my work – some of which were directly pointed at my physical body – adds an additional layer to my original study of rape as I focus now on myself as the studied subject, in what we can call the anthropology of the self. By discussing my own experiences, I hope to provide self-reflexive insights into the implications and consequences of studying rape, whether in peacetime or wartime.

As my work on the rarity of wartime rape in the Israeli–Palestinian conflict was interpreted by some as criticism of or even an attack on Israeli society,[3] I and my work were subjected to harsh reactions by the media. In this paper I consider the specific Israeli circumstances and context of these reactions, and my experiences as a woman scholar writing about (the rarity of wartime) rape in my own country. The reactions to my work taught me, in a very effective and tangible way, that wartime rape is one of the clearest manifestations of the relationship between the individual and the societal body. For me, it also served as a meeting point between my previous work on wartime rape and my current work on peacetime sexual violence, and demonstrated the extent to which wartime rape derives from peacetime sexual violence. My Master's thesis began by tracing global and historical incidents of wartime rape to get a better perspective on wartime rape's meaning and functions. Similarly, this essay begins by establishing the functions of peacetime and wartime rape through global and local examples, in order to understand the meaning of rape as a public statement.

The politics of wartime and "peacetime" rape

Analysing my own experience relies on understanding the more general phenomenon of rape as a violent human practice throughout human history.[4] Rape prevalence in both peace and war times calls for questioning the phrase peacetime, as for women, both victims and those terrorised by the thought that "it" may happen to them, there is no peace in these "times of peace". Writing about both "peacetime" and wartime rape, feminist authors, mostly women, uncover the views that enable, facilitate and normalise seeing and using women's bodies as penetrable beings, as penetrable commodities.[5] In so doing, they expose and proclaim rape's political dimensions, and challenge a powerful hegemony that naturalised the ways in which women's bodies are seen and consumed.[6] The intensity of the responses to their work attest to the greatness of the threat they pose to these powers.

For many ethnic and nationalist groups, women's bodies lie at the intersections of the group's boundaries, marking the frontier land. As such, women's bodies are constantly supervised and surveilled, patrolled and policed, regulated and restricted, to make sure that their bodies, the gate to the nation's body, are not penetrated by alien individuals.[7] Raping women of the opponent group by combatants or civilians during armed conflicts, once seen as simply another atrocity of war, is now also acknowledged as a political act, meant to terrorise, degrade and demoralise the defeated enemy while symbolically and sexually reward the victors.[8] It is an act in which women's bodies are turned into a medium through which one group of men conveys a potent message to another group of men.[9]

At the same time, wartime rape and sexual violence is also committed by men against women of their own group when they are viewed as subversive, traitors or collaborators, that is as national security threats. As such, in these periods of crisis, women's bodies and their sexuality become a way in which national and ideological identity can be both threatened and maintained. Sexually hurting individual's bodies sends three sets of messages to these women, their allies and the society as a whole: (1) a disciplining message: any resistance will be ruthlessly crushed; (2) a reminder of status: they are penetrable beings, a message that reinforces the prevailing patriarchal social order; and (3) a public proclamation of propriety that delineates proper sexual demeanour and approved ethnosexual partners.[10] Therefore, whether within or without group boundaries, sexual abuse of women's bodies during wartime sends a greater political message to the wider society much beyond affirmation of manhood.[11]

Studying wartime rape marks its roots in "peacetime" rape, as well as the latter's political dimensions. All of the sexual atrocities that take place during wartime against women of a specific group, such as rape, sexual slavery, forced pregnancy and abortion or pornography, now seen as political acts, are inflicted every day on individuals belonging to the group "women" in what we call "peacetime".[12] The equation is simple – without viewing women's bodies as commodities, without men experiencing a sense of entitlement, possessiveness and/or a sense of superiority in "peacetime", women's bodies cannot be seen as spoils of war, or as a means of communication with other men during wartime. Interestingly, acknowledging the political dimensions of wartime rape helps us to recognise the political dimensions of "peacetime" rape. Rape in "peacetime" works the same way that wartime rape works – it creates dominance of men of one group over the men and women of another by destroying the target group's self-conception as dignified, secure and self-determined, replacing it instead with fear, self-revulsion and degraded identity. It is a means of creating fear and maintaining dominancy. Studying rape critically, as a social phenomenon, poses a clear challenge to those who benefit from it.

Controlled occupation: the rarity of military rape in the Israeli–Palestinian conflict

Between the years 2003 and 2006 I worked on my Masters thesis at the Department of Anthropology at the Hebrew University in Jerusalem. The topic was "The Rarity of Military Rape in the Israeli–Palestinian Conflict".[13] It was the product of a personal quest for an answer to a question I found fascinating, one that led me to forsake my original

MA thesis project.[14] Based on interviews with Israeli reserve soldiers and literature about wartime and ethnic rape, the purpose of my paper was not to provide a decisive, report-like answer to the question of why wartime rape is so rare in the Israeli–Palestinian conflict, but to explore and describe the social situation in which wartime rape seems to not happen. How is it that it is so rare? What are the organisational and cultural mechanisms and practices that prevent the rape of Palestinians by Israelis in this specific conflict?

In my study I suggested a model according to which military rape is a product of group boundaries management; that is, it is a result of a social situation in which socio-cultural, physical-spatial and behavioural boundaries are vague, while simultaneously gender boundaries are clear and solid. I then discussed two types of military rape. The first type, a political, intentional military rape, is motivated by society's need to create concrete boundaries. These acts of rape mark an almost tangible borderline between the two groups – the penetrating vs the penetrated, the dominating vs the dominated. The second type is a symptomatic consequence of these same blurred physical-spatial boundaries when combined with clear ethno-, national and hierarchic boundaries. In this situation combatants of a well-distinguished dominant group are exercising power in a space inhabited by a well-distinguished dominated group. This type of rape is employed by individual combatants to accomplish their own personal aims.

In the analysis chapters of my thesis I described a clear feeling of group belonging among the Israeli soldiers, as well as clear power relations between the two groups: Israeli soldiers and the occupied Palestinian population. At the same time I demonstrated the Israeli soldiers' complex understanding of gender roles. Their elaborated views of women, men and society resulted in blurry and vague gender boundaries, ones that did not necessarily support hurting women sexually as a mode of wounding a society as a whole. However, the Israeli soldiers (men and women), a well-distinguished dominant group, were and still are exercising power in a space inhabited by a well-distinguished dominated group. Therefore, I claimed that in the Israeli–Palestinian conflict, rapes of Palestinian women by Israeli soldiers, committed in the past and maybe also in present times, were examples of symptomatic military rape rather than political, intentional military rape.

To explain how these symptomatic rapes are prevented in the Israeli army, I explored the ways in which the Israeli soldiers' behavioural, professional and moral boundaries are constructed, bequeathed and disciplined, as well as the practices which are used by the army to manage and maintain the physical-spatial boundaries between Israelis and Palestinians. I found that the vagueness of the spatial boundary in the Israeli–Palestinian conflict results in the engraving of the ethno-national boundaries within the soldiers' bodies. This serves as a self-disciplining mechanism, accompanying them wherever they go and, consequently, leading to physical rejection of the mere idea of trespassing these boundaries. Intentional military rape avoidance in this conflict thereby stands as an alternative way of realising the same political ends usually gained by employing intentional military rape: that is, establishing concrete group boundaries.

As I showed in my thesis, the rarity of military rape in the Israeli–Palestinian conflict reflects and reinforces group boundaries. The political objectives accomplished through intentional military rape in other conflicts are achieved by the Israeli army through rape avoidance. The rarity of symptomatic military rape, however, does not embody an alternative way of realising the individual aims of rape. Instead, it indicates a clear policy that rejects military rape as a social, collective hazard. That is to say, while intentional military rape embodies the recruitment of the individual's behaviour to the needs of the collective, the rarity of symptomatic military rape represents society's ability to penetrate the individual's body and design his or her desires in accordance with society's needs.

My thesis had three main conclusions. The first was that in order to explain the rarity of wartime rape in this conflict we need to consider a complex combination of practices, mechanisms and circumstances that I describe at length in my MA thesis; this complex combination relies on a distinction between symptomatic and politically intentional wartime rape and questions of social and physical boundaries between groups. Second, politically intentional wartime rape has clear political objectives, mostly the separation of one group from the other(s) and the establishment of clear dominancy. In the Israeli–Palestinian conflict, I claimed, the same objective is achieved not by rape, but by rape avoidance. Third, the fact that there is no clear physical border between Israelis and Palestinians creates a situation in which individual-based, opportunistic wartime rape is much harder to prevent. I claimed that the lack of a clear physical border is bridged by inscribing an inner boundary within people's bodies, an internal uncrossable barrier the soldiers carry within themselves wherever they go.

It is important to emphasise that the cultural mechanisms I discuss are not the sole mechanisms affecting the rarity of wartime rape in this conflict. The relative absence of wartime rape, or the restraint exercised by the Israeli military in this case, is strongly tied to varied mechanisms of discipline, regulation and control endorsed by the Israeli army.

My thesis was very well received in Israeli academia, as well as in the Israeli Defense Forces (IDF). It received two important prizes and was published as a book as part of one of these prizes.[15] It was, and still is, studied among high ranks in the IDF, and it led to two job offers from different research divisions in the IDF. However, I was actually trained as a Latin-Americanist scholar, and upon completing my Masters degree, I returned to my original field of studies, leaving the topic of the Israeli–Palestinian conflict, as well as Israel, to pursue a PhD degree in Vancouver, Canada. My doctoral research focuses on "peacetime" sexual violence in Guatemala. I soon found, however, that my Masters thesis refused to leave me.

Uncontrolled reaction: the rarity of restraint in public discussion

In December 2007, *Makor Rishon*, an Israeli right-wing newspaper, published a cover-page story about my thesis, entitled "Rape Refusers Are Compared to War Criminals".[16] The article claimed that I blame Israeli soldiers for being racists because they refuse to rape Palestinian women. In Canada at the time, I learned about the article through an email from one of the soldiers I had interviewed. What appeared to be an insignificant, minor episode of bad journalism developed within that weekend into an unpredictable media and academic crisis that to date, five years later, has not completely died out. My thesis, the one so many people assured me would rot on a library shelf, unexpectedly became a very public document. Or, more accurately, *Makor Rishon*'s version of my thesis.[17] Two sentences extracted from my paper and another from the paper's abstract became the public version of my thesis. This version was far less well received by the general public, who was never the intended audience of my project.

The next morning an intensive public discussion about the "racist soldiers" version of the paper began, mostly on the Internet. My work was discussed in electronic news articles, opinion columns, countless blog posts and internet forums. There were also articles and responses in the written media and several discussions on radio shows. In addition to modifying the content of my thesis, the media reports were packed with inaccurate details regarding my life, including the university I now attend, the stage of my studies, the identity of my supervisors and even the proper spelling of my name.

Thanks to the fact that my name was misspelled, and that I lived in Canada, I was mostly able to maintain my privacy. Still, a few people were able to find my contact information and soon enough the emails started to arrive. Most of these emails were silly, some mean, but generally this invasion of my privacy, though unpleasant, was not too onerous. The more offensive comments were the ones posted publicly, mostly online. *Makor Rishon* published a follow-up article entitled "On Rape and Prejudices" by the psychiatrist Kent Levin,[18] a man whom I have never met, in which he attempted to analyse my problematic, self-hating character, as demonstrated by my "anti-Israel/Jewish/women" views. Lawyers on a law internet forum considered whether there were legal grounds to sue me for libel or for endangering national security. Most responses were posted by furious citizens who read *Makor Rishon*'s version of my thesis, or its sequels, and were so angry with me that they thought I should be physically punished. The level of stated violence against me was so high that the head of my department at UBC thought I needed full-time security.

The most prevalent suggestion of punishment was rape. Comments like this, posted on a Ben Gurion University website, were common: "I guess the researcher needs to be raped by a Japanese/Arabic/American soldier to feel politically correct and normal."[19] Another internet forum posted a picture of the poet and translator Tal Nitzan and started a discussion around the question, "is she pretty enough to be raped?"[20] My body disguised under that of this other Tal Nitzan, became an objectified item in public discussion. I found this process fascinating and thought-provoking and tried to understand, through other local and global incidents, what there is in the study of rape that produces these reactions.

Wartime rape as a terror-inflicting method

The practice of wartime rape has a great impact, far beyond its momentary implementation, on both the victims and perpetrators. Just like "peacetime" rape, it is a means used to perpetuate dominance by keeping all women (and in the case of wartime rape, their communities) in a constant state of fear.[21]

Wartime rape was frequently used in Bosnia as a means of terrorising civilian populations and forcing ethnic groups to leave.[22] Sexual violence as punishment against same-group women is also used to have a greater impact beyond the actual act and victim. Many times it is not carried out by (self-appointed) state agents, but by "concerned, patriotic citizens". A prominent example for this practice is the public shaving of French women accused of collaborating with Nazi Germany. These women were humiliated as an act of revenge, and reactions to this symbolic act resonated with views and reactions to acts of rape. Girls watching stated that this punishment was worse than death, and the actual victims left places where they had been humiliated to try to rebuild their lives elsewhere.[23] Although most of these women were not raped,[24] the shaving of their hair, closely related to femininity and sexuality, was an act of sexual violence. Overall, these shavings reflected the willingness of the general public to watch traitors being punished, and their visibility allowed people to state their (rediscovered) patriotism.[25]

Media(ted) rape as a terror-inflicting method

From my distanced position in Canada, the public responses to my thesis seemed, in a way, similar. Obviously, the effect on my life was not even remotely similar to the physical and mental suffering these women and their relatives went through. Yet the mechanism used and the cultural logic behind it were quite similar. A crowd of self-appointed state representatives, joined by a mob of concerned, patriotic citizens gathered to defame my problematic character and disturbed personality. Yet this wasn't enough. A body had to be dragged into the main square. It was examined, evaluated, mocked, ridiculed and then publicly and repeatedly raped as a combined act of punishing me and terrorising others.

Modern technology allows public events to be seen beyond the traditional spatial and temporal limitations that affect our visibility. It enables incidents to be stretched beyond the places and times they are situated in, and for them to be replayed over and over again. Additionally, new technological modes create an interactional approach to communication media,[26] one that allows viewers to take part in creating the reality rather than remain silent information consumers. Consequently, technology allowed a much greater and more active crowd in the public rite of my judging and punishing.

Hundreds of people, maybe more, gathered to witness and defame me and my work. This, of course, had nothing to do with my actual work, which, as I mentioned, is well valued by the IDF. Under an enraged banner of morality, they violently proclaimed and projected their nationalistic, patriarchal and at times racist views. Being the actual person represented, after which that virtual body was named, I insisted on viewing it as the unreal phenomenon it was. As an external, distanced observer I could see the terrorising and disciplining message it sent feminists, left-wing supporters and society as a whole. As a social scientist, however, I found their message fascinating: We are the most moral people in the world (indeed, we do not even rape our enemies) and because you are suggesting we are not, you should be raped.

Between the bloodthirsty mob and the cautious, self-protecting audience, no one jumped in to protect that (virtual) wounded body. No one. My friends and family, as well as my colleagues and professors in Vancouver, were there to support me through the whole process, although they themselves were quite traumatised and speechless. However, even though I had the academic support of the Hebrew University, which was itself attacked along with the Israeli Sociology Society that awarded my paper, there was no clear act of intervention intended to stop this media craze. No one was really prepared for dealing with such an attack, and the common view was that the topic would fade away soon enough so the best response was to keep quiet. However, the issue did not die out, and I was left looking from afar at this virtual body that was tagged with my name, unsure of what to do with all of this unexpected attention.

Like an uninvolved viewer watching a TV news report on a wartime rape somewhere far away, all I needed to do was to turn off my computer and the whole scene would be gone. But could I do that? As a scholar studying rape, I did not turn off the TV when rapes of other women were reported. Could I – should I? – turn off the screen, where my virtual, though "live", rape was taking place? At that point, the only thing I was able to do was to keep on consuming the "news" and do my best to make sense of it. Is this an attack on the woman (traitor) scholar? Is this an attack on the feminist (traitor) scholar? Is this an attack on the Israeli (traitor) scholar?

A special treat(ment) for women traitors

Joane Nagel opens her discussion on ethnicity and sexuality[27] with two images of people accused as French traitors, published in a pictorial history of the Second World War. The first image is of two women carrying the physical marks of shorn women (shaved heads, shoeless feet, stripped clothing and swastikas tattooed on their foreheads). The second image is of a man on his knees with a blindfold on his eyes, who is about to be executed with a shot to the head.[28] Virgili claims that marking women's bodies is intended to degrade their image rather than to destroy them completely. It is a way to exclude women collaborators from society and externally mark their inner ugliness.[29] In France, this mode of violence allowed most accused women to escape a more permanent fate (for some it was just the initial punishment followed by graver acts). At the same time, one may claim that it was actually a kind of supplementary punishment directed at them alone. The difference in the images and the treatment of the women and the man, notes Nagle, display the sexualised and gendered nature of patriotism, treason, betrayal and the relation and relative importance of men and women to the nation.[30]

Different modes of sexual violence are used against women seen as traitors, to punish and humiliate them, to terrorise society and maintain its patriarchal order. Men can also be the victims of sexual abuse (an act that deprives them of their manhood). For instance, we hear of incidents of sexual abuse occurring in the course of interrogations. However, these acts are notably less frequent than acts of sexual violence exercised on women's bodies. Moreover, men seen as a national security threat are often punished, humiliated or interrogated through sexually abusing the bodies of women related to them.

At this point we can safely conclude that rape and other modes of sexual abuse are uniquely pointed towards women's bodies when seen as traitors, collaborators, subversives, or anyone else seen as posing a threat to national security. Likewise, it seems that as a practice the greatest strength of rape is its terrorising quality. As such, it is well translated to the virtual, media dimension of social life. "We will rape you" is, indeed, not as traumatic as "we are raping you", but as a publicly announced threat, it has a potent effect on both the threatened individual and society as a whole.

What feminists really want ...

I was not the first who went through a terrorising media(ted) rape. Looking back at those who stood there before me, I somehow find it quite flattering. During the feminist movement's anti- pornography campaign, leading feminist scholars and activists who opposed pornography were defamed by members of the pornography industry. In the case of Susan Brownmiller, the claim was made that she wrote *Against Our Will*, her groundbreaking book about rape,[31] because she wanted to be raped. This defamatory lie was proclaimed in pornography depicting a putative encounter between a man and woman in which, at the point of the sexual act, the woman started screaming, repeatedly begging the man to not rape her. Consequently, Brownmiller was depicted as a woman who wanted to be violated, whose no means yes.[32]

Brownmiller was not the only one to get this kind of attention. Following Gloria Steinem's significant feminist social and political activity, starting with an investigative report of the treatment of women in *Playboy*, *Hustler* magazine published a piece called "Hustler Interview: Gloria Steinem's Clit." On different occasions the magazine also published cartoons, articles and photos mocking the sexuality of Andrea Dworkin, a radical feminist well known for her criticism of pornography.[33] In a lawsuit against the magazine it was acknowledged that the persistent attacks on feminist anti-pornography leaders was meant to intimidate them, to discourage them from exercising their right to speak out against pornography, because if they did so they would risk such vile and cruel portrayals of themselves as Dworkin and Steinem experienced.[34]

By politicising pornography and violence against women, Dworkin, Steinem, and others challenged naturalised ideas about how women and their bodies should be seen and treated. This challenge meant that many men, who saw themselves as lawful, respectable citizens, could be seen as involved in acts of violence against women. Ironically, the backlash to this challenge, described above, confirmed the claims these feminist activists were making. As the heads of the porn industry depicted these women in pornography as a means to defame, humiliate and terrorise them, they actually asserted that pornography was a tool for the defamation and humiliation of women. It is clear that public threats of rape and sexual defaming are measures specifically directed towards feminists who dare to contest the way women's bodies are seen and used by men for pleasure and/or business, meant to terrorise and silence them and others.

An academic execution

Another important dimension for understanding the reaction to my work is the Israeli context. I was not the first Israeli scholar to go through such a media attack. A somewhat similar incident took place in February that same year, when Ariel Toaff, a professor of medieval and renaissance history at Bar Ilan University, published *Passovers of Blood: The Jews of Europe and Ritual Murders*. The book, published in Italy, was initially praised. In an extended review published two days before its publication, the book was described as a magnificent history book, in which the author "displays an extraordinary mastery in the fields of history, theology and anthropology", as well as "unheard [of] intellectual courage".[35] The following day, the medievalist Franco Cardini published another review, describing the book as "an exemplary historical research based on authentic sources and on an up to date reading of the critical literature", and he praised the author for his intellectual honesty.[36] Toaff himself was described as

> an historian perfectly qualified for addressing this question: an expert on Jewish dietary culture, including religious precepts and gastronomic habit, and as a product of interwoven fortunes of Jewish and anti-Semitic imagery: an Italian by birth (son of the former chief rabbi of Rome), but docent of Medieval history in Israel for some years now.[37]

Once released, the book sparked an intense controversy. The media depicted it as claiming that the blood libels against Italian Jews were based on actual practices of blood rituals, and as the book was published in Italian, most of the following responses were based on that interpretation.[38] Toaff was called a ridiculous researcher, a traitor of the Jewish people, a Jew-hater of himself, a stupid anti-Semite. The "Internet mob" called him a dirty leftist, a fool, a drunk with serious psychiatric problems. He received very serious threats to his life, and warm exhortations to commit suicide. The Israeli Parliament's Education Committee demanded to try him as an accomplice of anti-Semitism. Bar Ilan halted the distribution of his book and pulled it from circulation, removed Toaff from his position as head of department and forced him to stop his teaching activities.[39]

It is hard to ignore the similarities in the reactions that our (very different) works induced. Yet the differences are also quite striking. It seems that Toaff paid a much higher professional price. As a young female student I was depicted as a "silly little girl"; Professor Toaff, a fully grown-up male academic, had to carry the full burden of "responsibility for his actions". A comparison of the type of threats we received brings to mind the *French traitors'* pictures and returns us to Nagel's statement that the nature of patriotism and treason are sexualised and gendered, displaying the relative importance of men and women to the nation.[40] The *silly girl* doesn't pose the same threat to the nation as the *full professor*; hence she should be humiliated and terrorised, while he should be eliminated. At the same time, these unparalleled threats are an expression of the different ways society views fe/male bodies and the things that can be done to them. Both Toaff's and my work revolved around practices involving body penetration – blood rituals and rape. While I was to be physically punished by forced sexual penetration, no one suggested that Toaff's body should be penetrated for the purpose of blood extraction. No one posted his picture on a website and moderated discussions concerning the question from which body parts we should start extracting his blood.

(My) Body and (the Israeli) nation

The previous examples demonstrate that Israelis see and treat Israeli women in ways in which they are seen and treated elsewhere. Yet cultural phenomena have localised expressions. In *The Body of the Nation*, Weiss claims that Israeli nationalism represents an embodied discourse in which the national territory becomes equivalent to the personal body, and the body becomes a literal and metaphoric vehicle for collective fears, hopes and commitments. This deep structure of the nation is expressed in times of attack on the nation.[41] Moreover, Weiss shows how Israeli and Jewish identities, although sometimes discursively separated, are still closely tied in more fundamental, non-verbal practices of body identification.[42]

As I demonstrated in my thesis, morality is a central defining characteristic for group affiliation among the Jewish-Israeli collective.[43] By claiming that the rarity of wartime rape in the Israeli–Palestinian conflict does not attest to our morality, I challenged one of the deepest assertions many Israelis hold regarding themselves as individuals and as a nation. My thesis was therefore received as a vicious attack against the nation. This "attack" provoked that *deep structure* of the nation, mobilising a strong nationalistic reaction against me, my work and my body. In a way, my body became a space to deal with the challenge my work aroused.

The fact that the reaction to my work brought my body into the public discussion made me acknowledge the presence of *my body* in my thesis itself. I was well aware that my position as a young woman interviewing young men influenced the conversations I had with my interviewees, just as the fact that I am Israeli and had served in the army also had its effects.[44] However, re-reading some of the original interviews, I noticed that some of the interviewees clearly used my body as a measuring tool, comparing it to the female Palestinian body we were discussing. For them, my physical body represented a prototype of a generalised Israeli woman that they used to describe a generalised Palestinian female body. Considering the fact that my body was used as prototype of a generalised Israeli-Jewish body, it's not surprising that it was also used as a tool to punish and discipline me.

I never felt threatened by the public reactions to my thesis. I never thought that someone would actually come and rape me. Considering that, why bother dealing with these insinuated rape threats? The fact that I am attests to the power of the threats. Judith Butler suggests embedding the feminist discussion in the (female) body.[45] Bringing the body in as a method of intimidation is very powerful, yet using one's body to analyse the social situation in which this body is situated is also an extremely powerful tool.[46] Although a threat to the body is a symbolic act, it is almost tangible in the visceral response it evokes. Suggesting I should be raped was a powerful statement. It displayed wartime rape as a manifestation of the relationship between the individual and the societal body. Seen as traitorous or subversive, rape threats were to punish my specific body and to put me, a penetrable being, "in my place" in the nationalistic, patriarchal order. Through hurting (or threatening to hurt) my body, clear terrorising messages were sent to the collective nation about the limits of tolerance: neither resistance to the nationalistic ideological view of the collective as moral nor to the patriarchal order will be tolerated. Failure to conform will lead to grave consequences. It is important to note that, as far as I know, these reactions were not organised but seemed like the gut reactions of individuals and groups of self- appointed concerned citizens.

The commonness of these threats, the fact that Israelis simply see and treat (Israeli) women in the ways they are seen and treated elsewhere, confirms my claims regarding the rarity of wartime rape in the Israeli–Palestinian conflict. The Israeli collective, like other collectives, uses rape and rape threats to punish and terrorise, to discipline and maintain the social order. However, the Judeo-Israeli societal body experiences external penetrating as dangerous, thus creating cultural and organisational mechanisms meant to prevent this practice.[47]

Notes

1. Tal Nitsán, "Controlled Occupation: The Rarity of Military Rape in the Israeli–Palestinian Conflict", Jerusalem, The Shaine Center for Research in Social Science, 2007.
2. Mariza G. S. Peirano, "When Anthropology Is at Home: The Different Contexts of a Single Discipline", *Annual Review of Anthropology* 27 (1998), pp. 105–28.
3. Phyllis Chesler, "Refusing to Rape=Racism if you are an Israeli Soldier", *Pajamas Media*, 24 December 2007; "Tal Nitsán revisited", in Gudrun Eusser, *Simply Jews*, 25 December 2008; Hebrew University Paper Finds: Hillel Fendel, Arutz Sheva, "IDF Has Political Motives for Not Raping", *Israel*

National News, 23 December 2007; Ami Isseroff, "Help! Rape!", *ZioNation – Progressive Zionism and Israel Web Log*, 31 December 2007; Lee Kaplan, Arutz Sheva, "The Raping of Israeli Academia", *Israel National News*, 1 January 2008; Amnon Rubinstein, "Homemade Israel-bashers", *The Jerusalem Post*, 27 February 2008.

4. Susan Brownmiller, *Against Our Will: Men, Women, and Rape*, New York, Simon and Schuster, 1975, p. 15.
5. Judith Butler, *Bodies That Matter: On the Discursive Limits of "Sex"*, New York, Routledge, 1993, p. 50.
6. Susan F. Hirsch and Mindie Lazarus-Black, "Performance and Paradox: Exploring Law's Role in Hegemony and Resistance", in S. F. Hirsch and M. Lazarus-Black, eds, *Contested States: Law, Hegemony, and Resistance*, New York and London, Routledge, 1994, pp. 1–34.
7. Joane Nagel, "Ethnicity and Sexuality", *Annual Review of Sociology* 26 (2000), pp. 107–33.
8. In 1998, Judge Nanaethem Pillay of the ICTR said, "from time immemorial, rape has been regarded as spoils of war. Now it will be considered a war crime. We want to send out a strong message that rape is no longer a trophy of war."
9. "Genocide's Sexuality", in Catharine A. MacKinnon, ed., *Are Women Human? and Other International Dialogues*, Cambridge, MA, Belknap Press of Harvard University Press, 2006, pp. 209–33.
10. Nagel, "Ethnicity and Sexuality", p. 109.
11. "Genocide's Sexuality".
12. "Genocide's Sexuality", p. 225.
13. "The Rarity of Military Rape in the Israeli–Palestinian Conflict", MA dissertation, the Department of Sociology and Social Anthropology, Jerusalem, Hebrew University of Jerusalem, 2006.
14. For more about the writing process, see Tal Nitsán, "Reflections on Methodology and Ethics of Doing Anthropology of the Absence of Violence 'At Home'", in *Humans. Anthropological Perspectives on Holism*, Department of Anthropology, UBC, Vancouver, 2007.
15. Nitsán, "Controlled Occupation".
16. Amnon Lord, "Rape refusers are compared to War Criminals", *Makor Rishon*, 23 December 2007.
17. Another important source was the first article which was translated into English: Heb. U. Paper Finds: Hillel Fendel, Arutz Sheva, "IDF Has Political Motives for Not Raping", *Israel National News*, 23 December 2007.
18. Kent Levin, "On Rape and Prejudice", *Makor Rishon*, 21 January 2008.
19. At BGU Students' website.
20. This one was already removed, and can no longer be found on the Internet.
21. Susan Brownmiller, *Against Our Will*, p. 15.
22. Cynthia Enloe, "When Soldiers Rape", in idem, *Maneuvers. The International Politics of Militarizing Women's Lives*, Berkeley, University of California Press, 2000, p. 140. Similar practices were reported during the armed conflict in Guatemala as well as in other places.
23. Fabrice Virgili, *Shorn Women: Gender and Punishment in Liberation France*, Oxford and New York, Berg Publishers, 2002, p. 196.
24. Virgili, *Shorn Women*, p. 193.

25. Virgili, *Shorn Women*, p. 3.
26. John B. Thompson, "The New Visibility", *Culture & Society* 22:6 (2005), pp. 31–51.
27. Nagel, "Ethnicity and Sexuality".
28. Nagel, "Ethnicity and Sexuality", p. 107.
29. Virgili, *Shorn Women*, p. 195.
30. Nagel, "Ethnicity and Sexuality", p. 108.
31. Brownmiller, *Against Our Will.*
32. Catharine A. MacKinnon, "On Sex and Violence: Introducing the Antipornography Civil Rights Law in Sweden", in idem, ed., *Are Women Human?*, pp. 91–104.
33. Andrea Dworkin v. Hustler Magazine, Inc. Case No. 867 F.2d 1188 (9th Cir. 1989), 1987, Clause # 3,15.
34. Andrea Dworkin v. Hustler Magazine, Clause #52.
35. Sergio Luzzatto, "Quelle Pasque di Sangre, Il fondamentalismo ebracio nelle tenebre del Medioevo", *Corriere della Sera*, 6 February 2007.
36. Franco Cardini, "Pasque di Sangre. Il coraggio della storia", *Avvenire*, 7 February 2007.
37. Luzzatto, "Quelle Pasque di Sangre".
38. For more about the unfolding of the controversy see Sabina Loriga, "The Controversies over the Publication of Ariel Toaff's 'Bloody Passovers'", *Journal of The Historical Society* 8:4 (2008), pp. 469–502. For Toaff's response to these accusations, see Ariel Toaff, "Postface", in idem, *Trials and Historical Methodology in Defense of Pasque di Sangue*, Bologne, Il Mulino, 2008, pp. 363–98.
39. Ariel Toaff, personal communication, August 2009.
40. Nagel, "Ethnicity and Sexuality", p. 108.
41. Meira Weiss, "The Body of the Nation: Terrorism and the Embodiment of Nationalism in Contemporary Israel", *Anthropological Quarterly* 75:1 (2001), pp. 37–62.
42. Weiss, "The Body of the Nation", p. 53.
43. Nitsán, "Controlled Occupation", pp. 150–82.
44. Nitsán, "Controlled Occupation", pp. 7–8.
45. Butler, *Bodies That Matter*, p. 28.
46. Nancy Scheper-Hughes and Margaret M. Lock, "The Mindful Body: A Prolegomenon to Future Work in Medical Anthropology", *Medical Anthropology Quarterly* NS 1:1 (1987), pp. 6–41.
47. I owe a great many thanks to my family, friends and colleagues who supported me in the winter of 2008, as well as in the following writing process. I would like to thank Brendan Naef for his encouragement and feedback in the first stages of this project, Eric Sorenson and Nir Nitzani for their support during the writing process itself, and Lainie Schultz, Natalie Baloy and Solen Roth for their help in the different editing stages.

12

The Nigerian Civil War of 1967 and the Stigmatisation of Children Born of Rape Victims in Edo State

Adediran Daniel Ikuomola

The history of the Nigerian Civil War of 1967–70 still lingers in the memory of many Nigerians. This is especially true in ethnic communities that didn't participate in the war and hence that were seen as "saboteurs" by the belligerents. For this reason, many atrocities were perpetrated against these populations; rape was one of them.

War is generally referred to as the business of men because of the popular definition of war as "being in combat".[1] But warfare involves many activities besides the exact contact between armed men. Confessions of women from countries that have known civil disturbances help to illustrate the ordeal of the female gender and the challenges they grapple with during episodes of violence and civil strife.[2] War situations generate conditions for rape and mental suffering for women in addition to obvious physical trauma thereafter. Some of these traumas are evident in the recorded history of the armed violence in Nigeria.[3]

During the years of the Civil War, sexual aggressions were committed by the Biafran and the Federal Nigerian armies upon civilian populations. However, pride, shame and the African culture of silence on rape and other sexual atrocities still discourage recent victims, because legal authorities in Africa seldom take appropriate action; many women are unaware of their legal rights; and women may be victimised, either by insensitive, accusatory questions or by actual assault.[4]

On the other hand, scholars and researchers have been effective in unveiling some of the silent issues in the aftermath of the Nigerian Civil War. Generally the academic literature dealing with this armed conflict emphasises the causes of the war, the losses and other trajectories.[5] It is only in recent times that the role of women has come to be highlighted in terms of support and recruitment in the Biafran (secessionist) army, which tend to show the bravado of women. The few negative aspects of the war against women – quite apart from the suffering relating to their roles as mothers who had to cater for the children while their husbands were gone – was limited to the abduction and forceful marriages of beautiful young women by federal soldiers.[6] This account has, however, been looked down upon as defeatist, because it was coming from the Biafran vanquished camp. Until today, there is no literature on the consequences of the sexual violence in the Nigerian Civil War, especially about the stigmatisation of children born of rape victims originating from communities living in the defunct Mid-Western State in Nigeria.[7] Evidence of these tragic events abounds, even today in many of these communities and among families who were caught up in the war and had to return home with their impregnated daughters and wives raped by belligerents. Traditionally, African society disapproves of rape, but also vehemently dislikes the act of having children outside wedlock. The repercussions are enormous and the suitability of unmarried women to potential suitors tends to be reduced and even negated. The dislike of the community members of the victims' children as well as their families extends the repercussions of non-marital births beyond the personal stigma. The negative effect of such attitudes is usually more on single girls than married women.

This study therefore seeks to observe the attitude of children (and now adults) born of rape victims during the Nigerian Civil War of 1967–70, as a result of the stigmatisation attached to their names. It also examines community responses to incidence of rape and the level of compensation for mothers and the resultant children born after the war. This study is focused on victims in Edo State, which is a part of the former Mid-Western State.

Adults, but born from rape

The Edo is a "generic name given to a group of people who have a common ancestor and have a common language, with some different variants, depending on the distance between the group and the 'tap root'", and who are resident in and around present-day Benin City, the capital and principal city of the State.[8] In short, the land, the political state, the people, tribe and language are called Edo. The Edo-speaking people are today divided into the following clans: the Bini, the Esan/Ishan, the Afemai, the Akoko Edo and the Owan Oras. This study was based on information collected from 1985 to 2005 among some elderly Bini family members and war veterans in the traditional quarters of Ibiwe Ogbe, Oliha and Ogida, which are located in the ancient Bini Kingdom (today Edo State). Through snowballing techniques and key informants mostly from family sources, respondents and victims were traced from Bini city (Oredo Council Area) down to two other clans in Ikpoba Okha and Ovia Councils in areas surrounding these cities.

Data pertaining to this study were collected in bits, separately from respondents while their family members were involved in focus-group discussions. This study started in March 2007 and lasted until to the end of 2008. It was conceived first as an independent enquiry to document the suffering of Edo and Anioma Igbos people during the Nigerian Civil War; and later as a study on African people and culture carried out for the Nigerian Anthropological Association, University of Benin chapter. Like every other study relating to sexuality and memories of war, the responses to questions linked specifically to rape were difficult to obtain; on the other hand, several among the people met were unwilling to participate in group discussions and in personal interviews. There were also difficulties in locating all respondents within the Bini metropolis as was initially envisaged, where the study extended to other suburbs and villages. Ethics-guided research was highly emphasised especially on voluntary participation. Some of these problems were solved thanks to a Civil War veteran family background researcher who facilitated the implementation of the fieldwork.

The research sample comprised of 50 respondents: 41 were females and 9 were males, all drawn from a survey of 50 households in three Local Government Areas of Oredo, Ovia and Ikpoba Ohka, in the Edo State. The ages of the respondents showed that the oldest among them – 13 people – were born in 1968 while the youngest, who constituted the majority (and over two-thirds of the respondents), were born in 1969. Educational attainment of the respondents showed that 16 of the female respondents had no formal education. Marital status showed that 32 female respondents and 7 males were married. The occupation status shows that more than half of respondents were traders and 10 of these worked as civil servants.

Names in African settings are usually attached to events, supernatural, natural and other divinely inspired connotations.[9] It is the same scheme among the Bini, in Edo State, as the study revealed.[10] Among families who experienced the Nigerian Civil War, various names linked with this event were given to the respondents at birth. A few names are directly recalling the rapes in the Nigerian Civil war of 1967, as shown in

Table 12.1 Socio-Demographic Characteristics of the Respondents

Year of birth	**1968**	**1969**
Male	10%	8%
Female	16%	66%
Total	26%	74%
Educational Qualification	**Male**	**Female**
Primary	4%	22%
Secondary	8%	18%
Tertiary	6%	6%
None	–	32%
NR	–	4%
Total	18%	82%
Marital status	**Male**	**Female**
Single	4%	–
Married	14%	64%
Divorced	–	18%
Total	18%	82%
Occupation	**Male**	**Female**
Traders	12%	40%
Civil servants	6%	14%
Housewife	–	18%
Unspecified	–	10%
Total	18%	82%

Source: Field Survey, 2008.

Table 12.2. Like in other parts of Nigeria, and in Africa generally, the names were usually given by a male head in the immediate family or by the eldest male in the extended family; women are usually not allowed to name a child in African culture.[11] This is a form of hegemonic masculinity[12] which has continued to sustain the systemic dominance by African men of women culturally and socially in both the private and public domain.

The percentage representation above shows that among the interviewed and sampled respondents, 15 of the female and 3 of the male respondents were named Okwuoeimose (the ugly face of war) at birth, which recalls the sexual violence which occurred during the Civil War. The other names, even if they also make reference to this topic, are more elusive.

Table 12.2 Some of the African Names Given to Respondents at Birth

Names	Abbreviation	Meanings	Male	Female
Okwuoeimose	Imose	War is ugly	6%	30%
Okwodiaghe	Diaghe	War is not worth watching	2%	14%
Okwoeinata	Nata	Not to be told	4%	–
Okwoienoma	Enoma	War is not to be desired	2%	12%
Naimie	Imie	Not to be experienced	–	14%
Okwoba	Iba	Red is the colour of war	4%	12%
Total			18%	82%

Source: Field Survey, 2008.

The meanings and circumstances surrounding the above-mentioned names were explained by an Ovia female interviewee:

> I was named at birth Okwuoeimose meaning the face of war is ugly. I later got to know the meaning, quite late while I was in school in the 1980s. So after secondary school I decided to abbreviate the name from Okwuoeimose to Imose which gave it a different meaning entirely. Imose in Bini dialect simply means beauty.

The focus group discussion highlighted some of the reasons why such names were given to children born during that period. For names such as Okwuoeimose, Okwuoria, Naimie and Okwoienoma, people were told that these names were given to them to remind people of what happened in the past and to stop such things from happening again.

Second, the word Okwuo – which means war – is, since the end of the Civil War, not mentioned among the Bini communities, except in times of provocation and communal conflict. Third, for those bearing such names, it becomes a living reminder for the community of events that once occurred, especially among the elders, and a form of mockery for youths and aggrieved persons. Lamenting the stigmatisation resulting from her name, an interviewee noted that

> So those of us whose pregnancy came up during this period and were born shortly after, mostly we had names beginning with the word "Okwuo"; in other instances if the events or circumstances were nice, names were also given to mark such events and their importance to society, but many have come to use it against us. Thus these names we are bearing ... Stigmatisation is a big problem we faced while growing up.

On the contrary, eight of the male respondents tend to disagree with the above point, and rather see names containing Okwuo as prefix as symbolising masculinity. It is important to note that this point of view is prevalent in the majority of male respondents. One of them explained during the group discussion that war-names teach lessons to the people: "so we all should be proud of our names and forget about what people are saying". For another participant, "the names signify a period of wars and depict the strength of warriors. So that is why we were given such names by our parents."

Stigmatisation attached to the names given to children born of rape victims

The study demonstrated an overwhelming response, most especially from the female respondents who asserted that they were being punished by receiving such names and that they are still suffering indirectly with the stigma associated with the circumstance surrounding their births. A male respondent – a school teacher at Ikpoba-Okha – commented that "the stigmatisation is even worse in circumstances where either parent is unknown". Narrating a death scenario of a parent, he went further, saying that

> In my own case, as my mother died a few months after my birth, I have come to realise that when one is not educated or not doing well in society, the stigma is heightened. People see some of us as a bad omen [he burst into tears]. This has made many of us to go on self-exile in cities where less is known of us.

Corroborating the issue above, a response from a mother in one of the focus-group discussion sessions in Ikpoba-Okha revealed that stigmatisation was greater among women, coming from the general public, their husbands and even from fellow women:

> The major problem with us, women born this time in question, is the way we are referred to especially among families that are in the know. For example a neighbour called me names just because I was not in support of her opinion to impeach the president of our Street Landlord Wives Association; saying that my attitude is related to the circumstance of my birth, after a heated argument. You can imagine how I felt that day, saying it in our local dialect. To date I still feel it anytime I set my eyes on this lady, who incidentally is from my mother's clan.

Table 12.3 The Effect of Stigmatisation on Respondents Born of Raped Mothers

Effect of stigmatisation	Male	Female
Late marriage	11.1%	36.6%
Leaving the community	33.3%	53.6%
Depression	11.1%	46.3%
Changing of names	67%	34%

Source: Field Survey, 2008.

Among some of the women, 12 of them also noted that on a few occasions they have been stigmatised in their very own matrimonial home by their own husbands and in-laws, sometimes jokingly and other times with all seriousness. A lady participant in Oliha-Oredo concluded that African "culture does not permit us to complain. I remember the day my husband was furious simply because I came back home late to prepare his meal for that evening; he abused me with the meaning of my name." Further, she noted that this happened

> not only once: another instance was a day we had a quarrel about whose responsibility it is to pay the children's school fees which I have been paying for some time now, just because I told him it was not my duty as a wife, he flared up and said, "I am not surprised. It's typical of those born of unidentified parents." To crown it all, I was called a bastard by my own very husband ... When I remember that day, I always feel sad.

This particular notion of names and their influence on character and behaviour of the bearer is an aspect of African culture inherently built into individuals consciously or unconsciously through everyday socialisation.[13] A particular example in South Africa shows that among the Basotho people, names are seldom chosen at random and usually recall a grandfather, or other important relation. Sometimes they commemorate an important or unusual event or personage, and other times an abuse.[14]

The effect of stigmatisation on children born of rape victims

It was observed that the majority of male respondents agreed that stigmatisation has caused them to change their names from war-related meanings to other meanings that suit their personality or new status. One third of the female respondents did the same. In Ikpoba-Okha, a male participant, a civil servant working in a local secondary school, said that with life experience

> there are better ways to cope with such anomalies. For example, for the simple fact that I am now a born-again Christian, I had a vision to change my name to suit my new found religion. So I choose Emmanuel [his former name was Okwuodiaghe] to avoid anybody asking me what circumstance brought about the name. Because this is a work of research and because I am an educated person, I have sworn not to talk about it anymore.

Another effect of stigmatisation was the enthusiasm to leave the community where these people were born. This decision was mostly taken by the women who experienced major stigmatisation in their community. That's why many of them were forced to leave their villages. This argument was captured during the group discussion session: an Ovia female respondent mentioned that "stigmatisation is responsible for a lot of the respondents moving out of their place of birth and migrating farther, especially to big cities where their identity is secured and there was the possibility of starting anew." It was also noted that change of name was a common practice among ladies.

This view was supported by 19 other respondents. Similarly, it was also noted by 62% of the interviewees the role marriage plays in reducing the stigma attached to names and conditions of their birth. As two participants, named Okwoeimose and Okwuodiaghe, concluded:

> If not for marriage I wonder how my life would have been in my small village where everyone seems to know about the rape incidence of my mum during the Civil War. Marriage has helped a lot, taking away to some extent the stigma, but there are continuous ties with those I grew up with, especially the older ones, who still look at us with pity and disdain. This, to a large extent, annoys me anytime I come across some of them. This has prevented me and my family from going to my only home, which is my maternal home.

A male respondent commented on the issue of gossip in the community, a reason also associated with the exodus of victims from the community as well as the increasing number of migrants who never returned. This participant, named Okwoba, has been living in Benin city but was present in one of the discussion sessions:

> I was told that the war caught up with my grandparents who were itinerant traders in the East before the war, and the incidence of rape frustrated them back home in Orionmwon. But as time went on my mum had to leave when I was ten years old – that was in the 1980s – to Benin as a result of gossip about her and me her [son] and also because of the inability to settle down in terms of marriage.

Stigmatisation and late marriage

Late marriage and the inability of rape victims to get married to their peers (age, grade) or to men within the same community had been noted by scholars.[15] The study reveals that about 37 per cent of the female respondents were affected in the form of settling down into matrimony. This was also inferred from the age difference between respondents and their siblings on one hand, and, on the other, from being the only child of their parent, which signifies that some of the respondents' mothers were never married, or had delayed marriage, or even lost interest in marriage after the incidence. Over 25 respondents attested to this. For instance, a female respondent commented that she was 13 years older than her stepsister, because her mother could not marry in her own village, and was forced to go to the city in search of a husband: "I was in secondary school before she left for Benin in search of suitors. She must have been in their thirties at the time, which is quite late for marriage ... for an Edo lady without Western education. Luckily for her she met my stepfather."

A male respondent, who was an only child, told how his mother died without getting married:

> My own case of being an only child shows clearly that my mum was never married. I know that this continued until she died last year. Although she told me she would have love to marry, her tribal men were always looking at her with disdain. And that there was nobody to stay within the city [Benin], as she also lost her father [my maternal grandfather] to the war.

A female interviewee, Enoma, noted in support that stigmatisation went beyond her mother down to her, a situation she concluded was

Table 12.4 Community Responses after the War to Incidence of Rape

Responses	Percentage
Parents were welcomed	46%
Causes were attributed to the rapist	70%
Incidence reported to the government to find and punish offenders (military or civilian) of rape during the war	92%

Source: Field Survey, 2008.

the reason why her mother died early a few years after her birth, and why she, Enoma, is still not married at the age of 40:

> It is not only our parents that were affected. It is a problem we are also facing. Take myself as an example. I am still single at 40, not because I love to remain single but the attitude of men, ego and our belief system about the war (I'm sorry to say) put us women of such circumstances at a disadvantage since most times investigations were made about one's family and circumstances surrounding one's birth. The same thing happens to a young girl if she is raped today by fellow community men; they talk less of not knowing the rapist in the case of the Civil War of 1967.

She explained further that it was not as if there were no suitors coming for her while she was much younger. In simple terms, she told of one such relationship she was involved in and how the man in question asked her to give an account of her birth: "I was quite embarrassed. I knew then he must have been told by someone in the village. I felt teased and told him the whole story, then he said his parents were not in support of him marrying me." She concluded that the community were in the know about all that ever happened: "It was easy for them to know because my mother died early and without a grandmother. I grew up with my grandfather, and the community knew he was not my biological father."

Community responses after the war to incidence of rape

The responses from the study showed that the examined three communities made attempts to welcome back the parents and victims of the Civil War. From Table 12.4, 23 respondents noted that their parents were welcomed back to their community. This was necessary because most communities were happy to see the survivors of the war, especially those who were trapped in the eastern part of the country. This was narrated by an Ikpoba-Okha female interviewee:

> Like most wars, survivors were usually welcomed as we were told it was a celebration galore, joy and happiness after their arrival [referring to the mother]. The community rejoiced and gave thanks to God. Although I was not born then, the story was told by my maternal grandfather. He said this was immediately after they returned from where they were trapped. However, he said after everything settled down, about a year later, another reality set in as children were born, children whose paternity could not be determined as a result of the incidence of rape during the war. They became victims as well as their family.

The community saw this as something strange and as ill luck for society.

As it was then in most rural communities in traditional African societies, events or cases viewed as evil were usually taken to the shrine where the entire community gathered and asked the gods to avenge the situations which individuals cannot redress.[16] Respondents noted that abuses, spells and curses were heaped and cast on the perpetrators of such evils as rape during the war. This account was mentioned and asserted by 35 of the 50 respondents in the study: "To date the evildoers, especially the rapists who placed an everlasting stigma and name on us and the people of this community, have not been forgiven and continuously the community will forever be heaping curses upon curses on them and their families."

Responses show that almost all respondents agreed that effort was made by the parents and community to inform the government agencies in order to locate and punish military or civilian offenders of rapes committed during the Civil War, but nothing was done to ameliorate problems resulting from the war. The requests seem to have fallen on deaf ears, because, at that time, emphasis was put on how to rebuild infrastructures destroyed by the conflict, and all the national policy was led by the slogan "Every man should forgive and forget, because we are brothers and brothers fight and reconcile." So, after the war, reconciliation and rebuilding, as noted by literature and government gazettes, was predominantly aired on radios, in print and on television, publications and programmes running continuously.[17]

> No reasonable effort could be achieved after the war and even to date, because emphasis was on reconciliation and everything was done to reunite the country. And any attempt to dig into rape cases

Table 12.5 Compensations for Rape Victims and the Resultant Children

Responses	Percentage
Free medical treatment in government/military hospitals	36%
No compensation in any form	64%

Source: Field Survey, 2008.

> was seen as "reopening the wounds" of the Civil War. This was basically the government reply to the community as we were told. It is important to state here that the era in question was militaristic and not a democratic regime ... so everywhere could have been tense at that time, particularly the people affected.

Compensation

The last objective of this study was to examine the level of compensation for the rape victims and the resultant children of the Nigerian Civil War. It was observed from 18 respondents that if some victims were compensated, it was only with free medical treatment in government and military hospitals. But the majority of the respondents noted that their parents did not receive compensation in any form whatsoever. A female respondent captured this in her annoyance with those who answered in the affirmative during the focus-group discussions, by saying,

> If there was any compensation my mother would have told me. It was only those who were in the big cities that enjoyed such benefit, if there was any at all. Come to think of it the only major government hospital then was in far-away Ibadan; others were mere clinics probably in the military barracks in Benin city. How many people would have gone closer to the hospitals in the barracks with the memory of the Civil War still fresh in their heads? Again most people then were said to have gone to their villages in fear that the war may continue, so tell me what kind of compensation was there?

Another respondent, among those who answered in the affirmative way, concurred:

> Really there were few hospitals then, and mostly in the cities, and only those around Benin city benefited. But to say it was only in Ibadan is an exaggeration because there was a military hospital in Benin, the capital of the old Mid-Western region. For me I was told

> that there was free medical treatment, maternity care and child delivery in government and military hospitals. These were what looked like compensations.

This shows, more or less, that the possible compensation for the effects of the war was only limited to physical or material losses, other quantifiable and personal belongings and effects. Injuries like loss of life and breadwinners; increased number of orphans, disabled men, women and children; rape victims and the resultant children and other long-lasting psychological injuries and tortures caused by warring factions were not compensated, and will certainly not be for years to come, because of the stronghold of African tradition and cultural practices which still place a stigma on rape and its female victims, and children whose paternity is not known.

This study to a reasonable extent exposed some of the problems faced by children born as a result of rape in wartime. Rape in wartime has been left unchecked in many forgotten conflicts. It would seem today that sexual violence during wars has become too banal to provoke a response. Nevertheless, until an international legal framework is firmly established, ad hoc advocacy efforts, human rights and humanitarian law will go a long way and remain crucial in preventing sexual violence in war. The international court of justice as well as the local judicial system should help transform the legal and cultural acceptance of sexual violence, from a norm acceptable as part of military and domestic laws. Perpetrators of sexual violence will then no longer be exempted from punishment, as most cases have shown they are. Proper education and enlightenment about the aftermath of rape should be given to soldiers preparing for war either on the side of the ruling government, oppositions or rebels. This is crucial to legitimating norms of gender justice and shifting both blame and shame from victim to perpetrator, although this also requires committed, knowledgeable and sensitised judicial personnel as well as persistent civil-society engagement. Women's NGOs must remain vigilant, supporting efforts to ensure sexual violence is no longer treated with levity, empowering women and men whose paternity are not known to reject the socially imposed stigma and to obtain redress and to participate fully in peacebuilding. Women's right to control their bodies and their sexuality must be respected at all times, war or no war.

Lastly, the Nigerian government should come out openly and specifically apologise to communities and families with children born of unknown soldiers of the Biafran and Nigerian army during the Civil War. This will serve as a first step in the right direction to ameliorate the psychological trauma they have and are experiencing in their various communities as well as bring to bear other communities other than Edo people to give their accounts, because this is far beyond the Binis, whose accounts this study has captured for future reflection and research.

Notes

1. Jeffrey A. Sluka, Carolyn Nordstrom and Joann Martin, eds, *The Anthropology of Conflict in the Path to Domination, Resistance and Terror*, Berkeley, University of California Press, 1992.
2. Alexander A Madiebo, *The Nigerian Revolution and the Biafran War*, Enugu, Fourth Dimension, 1980.
3. J. Akande, K. Awosika and I. O. Albert, "Community Conflicts and Violence against Women in Nigeria", in Aïcha Tamboura-Diawara, ed., *Women and Violence in Africa*, Dakar, Association of African Women in Research and Development (AAWORD), 2005.
4. United Nations Population Fund (UNFPA), Programme Advisory Note, Reproductive Health Effects of Gender-Based Violence; Policy and Programme Implementations, 1998.
5. Hilary M. Njoku, *A Tragedy without Heroes. The Nigeria–Biafra War*, Enugu, Fourth Dimension, 1987.
6. Egodi Uchendu, *Women and Conflict in the Nigerian Civil War*, Trenton, NJ, Africa World Press, 2007.
7. The Mid-Western State was formed in 1963 from Benin and Delta provinces of the Nigeria Western Region. Its capital was Benin City. The Biafran forces invaded the new Mid-Western State, en route to Lagos, in an attempt to force a quick end to the war. While under Biafran occupation, the State was declared the "Republic of Benin". The "Republic" collapsed a day after the declaration as Nigerian troops overtook Benin city. The Mid-Western State was renamed Bendel State in 1976. In 1991, the Bendel State was split into the Edo and the Delta States.
8. Allan F. C. Ryder, *Benin and the Europeans. 1485–1897*, London, Longman, 1977.
9. Ogonna Chuks-Orji, *Names from Africa. Their Origin, Meaning and Pronunciation*, Chicago, Johnson Publishing Company, 1972; C. Nze, "The Art of Naming among the Igbo", *Ikenga* 6 (1984), pp. 1–2; Susan M. Suzman, "Names as Pointers : Zulu Personal Naming Practices", *Language in Society* 23 (1994), pp. 253–72; Samuel Gyasi Obeng, "From Morphophonology to Sociolinguistics: The Case of Akan Hypocoristic Day-Names", *Multilingua* 16:1 (1997), pp. 39–56; Louise Crane, *African Names. People and Places*, Urbana-Champaign, University of Illinois, 1982.
10. Ota Ogie, *Edo Culture. Modern Essays*, Edo Publications, 1974.

11. Sharifa, M. Zawawi, "*What's in a Name?*", *Unaitwaje? A Swahili Book of Names*, Trenton, NJ, Africa World Press, 1993.
12. Sanit Gac, "Patriarchy, Masculinities and Health Inequalities, *Elsevier* 23:2 (2009), pp. 159–60.
13. E. Goody, "Delegation of Parental Roles in West Africa and West Indies," in Thomas R. Williams, ed., *Socialization and Communication in Primary Groups*, The Hague, Mouton, 1975, pp. 125–58.
14. Hugh Ashton, *The Basuto. A Social Study of Traditional and Modern Lesotho*, London, Oxford University Press, 1967.
15. Thomas McCahill, Linda Meyer and Arthur Fischman, *The Aftermath of Rape*, Lexington, MA, Lexington Books, 1979.
16. Ogie, *Edo Culture.*
17. Olusegun Obasanjo, *My Command. An Account of the Nigerian Civil War 1967–1979*, London, Heinemann, 1980.

13
"Special Decisions" Children Born as the Result of German Rape and Handed Over to Public Assistance during the Great War (1914–18)

Antoine Rivière
Translated by Helen McPhail

At the end of 1914, the first official reports on the exactions inflicted by German soldiers in the invaded regions of eastern and northern France confirmed that women and young girls had been raped "with unbelievable frequency".[1] In the first months of 1915 this provoked violent controversy, which developed in the popular press as well as in medical and legal journals, and which could be expressed in a single question: What to do with the children who would be born as a result of these rapes? With the aim of separating *enfants de boches* from French families and society, one section of opinion preached abortion, and went so far as to excuse infanticide. According to supporters of these extreme measures, if these children were allowed to be born their German heredity would represent a danger of mortal degeneration for the "French race".[2] They were confronted either by those who rejected abortion absolutely, for religious or pronatalist convictions, or by those who argued for nurture over heredity and considered that the way to take revenge on German and criminal fathers would be to bring up their children and make true French citizens of them.[3]

The government was quick to perceive the danger in allowing the development of arguments in favour of abortion, and was anxious that such arguments might gain audience even as far as parliamentary circles, where Louis Martin, a Radical senator from the Var, proposed – without success – a law designed to authorise abortion for women raped by the enemy.[4] Determined to "react against [this] trend of opinion",[5] in a circular dated 24 March 1915, Louis Malvy, Minister for the Interior, took measures which were designed to "offer mothers every facility to give birth in secret and to give up their child"[6] to the Parisian *Assistance publique* (Child

Welfare Authority). Thus orchestrated by the public authorities, the concealment of "the barbarian's child"[7] in the anonymous mass of wards in state care, in the midst of abandoned children, orphans or children found, taken in and brought up by social services, seemed to satisfy both camps, at least as a last resort: the outcry died away within a few days.

Between 1915 and 1921, 403 children "born as a result of German acts of violence"[8] were thus taken in by the service of Children in Care in the department of Seine (Paris and its close suburb), and registered under the ad hoc category of "special decisions": a denomination which had the advantage of revealing nothing explicit about the origins of these particular wards,[9] and which in bureaucratic practice soon came to designate not only the circumstances of their admission but the children themselves. In all likelihood, this figure makes it possible to estimate the total number of children born following the rape of a French woman by a German soldier during the First World War at between 1000 and 5000;[10] the figure of "10,000 German births",[11] the only numerical estimate put forward at the time by some newspapers, would thus be an over-estimate but would indicate a figure of some size – several thousand – which was not purely imaginary.

The personal files of children taken into public care by "special decision"[12] now throw fresh light on some elements in the history of the German occupation during the Great War. The mothers recounted the circumstances of the rape and their relations with the occupying forces, before and after the attack, to the Assistance official who dealt with their statements. They also spoke of their reasons for giving up the child, and in most cases their reasons had nothing to do with either the father's German identity or the violent and criminal circumstances of the conception. In most cases, in fact, it was the urgings of a family circle anxious at the disgrace and shame hovering over the girl-mothers and children born of adultery that overcame them; under constraint and overwhelming persuasion they resigned themselves to give up the state of motherhood which, they said, they were ready to take on. Through these singular stories the attitude of French society vis-à-vis the children born of German rapes thus emerges as much more complex than might appear from the patriotic warrior discourse on the "children of the enemy"[13] at the beginning of 1915, and which initially posed the debate in terms of race.

The Public Assistance solution: abandonment and secrecy

When they decided to intervene in March 1915, the Minister for the Interior and its director of Public Assistance and Health, Jules Brisac, wished to persuade the victims of German rapes not to seek abortion or infanticide. Largely inspired by the doctrines and operations of the Public Assistance system, they addressed a circular to Prefects containing measures to allow these women to conceal their pregnancy and then to dispose of the child in total secrecy, without recourse to criminal means. The governmental solution thus consisted of concealing first the women and then the children.

First, victims of rape by German soldiers were to be moved from their home setting. The circular therefore provided for their removal to Paris and their admission into a maternity clinic in the capital where, as Brisac reiterated, they "have every opportunity of giving birth without the knowledge of their ordinary circle".[14] After the birth came the handover, the keystone of the system devised by the government to create a definite break in the links between child and mother, giving her the confidence that her secret would never be made known.

In the terms of the ministerial arrangements, whether the children were born in a clinic in Paris or in the provinces, all newborns destined to be handed over were sent to the centre for Children in Care in the Seine, in the Rue Denfert-Rochereau in Paris, in order to be registered there as Public Assistance wards. This delocalisation of admissions was designed to take children away from the invaded regions and to put them beyond the reach of any future reprisals from a population living under the severe challenges of battle and occupation – it was feared that they would be too quick to identify the invader's child with the invaders themselves. But the key factor lay elsewhere: this measure of dislocation was supposed to lose the "German births" in the considerable total of 50,000 children who were then wards of the Seine service, and to distribute them throughout the territory: the Paris authority, unlike most provincial services which recruited their wet nurses locally, placed its tiny protégés across some thirty departments. By removing the newborns from the place of their conception and blurring the tracks, suspicion was avoided concerning the place to which they were taken – local officials, the wet-nursing family, the village community – this pattern also ensured, in their own more or less well-understood interests, that the children themselves would never know, or even suspect, their origins.

The circular provided for a handover within the three days after the birth in order "that the declaration at the civil register can be made in Paris within the time limit established by law".[15] In the final part of the system created by the government, the children should in effect be entered in the civil registers as "born of father and mother unnamed", without indication of the place of birth and under a name unconnected with the names of the biological parents. If the handover enabled the child of a German rape to be distanced from village society and the family, their vital record created by the authorities was designed to remove the child from the legal family, in particular preventing any claim as an eventual inheritor.

This measure set in place a set of skills that was frequently tested: the service for Children in Care was in the habit of requesting the City hall of the 14th arrondissement in Paris to create a vital record for each child handed over without knowledge of parental identity, but very specific precautions were necessary in dealing with these "special decisions". Deliberately rejecting a custom which had long been accepted for abandoned children,[16] the management of Public Assistance in effect recommended the director of the home in the Rue Denfert-Rochereau "to create a vital record [for the child] with a surname and not only first names: this is intended to avoid the possibility that an incomplete description might subsequently leave the origin of the child open to supposition".[17] Tradition, however, is hard to destroy, and several wards taken on through a "special decision" received only a further first name in the guise of a family name. But when he agreed to follow the recommendations of the director of the Assistance, the official dealing with vital records was able to take inspiration from the calendar or from geography; for example, two children arriving at the same time from the Meuse were given the names of Bard and Leduc.[18] At the end of 1918, some of his choices, dictated by the outcome of the war, show signs of light-heartedness and national pride: a small girl was given the first name of France-Aimée;[19] another was entered in the civil registry under the first name and family name of Victoire Metz.[20] Some months later, although some family names still celebrated the end of the war, they no longer reflected the same warlike and patriotic register but appeared to represent a new pacific spirit. This was the case with the little girl named France Pax, who was accepted by "special decision" in July 1919 – but who did not enjoy this fresh world of peacetime for long, for she died a month later.[21] This pattern of naming, which was also a way of celebrating the armistice and acting as a reminder of the event, affected not only children born of German rapes but also other wards of the Assistance and even, for first names, the sons and daughters of ordinary families: none the less, in the case of the "special decisions" it no doubt took on particular significance as if, in symbolic revenge for the atrocities of the invasion, the choice of name should also ward off the anguish of defeat and enslavement that these children represented.

As noted by Stéphane Audoin-Rouzeau, "the measures taken by the government did not [unleash] the hostility of those who favoured the suspension of the laws on abortion".[22] In a few weeks the matter of the fate of these children vanished from newspaper columns, and the debate ended definitively, even though rape by German soldiers continued in the occupied territories after the period of invasion (80 per cent of children admitted by "special decision" were born of assaults committed after the first quarter of 1915). If we can judge cultural mobilisation against "the child of the enemy" through the press coverage given to the arguments from proponents of abortion or justified infanticide, it must be accepted, using the same sources, that the demobilisation was even more spectacular because it was complete and virtually immediate.

How to explain that the intolerable intrusion of these children of German origin into French families was finally tolerated by these partisans of the most extreme measures? It is possible – this at least is the hypothesis that I put forward – that the governmental decision was acceptable because it retained the essential factor: by ensuring that the children would no longer be identifiable as the offspring of a German father, it removed the most visible stigmas of the rape, and eliminated the most tangible signs of virile France's inability to protect its women.[23] At the end of the handing-over procedure, the real story of the origin of these children was in effect buried under the seal of secrecy, in the most remote of Public Assistance registers; it was replaced by a single narrative, that of the vital record in which the father is shown as unknown. In other words, German paternity was officially supposed never to have existed. Everything happened as if the public authorities were responding to the biological paternity imposed by the rape through their capacity to designate the father legally or, in particular circumstances, to indicate the absence of a known father. What the success of the governmental intervention reveals is, it seems, the true source of the controversy at the beginning of 1915: behind the façade of a discourse posing the debate solely in terms of biological origin, another (hidden) stake was advanced, which indeed included the question of race and blood, but which exceeded and transcended it, that of affiliation.

Silence and dissimulation: therein lay the full effectiveness of the solution of handing a child over to the Public Assistance. In June 1915, in a letter addressed to *La Chronique médicale*, a certain F. Clavier rejected the proposition that children born of German rapes should be allowed to live; in his view, the only response imaginable to this form of enemy aggression was abortion, which should ensure "the elimination of these sad bits of wreckage from a cataclysmic time".[24] In the eyes of certain of his contemporaries who, like him, had for a time defended radical solutions, the governmental measures were finally acceptable, if not desirable, because they delivered the children to another form of nothingness, that of being without family or origins, of being children in the care of the Public Assistance.

The first admission by "special decision" was registered in May 1915; others were not slow to follow, in an irregular pattern. The atrocities of the invasion were followed by the assaults during the occupation, then the reprisals of the retreat, so that until the end of hostilities each liberated territory delivered to the Assistance its batches of women made pregnant by the enemy, and children of the war.

The circumstances of rape and the chronology of handing over

French women continued to suffer sexually throughout the war which apparently alternated between moments of calm and periods of brutal outbursts. The chronology of handovers under "special decision" depended only partly on such fluctuations, which defined the pattern of births, for it was also linked to the evolving German territorial seizure and the possibilities open to victims to flee the invaded regions and then hand their child over to a French authority.

The first peak in the curve of admissions to the Paris reception centre corresponds with the period from August to December 1915. These were handovers by women from the regions that were invaded in the summer of 1914, then liberated between September 1914 and the beginning of 1915 by the French counter-offensive. From January 1916 to February 1917, in the setting of the German occupation which remained fixed from the end of 1914, few fresh "special decisions" were taken although children continued to be born from German rapes. The mothers who then succeeded in getting back to territory under French control were very rare. A few arrived at the end of a long and complicated journey, such as the woman who, from her village in the Somme, was sent with her newborn to Belgium, then to Germany, before finally reaching France "repatriated via Switzerland";[25] others formed part of a few convoys in which the German authorities organised "the return of civilian internees [...] to France".[26] From February to November 1917, on the other hand, we can see a spectacular rise in admissions, which coincides with the German troops' strategic withdrawal to the Hindenburg Line. This retreat in February–March 1917 liberated a stretch of territory from Arras to Soissons which had been occupied since the summer of 1914, and offered mothers the possibility of achieving a handover which some, raped in the earliest days of the occupation, had been forced to delay for a long time. The number of "special admissions" reached its peak at the end of 1918 and during the first half of 1919: this, too, reflects the liberation of the invaded regions. In 1917, as in 1918–19, when they finally escaped from German power some women followed the flood of refugees and arrived independently to abandon their children in the Rue Denfert-Rochereau; others, who chose to remain in their own region, gave up the child to the prefectoral services which undertook to transport the child to Paris.

It seems then that, contrary to what was originally foreseen by the authors of the circular in March 1915, a fair number of the victims of German rapes could not be taken into care during their pregnancy and that, far from being able to hand over their child immediately after the birth, some had to wait for the end of the occupation before they could separate themselves from the child. Although nearly one child in two was aged less than two weeks at the moment of its registration under the "special decisions", more than one in four arrived at the reception centre in this way after the age of twelve months.

The majority of children who were conceived during the "invasion rapes" of August 1914 were dealt with very nearly as set out in the terms of the ministerial circular. Raped by soldiers whom they never saw after the attack, the mothers could take refuge in Paris after the departure of the German forces, give birth there and hand over the child immediately. The same applied to giving up the children born as a result of the "retreat rapes", whether this related to rapes committed from the summer of 1918 onwards or those perpetrated in 1917. Evidence of this came from a woman who was attacked near Soissons in February 1917: "The Germans, furious at their retreat, took revenge on the women."[27] On the other hand, some women who were raped during the invasion, for example in the Ardennes, and others, victims of the occupation rapes, remained for long months – and some throughout the entire war – in submission to enemy soldiers.

In the occupied towns and villages, where the male population was away in the French army or in a German prison, the women were both very vulnerable and forced to live in proximity to the occupying enemy. Women were requisitioned for work in the fields or factories, as well as living under the same roof as soldiers – circumstances particularly favourable to an attack. This often happened after a period – a few days or several months – of living at close quarters without violence.

The context of the occupation also favoured the post-rape pursuit of coexistence between victim and aggressor. In an Ardennes village, for example, a woman was required to provide accommodation for a German soldier from January 1918, at a time when her husband had just been sent to incarceration; five months passed before the rape, then unavoidable cohabitation continued for several weeks more without a fresh attack.[28] When terror and the victim's silence, or inaction on the part of the military hierarchy, backed the aggressor in his feeling of impunity, the rapes might be repeated, as in the case of a woman living in Meurthe-et-Moselle who was abused regularly by a German soldier during the six months from January to June 1917.[29]

Sometimes these forced cohabitations turned into a sort of resemblance to conjugal and domestic life. A woman in an Aisne village described how the German soldier who was billeted in her house came into her room at night and raped her in the autumn of 1916. After this attack, "relations, to some extent forced, but without violence"[30] continued until the liberation of the area in April 1917: the victim said she had accepted the situation in order to avoid being brutalised again and "in order to have supplies"[31] – food and fuel – for herself and her two legitimate children. Sexual relations without repetition of the initial physical violence and shared participation in household management, cohabitation over several months and then the pregnancy of the young woman appeared to imitate the life of an ordinary household. Despite the fear and sufferings endured by their victims, some German soldiers were undoubtedly able to persuade themselves in this way that in the occupied region they were constructing a substitute conjugal life.

It also happened that the rapist, once his crime was committed, was transformed into a protector of his own victim, enabling her to avoid suffering violence at the hands of other soldiers or the looting of her house. The aggressor could thus comfort himself with the illusion that the relations with his victim had changed their nature, and that they no longer fell under the sign of force.

After the rape, the physical and emotional submission of the victim could also reach its peak. A young woman from the Ardennes who had been raped by several Germans was "taken along with the battalion wherever it [went]":[32] beaten and humiliated, she was for several days the sex object and scapegoat for the soldiers. These cases of extreme violence, rare in the files, are certainly under-represented in our sources: the privations and brutality inflicted on the victim are such that one may suppose that these rapes were less frequent than those followed by a pregnancy to full term with the birth of a viable child.

If the journey towards a definitive handover was part of the evolving geographical pattern of the occupation, it was not reduced thereby, since it also depended on the wishes of the mothers or, in many cases, of their family circle.

Motives for giving up a child: traditional morals and combatant moral authority

In the eyes of those who spoke out in favour of abortion in 1915, it was useless to let beings live whose origins would inevitably prevent their mothers from ever feeling affection or attachment for them. In fact, 14 files of "special decisions" show mothers who rejected their child precisely because of its German origin and the violent circumstances of its conception. One woman ended her account with the confession that she "could not love [her child] given that he came from a German".[33] Or consider another who, in October 1918, explained to the staff in the reception centre, "I refuse to bring up a child from such a race";[34] the mother's explanation revealed the violence of this rejection, her adherence to the patriotic values of the time, and her capacity to pick up some of the most striking topoi of combatant discourse. If the intensity of the rejection of the child forced on her by the enemy is sometimes striking, what strikes the reader of these testimonies is that such cases are very rare. Only four per cent of mothers evoked their aversion to a child of German origin as the motive for giving it up. In contrast, many women, despite the circumstances of the conception and the origin of the father, expressed themselves as strongly attached to their child and only gave in to the separation with great reluctance.

More than a third of the cases of abandonment via "special decision" originated in constraint applied to the mother by her immediate family. For 38 of these women, all aged under 30, it was their circumstances as an "unmarried mother" which imposed on them the separation from their child. Half of them wanted to hide the existence of the newborn child from the family; the other half obeyed parents who insisted that the "the unwanted little thing" must be given up.[35]

Although the German identity of the father sometimes lay behind the parental injunction, in most cases it seems that the parents insisted that the child be given up because they feared above all that if it were revealed, the existence of the child would prevent their daughter from ever finding a husband and would dishonour the whole family in social terms. Thus guided by the sole preoccupation of their family's respectability and reputation, the parents established their insistence within a framework of fault and reparation: despite the fact that the fault was forced by violence, their daughter must hide her "lapse" and "make up for her shame".[36] That the child's father was German certainly added to the parents' fear of being the object of popular gossip and disapproval, but this was never anything more than a further reason for insisting on the child being given up.

When it did not come from the parents, it was constraint applied by the husband which won the day: among the 150 married women who handed over to the Public Assistance a child born after a German rape, two out of three gave this as the motive for abandonment. Twenty of them abandoned their child so that their husbands, mobilised and unaware of their situation, could never know of the child's existence and would learn nothing of the violence that they had suffered. In nearly 80 cases, on the other hand, the husband discovered the birth and circumstances of the conception, either when on leave or after demobilisation; in such cases, it was he who insisted that the child be given up. To force his wife to obey him, he could threaten to withdraw his military allowance from her which, although modest, was often an indispensable income in the families of mobilised men; but in most cases he threatened divorce, combined with a form of blackmail over their legitimate children: if she refused to give up her "German kid"[37] the mother risked being deprived of her other children. This is what happened to a woman whose husband discovered her pregnancy on his return from captivity at the end of November 1918: he urged her to give up the child to the Public Assistance immediately after the birth – but when the time came, in February 1919, she "could not bring herself to do so, and kept the newborn".[38] This caused her to be "banished from the conjugal roof"[39] and for several months, she lived alone with her baby. In the end, worn out by difficult and uncertain living conditions, in despair at being separated for eight months from her other child who was "kept by the father",[40] she gave way and in October 1919 she gave up her little girl.

A few of these men appeared to obey the precepts of combatant moral authority and asserted that if they refused to welcome the *enfant du boche*[41] into their family, it was because it "owed its life to the hated race".[42] One such man, mobilised in his factory had, for example, warned his wife "that he did not accept the presence of the child; and that the memory of a little girl of 8 years old raped at the same time as the mother by the Germans, and who died as the result of this rape, would perhaps incite him to take vengeance on the little child".[43] As a consequence of its origin, the child was here irredeemably part of an enemy group responsible for the disasters endured by the family. In a few cases, however, the masculine motivations did not amount to this anti-German aversion, and appeared to be based primarily on non-specific war-time moral norms and social conformism. In their letters to the Public Assistance, as in their oral evidence collected by the authorities, a good number of these men designated the child to which their wives had given birth following a German rape as "the product of adultery" or "the illegitimate one". These expressions could be seen as no more than the effect of a reluctance to speak too crudely of a distressing reality: but it seems to reveal, at least in around 15 of the files, one of the fundamental sources of this masculine attitude – the foreign child rejected by these men was not so much the child of another race as the child of another man.

Some of these husbands wanted the child to be given up because they suspected their wives of having had sexual relations voluntarily with the German father, without force. The peak of this reversal of perspective can be seen – as visible in three files – when the husband, who wanted the child to be handed over, gave up his insistence because in the end he was firmly convinced that the child was indeed born as the result of rape – and therefore no longer saw his wife as guilty but as a genuine victim. A man from the Somme who served in the infantry throughout the war learned in the summer of 1918 that his wife had apparently been raped by a German soldier three years earlier and that a little girl had been born as a consequence. By threatening divorce, he persuaded his wife to give up the child. After the armistice the couple resumed life together and, in March 1919, made a joint request to the Public Assistance to have the girl returned to them: the husband explained that "having had proof that his wife was a victim" and that the child "was indeed born as the result of German assaults" he "agreed to take [her] back into the family household".[44] In such – no doubt exceptional – cases, the German rape, when confirmed, was no longer the cause of abandonment but quite the contrary – it was what prevented it, because it dispelled any suspicion of adultery; this helps to show on the other hand that certain cases of abandonment by "special decision" were no different from the abandonment of children born of adultery which, in wartime as well as in peace, was the usual cause for admissions to the Assistance system.

Parental or marital influence can also be perceived in the fifty files – more than one in eight – in which at the moment of handover to the reception centre the mother asserted that she would take the child back if her husband failed to return from the front or if she managed to get away from her family. Thirty-five children were in fact the object of a demand for restitution by the mother, generally within less than three years from the end of the war. Divorce, the death of the husband, the deep depression which sometimes overwhelmed the mother after giving up her child and which led those close to her to take a more flexible attitude, were circumstances which created favourable conditions for these requests for restitution. Sometimes it was the fear of scandal or fear of stigmatisation which faded and made it possible to envisage the return of the child to the bosom of the family. In December 1918 an inhabitant of the Aisne, who had been mobilised since the outbreak of the war, wrote to the director of the Assistance bureau in the hope of taking back the child which his wife had abandoned a few months earlier on his instructions: "As I expect to be liberated soon [...] I have been thinking: [since] this child is a victim of the war and the mother is not alone in such circumstances, I consent to take the child back."[45] The important point here is indeed the matter of reputation: convinced that his wife was not the only French woman to have been raped by a German soldier, recognising that his family would not have to suffer being pointed at but, on the contrary, should be regarded with all the compassion due to victims of the war, this man gave in to the wish of his wife to take back the abandoned child. In all, 14 of these children were reclaimed and returned to their mother after being given up – a moderately high proportion of more than 40 per cent of favourable decisions.

Although after the separation the mothers were full of remorse or painful silence over a secret which they alone had to bear, the children themselves had to face another ordeal, that of a dreadful mortality which the public authorities certainly did not intend but for which they bear a measure of responsibility.

The raised death rate among children: the price of secrecy?

Following their abandonment, drowning in the anonymous mass of children in the Assistance system, soon despatched to a rural wet nurse, the children born of German rapes were wards like any others; yet they had to overcome a death rate which, compared to that of other children in care, was by no means ordinary.

Of the 393 children registered under the "special decision" category between 1915 and 1921, 186 – nearly half – died within six months of their admission. This high death-rate chiefly reflects the population age-structure represented in "special decisions", since three-quarters of the children reached the reception centre before the age of twelve months – that is at an age when mortality was normally very high. As in the case of other young Assistance wards, the deaths were mainly due to "congenital weaknesses", conditions of the digestive system, infectious disease (flu, meningitis, tuberculosis, cholera) or poor living conditions in the receiving families.[46] From the death certificates prepared by the authority there was thus no reason for morbidity specific to children born of German rapes; however, at the same age, a ward of the Seine had a greater chance of survival if he or she was an ordinary abandoned child than if admitted under the "special decisions". Over the whole period 1915–20, the death rate among children in care under the age of two was indeed 40 per cent, while for children born of enemy rape the rate was 54 per cent.

This excess death rate can be explained by the living conditions of the mothers between the rape and the abandonment of the child. Whether they had remained in the invaded regions or whether they had swollen the ranks of refugees, these women suffered numerous material difficulties: these privations, as well as the physical and psychological consequences of the rape, could undoubtedly have harmful effects on the child's health during gestation as well as after birth.

It seems, however, that some of the specific clauses for the Public Assistance "special decision" admissions also contributed to this higher mortality. The centralisation of admissions in the reception centre in the Seine which in the name of secrecy organised the circular of March 1915, thus imposed frequent and difficult journeys on more than half of these children – those whose mothers had not been able to come to Paris for the birth. First they were sent from the place of their birth to each department's reception hospices or the *préfectures*; from there, they were then taken to Paris; finally, about a week after their arrival, they left the centre in the Rue Denfert-Rochereau for a provincial destination, for example in the Nièvre, the Allier or the Creuse, to be handed over to a wet nurse. Fed along the way with food that was cold or barely warmed, from a badly sterilised bottle when they were not given solid food, exposed to cold and contagious disease, the chances of survival of these very young babies were substantially compromised by such travelling.

Faced with this situation, the Public Assistance remained almost silent, limiting itself to establishing this macabre accounting in its annual reports which, notably in 1919, bear some resemblance to the death rooms represented by shelters for abandoned children under the Ancien Régime. It is none the less certain that those responsible for children in public authority care did not fail to make the connection between the long and difficult journeys imposed on the "special decisions" and the high mortality recorded. The proof of this is that, since the end of the nineteenth century, directors and doctors in the service in the Seine, aware of the disastrous effects of the to-and-fro between Paris and the provinces on the health of the children given into their care, had been working constantly and actively to limit the travelling imposed on these babies. In 1904 in particular, during the great reform of child care services,[47] and then again in 1911,[48] they gained legal authority to modify the operation of the service to this end. Already in 1876 the director of Public Assistance in Paris wrote to the Prefet of the Seine: "Who does not see that these journeys imposed on children of a few months old are [...] a significant cause of death?"[49] Restriction on moving wards had thus been a constant preoccupation for the Public Assistance system in Paris, at least since the beginning of the Third Republic. In the name of a veritable crusade against infant mortality which was then under way in France,[50] it constituted one of the bedrocks of its institutional culture. From this point of view, its silence on the dangers that the special measures of 1915 forced on the children of German rapes is deafening. That the Minister for the Interior, the Director of the Paris Administration, Gustave Mesurer, as well as certain leaders of the medical world – from the doctor-midwives, and child-care specialists who, like Adolphe Pinard, had been the scientific authority for the circular of March 1915 – had, in full knowledge of the facts, assumed the risk that the admission system would increase the mortality of children born of German rape, leaves absolutely no doubt at all.

Thirty years later, in December 1944, when it had to regulate the fate of children born of rapes committed during the Occupation by Wehrmacht soldiers, the provisional government of the French Republic considered measures that were directly and explicitly inspired by those of March 1915. But this time – proof that all lessons had been taken from the experience of the "special decisions" – the public authorities decided to "avoid the danger that would be created for health or even the life of these children [by] an early transfer" to Paris and preferred "to provide for the move of the mother before the birth"[51] so that they could have the benefit of an establishment in the capital of the new procedure of "birth under X".[52]

The attitude of French society vis-à-vis children born of German rapes is complex and should not be reduced to the noise and fury of the 1915 debate. Some files indeed show the aversion, indeed the hatred, which, because of their origins, these children could arouse in certain French families. The vast enterprise of dissimulation entrusted to the Paris Assistance undeniably demonstrates that, without ceding to patriotic and racist extravagance, the public authorities wished to offer a solution which measured up to the distress that they could feel growing in public opinion. Their preferred choice of a procedure of secret abandonment, which endangered the life of the youngest and most fragile of these children, is sufficiently eloquent that, in their eyes, the "special decisions" were not children just like any others.

Yet the mothers' accounts and the statements of their husbands or their parents, often told another story than the straightforward rejection of an enemy-born child; they showed the long story of abandonment and of the Public Assistance, populated with illegitimate and adulterous children; they told of the violence suffered by many unmarried mothers, in times of war as in times of peace, by a society which handicapped them with great material dependence and the ban on becoming mothers because they were not married; finally, they recounted the tyranny of honour and reputation. Was "special decisions" ordinary giving up? In many cases, the files of these children reveal the gap which could exist between the norms borne by the ruling warrior morality of the day and by certain patterns of individual behaviour: behaviour, no doubt minority, in which the singular capacities seem to reveal much more of the weight of traditional morality and the weaknesses of this combatant magisterium than the undivided reign of a specific morality born of the war.

Notes

1. *Rapports et procès-verbaux d'enquête de la commission instituée en vue de constater les actes commis par l'ennemi en violation du droit des gens (décret du 23 septembre 1914)*, Paris, imprimerie nationale, 1915, vol. 1, p. 8.
2. *Le Matin*, 7 January 1915, quoted in Stéphane Audoin-Rouzeau, *L'enfant de l'ennemi (1914–1918), Viol, avortement, infanticide pendant la Grande Guerre*, Paris, Aubier, 1995, p. 99.
3. On the controversy of 1915, see Ruth Harris, "'The Child of the Barbarian': Rape, Race and Nationalism in France during the First World War", *Past and Present* 141 (November 1993), pp. 170–206; Judith Wishnia, "Natalisme et nationalisme pendant la Première Guerre mondiale", *Vingtième siècle Revue d'histoire* 45 (January–March 1995), pp. 30–9; Audoin-Rouzeau, *L'enfant de l'ennemi*.
4. The text was not examined by the Senate. *Documents parlementaires. Sénat, session du 18 février 1915, annexe n° 42.*
5. Letter from the Minister of the Interior to the Préfet for the Seine, 16 February 1915, Archives de l'Assistance publique de Paris, ref: Foss 603/125.
6. Ibid.
7. *Le Journal*, 17 December 1914, cited in Anne Cova, *Maternité et droits de femmes en France (xixe–xxe siècles)*, Paris, Anthropos, 1997, p. 197.

8. Frequently used expression in official reports for the admission of children.
9. Letter from the Minister of the Interior to the *Préfet* for the Seine, 27 May 1915, Archives de l'Assistance publique, ref: Foss 603/125.
10. Antoine Rivière, *La misère et la faute. Filles-mères et enfants abandonnés à Paris et dans le département de la Seine pendant la Grande Guerre (1914–1918)*, DEA under the direction of Serge Berstein, IEP de Paris, 2002, pp. 214–22.
11. Françoise Thébaud, *La femme au temps de la guerre de 14*, Paris, Stock, 1986, p. 59.
12. In the archives of the *Assistance publique*, ten files are missing; the other 393 are conserved, with those of the other wards of the Seine, in the Direction de l'Action Sociale de l'Enfance et de la Santé (DASES).
13. Audoin-Rouzeau, *L'enfant de l'ennemi*.
14. Letter from the Minister of the Interior to the Préfet for the Seine, signed by J. Brisac, 16 February 1915.
15. *Circulaire du 24 mars 1915, in Rapport sur le service des enfants assistés du département de la Seine pendant l'année 1915*, Paris, Administration générale de l'Assistance publique à Paris, 1916, p. 10.
16. Anne Lefebvre-Teillard, *Le Nom, droit et histoire*, Paris, PUF, 1990, pp. 69–70.
17. "Instructions du Directeur de l'Assistance publique au directeur de l'hospice des Enfants assistés", undated, quoted in *Directeur de l'Assistance Publique, Mémoire au Conseil de Surveillance de l'Assistance publique*, 20 May 1915, Archives de l'Assistance publique, ref: Foss 603/125.
18. File on two children admitted to the Public Assistance of Paris (AP) by "special decision" in April 1919, DASES. The name of the department taken as inspiration by the civil register officer has been changed.
19. AP file, "décision spéciale", November 1918, DASES.
20. AP file, "décision spéciale", November 1918, DASES; the child died in January 1919.
21. AP file, "décision spéciale", July 1919, DASES.
22. Audoin-Rouzeau, *L'enfant de l'ennemi*, p. 132.
23. On the "masculine traumatism" following the rape of women, see Audoin-Rouzeau, *L'enfant de l'ennemi*, pp. 90–8.
24. *La Chronique médicale* 6, 15 June 1915, p. 177.
25. AP file, "décision spéciale", February 1916, DASES.
26. *Rapport sur le service des Enfants assistés du département de la Seine pendant l'année 1917*, Paris, Administration générale de l'Assistance publique à Paris, 1918, p. 7.
27. AP file, "décision spéciale", November 1917, DASES.
28. AP file, "décision spéciale", October 1919, DASES.
29. AP file, "décision spéciale", January 1919, DASES.
30. AP file, "décision spéciale", July 1917, DASES.
31. AP file, "décision spéciale", July 1917, DASES.
32 AP file, "décision spéciale", November 1918, DASES.
33. AP file, "décision spéciale", April 1919, DASES.
34. AP file, "décision spéciale", October 1918, DASES.
35. AP file, "décision spéciale", June 1917, DASES.
36. AP file, "décision spéciale", March 1919, DASES.
37. AP file, "décision spéciale", May 1919, DASES.
38. AP file, "décision spéciale", October 1919, DASES.

39. AP file, "décision spéciale", October 1919, DASES.
40. AP file, "décision spéciale", October 1919, DASES.
41. AP file, "décision spéciale", February 1919, DASES.
42. AP file, "décision spéciale", June 1917, DASES.
43. AP file, "décision spéciale", March 1917, DASES.
44. AP file, "décision spéciale", September 1918, DASES
45. AP file, "décision spéciale", August 1918, DASES.
46. Ivan Jablonka, *Ni père ni mère. Histoire des enfants de l'Assistance publique (1874–1939)*, Paris, Seuil, 2006.
47. Law of 27 June 1904, *Service des Enfants assistés.*
48. Finance law of 13 July 1911, modifying the budgetary regulations of the Service des Enfants assistés.
49. *Rapport sur le service des Enfants assistés du département de la Seine pendant l'année 1875*, Paris, Administration générale de l'Assistance publique à Paris, 1876, p. 9.
50. Catherine Rollet-Echalier, *La Politique à l'égard de la petite enfance sous la IIIe République*, Paris, PUF-INED, 1990.
51. Letter from the minister for Public Health to the Minister for Justice, 13 December 1944, quoted in Fabrice Virgili, *Naître ennemi. Les enfants de couples franco-allemands nés pendant la Seconde Guerre mondiale*, Paris, Payot, 2009, p. 197.
52. These arrangements which combine giving birth anonymously and handing over the child in secret were created in three successive texts: the laws of 29 July 1939, 2 September 1941 and of 15 April 1943. Nadine Lefaucheur, "Accouchement sous X et mères de l'ombre", in Didier Le Gall and Yamina Bettehar, eds, *La pluriparentalité*, Paris, PUF, 2001, pp. 139–75.

14

The Russians and Germans: Rape during the War and Post-Soviet Memories

Norman M. Naimark

No one will ever know exactly how many German women were raped by Soviet soldiers at the end of the Second World War and the beginning of the peace. It may have been tens of thousands or more likely hundreds of thousands. If one includes all of the instances of rape, gang-rape, and rape murder during the Soviet offensives against and occupation of East Prussia, Silesia, Pomerania, Austria, the Czech lands and other German-inhabited areas of Eastern Europe, the numbers of victims might reach as many as two million. Some have suggested that over 125,000 women were raped in greater Berlin alone during and after the victorious offensive.[1]

The numbers of victims are important, but so was the ubiquitous fear of rape, and the ways in which rape permeated every aspect of women's lives in this period, from the fear of venereal disease and the demand for abortions, to the need for food and a roof over their heads. These women and girls *were* Germany, as millions of men had been killed on the battlefield, held in POW camps, and overwhelmed in face of the Russian onslaught. The women's stories became Germany's story: of total defeat, violation, occupation, accommodation and rebirth. These stories were told repeatedly by and among women during and immediately after the war. Many thousands were collected by Theodore Schieder and his team after the war and published in multi-volume collections about the *Vertreibung* (forced deportations) from the east.[2]

Diaries and memoirs by women about their experiences are scattered in archives and attic storage rooms around the world. Some are published (Anonyma, *Eine Frau in Berlin* – a primary subject of discussion later on – is a particularly insightful example); most are not. As historian Edith Repogle Scheffer has written, the diaries constitute attempts by German women to gain control of the chaos around them, provide their persons with a sense of agency, and create a narrative that allows them to emerge from the status of victimhood.[3] Sometimes the stories were about other women who were raped; sometimes they were about themselves. But there was a sense that all German women in the eastern part of the country shared this experience, while German men were left out. If the men were there at all, they were helpless, and when they returned from the war they often could and would not listen to the stories and did not understand. The women also sensed that they were forced to pay for the deeds of the men; rape in war is often about establishing ultimate domination over enemy soldiers by violating their women. At the same time, in these accounts, there is little acknowledgement among the women that their own government and army were to blame to a considerable extent for their suffering.

The diaries' authors seldom ask why the Soviet soldiers raped. In most cases, the women feared and even expected it, as a consequence of the high-pitched, incessant message of Goebbels and the Nazi propaganda machine that Soviet soldiers were barbaric hordes of Asiatics and their officers Jewish-Bolshevik rapists. When the first gang-rapes and rape murders took place in East Prussia in April 1944, Goebbels was quick to pounce on the opportunity to spread fear of Soviet occupation in order to bolster German defences. It is hard to know whether Nazi propaganda of this sort worked or not. It certainly sowed so much anxiety among the Germans faced with being overrun by Soviet troops that thousands of families followed through on suicide pacts.

There is no easy answer to the question why the Soviet troops raped so many German women. That soldiers rape in war is well known; the Second World War was not the first, nor will it be the last instance of mass rape in warfare. Allied soldiers in the western zones also raped German women, although the incidence was significantly lower, and the tenor of the occupation much less violent.[4] Soviet soldiers committed terrible depredations against women of other nationalities besides Germans. The Hungarian women and girls of Budapest were the first to feel the violence of the Soviet offensive on their persons after conquering Budapest in February 1945.[5] The "liberation" of Vienna and most of Austria by the Red Army was also accompanied by a violent outburst of rape.[6] Certainly in this regard, Soviet soldiers made no distinctions between the Austrians and the Germans.[7] All in all, German women in the Reich were particular targets, and the extent of rape by Soviet soldiers was unprecedented in any European war before or since.

Soviet soldiers sought revenge from the Germans: for what they had done to their homeland, to their towns and villages, and to their families, including extensive crimes of rape. At the outset of the offensive, the Soviet propaganda machine encouraged soldiers to exact revenge, to make Germans pay for what they had done, to search out and destroy "the beast in its lair". Photographs of piles of corpses at Majdanek (seldom identified as primarily Jews) were plastered on posters and newspapers to show the fiendishness of the Germans. The famous Soviet writer Ilya Ehrenburg wrote, "If you kill one German, kill another – there is nothing funnier for us than a pile of German corpses."[8]

Many Soviet soldiers experienced a furious rage as they encountered German civilians, some of it founded on their individual stories of family suffering, but some derived from the sheer brutality of the total war forced on the Soviet Union by the Nazis. The rage only intensified as Soviet soldiers moved into Germany, which even in the last stages of the war was vastly richer and more developed than the sometimes quite primitive circumstances from which they came. "Why in God's name did they attack us?", many soldiers asked. "We had nothing for them to take."[9] At the same time, semi-official Soviet war memoirs emphasised that goods from Russian and Ukrainian homes found their way to the cupboards of German households, that German prosperity, in other words, had been achieved at the expense of Soviet citizens.

Rage also had its origins in the deeper recesses of the Soviet collective consciousness. Even if soldiers yelled "for the homeland, for Stalin" as they charged the German lines, they led extremely hard lives and endured great privation at home. They rankled at the fierce discipline and unfair fines at work; they ate poorly and sometimes lived in hovels or even in the ground. There were few escapes from conformism and routine. Drink was one, and drink became a common aspect of the war and occupation that influenced the incidence and violence of rape. The same sober, good-natured soldiers who brought candy and food to young Germans girls during the day violated others at night during drunken rampages. During the 1930s, Soviet citizens were subjected to harsh Victorian inhibitions on sexual relations.[10] There was little talk of sex and no writing about sex; there were no condoms, no bordellos, no bawdy shows or movies. Many Soviet soldiers may well have been sexually repressed, which only contributed to their rage when confronting the supposedly free and easy Germans. Red Army soldiers, writes one British historian, vented "anger that had built up through decades of state oppression and endemic violence".[11]

East Prussia was completely devastated as a consequence of this mentality. No holds were barred; officers encouraged their men to rape and destroy. Alexander Solzhenitsyn described what he saw as a young officer in his prose poem "Prussian Nights": mothers raped, daughters violated and murdered, virgins turned into old women ("A girl's been turned into a woman. A woman into a corpse ...").[12] Lev Kopelev, who eventually published his memoirs in West German emigration, desperately tried to intervene when Soviet soldiers indiscriminately raped and brutalised German women in East Prussia. He was arrested, tried and sentenced to ten years in prison for engaging "in propaganda of bourgeois humanism, of pity for the enemy". His interrogator told him, "you engaged in agitation against vengeance and hatred – sacred hatred of the enemy".[13]

Official Soviet attitudes towards rape and the gross abuse of the German population changed in the spring of 1945 as the hate propaganda of Ilya Ehrenburg was formally condemned in *Pravda* (14 April 1945) and Soviet officers tried to reign in the wild behaviour of their troops. But the continuing fierce German resistance, the costly siege of Berlin and the realisation that so much had been lost despite the victory, did nothing to reduce the soldier's hatred of the Germans and inclination to exact revenge on the bodies of their women. In a recently published diary from the war, Vladimir Gelfand summarises the feelings of the Russian conquerors as Germany burned: "These haters of humanity, these animals, arouse no sympathy in me."[14]

Scholars argue about whether rape in war is primarily about sexual desire or violence.[15] In the case of the rape of German women by Soviet soldiers, the combustible mix of violence and sex was compounded by deep frustration on the part of the Russians that they had won the war against a people who claimed superiority even in defeat, lived in much better conditions and destroyed the very little they had at home. The contempt and disgust they sometimes exhibited for their rape victims reflected this psychology. Still, some Soviet officers and men became reliable partners for desperate German women. After the war, "occupation marriages" existed side by side with continuing outbursts of mass rape and pillage.[16]

By late 1946 Stalin and his satraps in Germany came to understand that they needed to eliminate rape if they were going to gain the allegiance of Germans to build a new "democratic" Germany according to Moscow's design. The only way they could do it was to isolate their troops by putting them in bases surrounded by barbed wire and military police. While the Western Allies quickly dropped the ban on fraternisation, instigating a period of freewheeling sexual relations between Allied soldiers and German women, the Soviets clamped down on all unofficial contact between their military and German civilians, a situation that continued almost until the collapse of the GDR.

The rape question in Germany

By the time of the establishment of the German Democratic Republic in 1949, stories of rape ceased to be discussed in public altogether, a situation that lasted half a century. After 1949 in West Germany, stories of rape were sometimes told as a way to undergird early Cold War anti-Soviet attitudes and policies. However, by the late 1960s, West Germans began to focus instead on confronting their responsibility for the Holocaust, the mass murder of Soviet POWs, and other genocidal actions of the Third Reich. The question of remembering the Second World War was highly political and generational. It also was related to foreign policy; during the period of *Ostpolitik* and détente, when Germany sought new and better relations with its eastern neighbours, it became almost impossible to talk about German victimhood without being accused of revanchism. The rape issue as such was confined to the right wing of the political spectrum and to apologists for the Nazi war in the east.

At the same time, the highly personal and ostensibly sexual character of rape also helped create a pall of silence over its perpetration. Men do not like to talk about rape when it relates to their wives and daughters because of the supposed "shame" it brings on them and on their families. Women avoid the subject for similar reasons. In some cultures, rape is equivalent to the desecration of a woman's purity and honour. The German word – *Schändung*, related to shame – (versus *Vergewaltigung*) – carries some of this meaning. At the same time, one needs to be careful of generalisations in this connection; over the decades since the war many German women have talked about their experiences, especially with other women, in remarkably forthright and unemotional fashion.

Taboo is too strong a word for the lack of attention to German victimisation between the late 1960s and the early 1990s. But the end of communism in Eastern Europe, the collapse of the Soviet Union, the reunification of Germany in the period 1989–90, and the demonstrable need of Germans to normalise their understanding of the Second World War, helped to remove the inhibitions to what was possible. The topics of the Allied fire-bombing, the destruction of German cities, the *Vertreibung* (the forced deportation of Germans from the east) and the problem of rape were belatedly reintroduced to the German public discourse about the war. Discussion of these important aspects of the war should not and cannot diffuse the centrality of the Third Reich's culpability for destroying the European continent by its genocidal war. But the Second World War also wrecked the lives of many millions of Germans, including a generation of rape victims. Germans still struggle with the problem of achieving the difficult and delicate balance between an understanding and acceptance of their ultimate responsibility for the horrors of the Second World War and their need to talk about and to acknowledge publicly the problems attached to their victimhood.

The public airing of the rape question received its first important impetus with the 1992 film (and subsequent book) by Helke Sander and Barbara Johr, *BeFreier und Befreite* (translated in English as *Liberators Take Liberties*). Sander answered the question how she came to the subject with the retort, "Why for nearly fifty years was it not a subject?"[17] While the success of the enterprise depended on the important changes in the European landscape in the period, 1989–91, feminist scholarship and activism also played an important role in providing a backdrop for the making of and interest in the film. In fact, Sander's impeccable feminist and leftist credentials made it possible for the film to be taken seriously. Media attention to mass rape in Bosnia from 1992–95 also provided impetus for the reconsideration of the German case. The film script states it at the outset: "Everyone knew about rape [after the war], but no one talked about it, as today in Kuwait, in Yugoslavia."[18]

The film itself focuses on interviews with German victims and Soviet soldiers with the idea of "unleashing memory" by allowing German women to recount the past, which they did with astonishing frankness in front of the cameras. The filmmakers interviewed 14 victims and witnesses; at least three had been young girls at the time who had no knowledge about sex. One woman, Inge Deutschkron, was a Jewess who tried to no avail to stop her rapists by showing her identity card. One woman was raped serially 26 times. How could she possibly keep count, Sander asked. She stopped counting, she answered, after the fourteenth time. Her family, who were forced to watch, told her the number later.

Significantly, the film provoked no serious reassessments of the rape issue in postwar Germany, as if a nasty secret had been aired in public, but it was time to get on to a different subject. There was, however, controversy and criticism, provoked by a larger discussion among feminists about the role of women in Nazi Germany. Some historians, Claudia Koonz among them, argued that German women had bought into the patriarchal Nazi system and fully supported it.[19] Although the crimes committed against German women were terrible and inexcusable, these could not be separated from the viciousness of the Nazis during and at the end of the war. Others, most prominently Gisela Bock, looked at the exploitation of German women by the Nazis, as they were forced against their will into housewifely and motherly roles. In this analysis, the war in the east was initiated, led and prosecuted by German men, not women. The women paid for the men's transgressions.[20]

One of the most trenchant critiques of *BeFreier und Befreite* came from Atina Grossmann, who thought not only that Sander allowed her German interviewees too much liberty to appear as victims, but that the film did not sufficiently contextualise the rape of German women within the larger picture of German depredations in the east. Grossman writes,

> The problem is that Sander's eagerness to integrate German women into the international transhistorical sisterhood of victims of male violence leads to a problematic historical slippage and displacement in which German women seem to become the victims primarily of National Socialism and the war, rather than of the failure of National Socialism and defeat in the war.[21]

Less appropriate were the criticisms that German women were portrayed yet again as victims "precisely at a historical moment when the most troubling victimization occurring in Germany was xenophobic violence against minorities".[22]

It really took until the beginning of the new century for Germans to deal openly with the subject of rape, and it came within the context of important, if controversial, efforts on the part of some Germans to give vent to aspects of their own victimhood at the end of the war and the beginning of the peace.[23] In his 2002 novel, *Im Krebsgang* (*Crabwalk*), Günter Grass explored the subject of the mass expulsion of Germans from the east and the tragic sinking of the refugee ship, the *Wilhelm Gustloff*, by the Soviets. Jörg Friedrich's *Der Brand* (*The Fire*) portrayed in melodramatic tones German victimhood during the purportedly gratuitous Allied bombing of German cities in the last year of the war. Meanwhile the positive reception in Germany of the translation of Antony Beevor's 2002 bestseller, *The Fall of Berlin 1945*, which focuses unsparingly, if perhaps a bit too floridly, on the widespread rape of German women, indicated something of a normalisation of the issue among the German public. At the same time, as James Mark notes in his study about memory and rape in the case of Hungary, the airing of the rape issue is more than just "post-Communist truth-telling".[24] Why, after all, were the first years of the new century so open to victimisation studies if not for a confluence of political and social agendas?

The re-publication of the diary by Anonyma, *Eine Frau in Berlin*, in 2003 should be understood in the same context. The history of this diary reflects a number of facets of the discussion (and lack of discussion) of the rape question in Germany since the war. In her early thirties, Anonyma is a lanky, blond journalist, well travelled and unmarried, though with a fiancé who is off at the front. She beings her diary when the Red Army conquers Berlin, writing at a sometimes frenzied pace for six weeks, between the end of May and mid-June 1945. Clear-eyed, unapologetic and unremorseful, she seeks out a sexual relationship with a Soviet officer to put a stop to her sufferings as *Freiwild* (open territory) for every sort of Russian soldier, and as the victim of gang-rapes, gratuitous violence and humiliating degradation. In one of the hardest parts of the book, one of her attackers – "wolves", as she calls them – completes the act of rape. Then, "Suddenly his finger is on my mouth, stinking of horse and tobacco. I open my eyes. A stranger's hands expertly pulling apart my jaws. Eye to eye. Then with great deliberation he drops a gob of gathered spit into my mouth."[25] Although her suffering is sometimes extreme, she assumes a highly pragmatic stance towards her survival, as do many of the women she describes around her. Her relationship with the Soviet officer serves her needs and his. Like so many other testimonies to the brutality of Soviet soldiers against German women, the "Woman in Berlin" does not understand what she is experiencing in the context of German aggression and depredations in the east. At the same time, she is unusually observant and canny when describing the individual characteristics of the Germans and Russians around her.

The diaries were first published in an English translation in New York in 1953, with the idea, in part, of serving as a useful addition to the barrage of popular Cold War images of Red Army soldiers as dangerous and rapacious. It was translated into seven other languages before a small Swiss publishing house issued the first German edition in 1958. But the book was mostly ignored in Germany, although sometimes criticised as ostensibly insulting "the honor of German women".[26] Not only was the woman raped, but she sought protection in a voluntary relationship with a Soviet officer. She was willing to grant some Russians too much character and individuality for Adenauer's Cold War West German society. Apparently, the author, who had insisted on anonymity because of the supposed shame of rape, was hurt by the criticisms and was not interested in further editions.

That the book was not republished until 2003 owes much more to the political and psychological tenor of the intervening period than to the anonymous author's wishes. As Hans-Magnus Enzensberger wrote in the introduction to the new edition, "German readers were obviously not ready [before the 1990s] to face some uncomfortable truths, and the book was met with either hostility or silence."[27] *Eine Frau in Berlin* was a bestseller in Germany the second time around and did much to bring the issue to the attention of the German public. However, a controversy broke out about investigative journalist Jens Bisky's story that disclosed the woman's name and biography. The public discussion focused on the identity of the woman and on the drafts of the diaries ostensibly altered by herself, her friends and editors. Bisky claimed that "the book is worthless as a document of contemporary history".[28] As Evelyn Finger of *Die Zeit* observed,

> In my opinion the German debate about the authenticity of the text ... was another way to avoid a real discussion of the topic ... It was amazing how some German journalists, when discussing the Anonyma-edition, gave the impression that the whole book was fake, and (implicitly) so were the mass rapes.[29]

It is hard to separate history and memory; they inevitably overlap and influence each other. But to the extent that political sensitivities about the war remain, it is difficult to analyse the rape issue as a significant chapter in the history of wartime and postwar Germany.

This is demonstrated as well by the critical reaction to the sensitive and nuanced 2003 short novel by Hans-Ulrich Treichel, *Der Verlorene* (*The Lost*). In almost every case, the critics skirt the central biographical event of the story, the rape by Russian soldiers of the chief protagonist, a German woman driven from the east with her husband. She herself never speaks of it. But, as narrated by her youngest son, born right after the war, "At some point, I understood this much, something terrible happened during the flight before the Russian advance. What it was, Mother never said, she only said over and over again that fleeing from the Russians something terrible happened to her and also that Father could not help her, and that no one could have helped her." In a moment of fear and panic at the appearance of the Russians, the woman passed her first born son, Arnold, to another woman on the trek, losing track of him and subsequently spending the rest of her life trying to find him. In this case, the novelist and the critics talk a lot about the *Vertreibung* and the heartrending quest to find Arnold, the lost son. But there is nothing about the rape, the *Schändung*, and the likelihood, strongly hinted at in the novel, that the remaining son was the product of the rape. "I was – in the truest sense of the world – *zum Heulen* [to wail about], only I understood much later why that was so."[30] The reader, however, never learns the truth, and like Germany itself, perhaps doesn't want to know it.

In September 2008, *Anonyma: Eine Frau in Berlin* was released as a feature-length film. Elaborately produced, expertly directed by Max Färberböck, and starring the famous and talented actress, Nina Hoss, the film represents, in some ways, the culmination of bringing the rape issue to the attention of the German public. But the reaction to the film has been strangely distant and uninterested, once again, as if the Germans want to put this history behind them. The criticism of the film is mostly technical, having to do with the timing, the lighting and the lack of realism in the film. More telling was the review of Joachim Kronsbein in *Spiegel online*. Here Kronsbein makes the important point that the director creates a kind of love relationship between the woman and her Soviet officer protector. This misses the point of these kinds of liaisons at this time; German women were forced to seek out reliable partners among Soviet officers as a way to protect themselves against marauders and rapists. But the border between rape and such relationships are hazy, just as the borders between rape and forced prostitution or even exchanging sexual relations for food and shelter cannot be so easily drawn. The movie has been a modest success as an "overripe Russian–German Ivan and Gretchen 'Romeo and Juliet'" story.[31] But the problem of rape itself has not been successfully explored.

Russia

That the Soviets and even Russians today, with very few exceptions, have refused to recognise the widespread and destructive nature of rape during the war has its roots in the romantic identification of the heroism of the Red Army during the Second World War – "the Great Patriotic War" – with the positive moral attributes of the Russian people. To stain the honour of Soviet soldiers during the war would be tantamount to insulting the dignity of the Russian people. The dynamics of history and memory in relationship to the war during the Soviet period also contribute to the denial of the rape issue among the overwhelming majority of Russian veterans and publicists. Not only were Soviet citizens not permitted to speak of such atrocities in connection with the campaigns against the Germans – as noted earlier both Solzhenitsyn and Kopelev were incarcerated for doing so – but, dating from the war itself, soldiers and then veterans were inculcated with a purely heroic version of their own actions, which they readily accepted, along with special awards, holidays, pensions and the like. Although there were thousands of books on the war that made up the favourite reading of Soviet citizens, none of them "ever mentioned panic, self-mutilation, cowardice or rape".[32]

In all circumstances, memory is selective, imperfect and, above all, deeply influenced by the social context in which it is elicited. In the Soviet Union, historical memory of the war was not only guided by state rituals and incantations of the Red Army's bravery and decency, but it remained unchallenged by dissonant voices or critical historiography. Family stories about the fallen reinforced an all-encompassing emotional attachment to the mythology of the war.[33] This powerful combination of state propaganda, the harsh censorship of challenging views and the proclivity of veterans to forget the shame of rape and remember the glory of victory continues to militate against the possibility of open discussion of the issue today. Based on interviews with more than 200 veterans, Merridale rightly notes that soldiers stories today "are a web of paradox, and sixty years of memory have only added to the confusion".[34]

Still, there have been challenges to the prevailing Russian view of the rape issue – in short, that it is not an issue at all – during the post-Soviet period. The partial opening of the archives in the early 1990s gave some impetus to discuss rape during the Yel'tsin period, as did the publication of Kopelev's memoirs in Russian in 1990. In his 1995 *Kak my upravliali Germanii* (*How We Ruled in Germany*), Mikhail Semiriaga, a military historian and veteran of the occupation, recognised that the German population suffered terribly in the east, although he claimed this was the result of the actions of Poles and Czechs, groups of bandits, remaining SS formations and some individual Soviet soldiers and officers. At the same time, he points to evidence that Germans actually sought and received protection from Soviet units against their pursuers. But in doing so, Semiriaga – for the first time that I know of in Russian historiography – gave credence in print to the problem itself and recognised, unlike the vast majority of his colleagues, that the rapes were more than "isolated incidents", although he claims they were then dealt with properly by the Red Army authorities and NKVD.[35] Similarly, Elena Seniavskaia's pioneering studies of the mentality of the Soviet soldiers at the front, their hatred for the Germans and their desire to take revenge, made it clear that acts of rape, even if not directly explored, were part and parcel of the "unstoppable acts of revenge."[36]

But it really took until relatively recently for the Russians to deal openly and without defensiveness with the wartime rape of German women. In an article striking for its unusual, even unique frankness about the rape problem, one veteran, Leonid Rabichev, in a 2005 issue of the literary journal, *Znamia*, writes in plain terms about what he saw in East Prussia as a young Soviet officer.[37] Rabichev recalls a particularly nasty scene, where "thousands" of Soviet soldiers attacked a trek of retreating German civilians, pushed aside the children and old folks and, "forgetting honor and obligation", threw themselves on the women and girls.

> The women, mothers and their daughters, lay right and left along the road; before each of them stood an uproarious armada of men with their pants half down. Those [women] who were bleeding or had lost consciousness were dragged by their hair to the side. The children who tried to help their mothers were shot at. Their commanders, majors, and colonels stood on the road, some laughed and some also directed – or better regulated. This was so that all of their soldiers without exception could participate.[38]

Rabichev's descriptions of the horrors of East Prussia go on. But this material in general is well known, at least in Western Europe and the United States. More interesting are his ruminations as a Soviet veteran, painter and writer about why he published this article. He relates that when he finally wrote down his experiences and showed the manuscript to his friend and fellow writer, Ol'ga Il'nitskaia, she told him to destroy it. It should never see the light of day, she insisted. "But I did not think at all about the reaction of the future reader or listener, I thought about how important it was not to leave out the details". In asking himself why, he comes up with the answer that this was not about "self-assertion, or any other goal", but rather about repentance (*pokaianiia*). "Like a thorn", he states,

> that sticks inside of me, and inside my entire generation ... This was ... a fragment of a criminal century, and with it as with the dekulakization of the 1930s, the Gulag, the deaths of tens of millions of innocent people, the occupation of Poland in 1939 – it is impossible to live with dignity, it is impossible to leave this life with dignity without repentance ... I was commander of a platoon, it sickened me, but I looked as if from a distance, but my soldiers stood in these awful criminal queues, laughed, when they should have burned with shame, and in fact committed crimes against humanity.

Rabichev might well have added that the Russian public, press and scholarship have done a much better job dealing with the Stalinist crimes of the 1930s than they have of confronting Soviet wartime atrocities.

Still, Russians are writing more openly and honestly about rape than during the Soviet period. Memoirs by the writers and veterans David Kaufman (Samoilov) (2002) and Boris Slutskii (2005) describe their wartime experiences and include substantial sections on the problem of rape in Soviet-occupied Europe.[39] Perhaps most surprising are the memoirs of the war by Nikolai Inozemstev, a prominent Soviet scholar of international relations, member of the Central Committee of the party and advisor to the Kremlin. Published in 1995, Inozemstev's memoir expresses his horror at the scenes of "mass rape", a term he frequently uses, in East Prussia. What most disturbed him and some of his fellow officers was the way "all of this rape lowered the dignity of the army as a whole and every Russian as an individual". He and his friends worried, with considerable justification as it turned out, that it would not be so easy to re-establish discipline and order once these "dissolute animal instincts" were allowed to be expressed.[40]

Although the sanctified memory of the war remains untouchable among the vast majority of Russian citizens, it is important to note that Russia today – despite the accusations of some of the country's detractors – cannot control all information or the way people write or think. True, in television and the press, with a couple of important exceptions, there is an "official" view of history that is promulgated in ways that remind one of the Soviet past. Yet, uninhibited online publications and exchanges are fully accessible, and commercial publishers can translate and issue books that cut against the grain of the dominant mythologies of the past. Similarly, it is important to register the fact that trends in Western historiography and cultural life are taken seriously by Russian intellectuals who are anxious to be considered a part of the European memory landscape. Despite howls of protest, Antony Beevor's *The Fall of Berlin* was translated and printed in Russian in 2004, this after the Russian ambassador in London had railed against the book as "an act of blasphemy" and "a case of slander".[41]

Similarly, the Russian reaction to the premier of the film *Anonyma, Eine Frau in Berlin* was bitter and hostile. *Pravda online* accused the film of reopening old wounds and arousing grudges against the Russians.[42] The *RBK Daily* was even more outraged. "Germany is trying to remove from itself the feelings of guilt for the Second World War" with this film. There is no documentary evidence, the online newspaper states, for the allegation of mass rape of the citizens of Berlin by Soviet soldiers. "That the diaries of the anonymous woman have been turned into a film at this precise moment should be seen as an attempt of some western forces to pour oil on the fire igniting a new 'Cold War'."[43] Although *Anonyma, Eine Frau in Berlin* was not invited to be shown at the German film festival in Moscow, there were online articles criticising the organisers for closing off uncomfortable renditions of the past to the Russian public. The respected historian Gennadii Bordiugov wrote, for example, that veterans groups had protested against the film even before any of them could possibly have seen it: "The movie is a diversion and provocation. This is an attempt to blacken the picture of the Soviet warrior, soldier, emancipator! As such, it denigrates Russia." But how can one learn about these events, asks Bordiugov, if Russians won't even be able to see the film and discuss it with the director? He makes the important point that even the horrible acts of the Wehrmacht on Soviet soil are understudied in Russia, since everyone wants to clean up memories of the glorious victory. He aptly concludes that "The Russians survived the test of the war. Can they survive the test of knowing the truth about the war?"[44]

One of the most interesting phenomena associated with the development of an online free press in Russia is the determination of a younger generation of Russians to get the story of the war straight from veterans themselves. Particularly impressive is the Russian website *I Remember* (*Ia pomniu*), which is comprised of a series of long interviews, conducted over the past several years with hundreds of Soviet war veterans from all over Russia and in the West.[45] The interviews, mostly in Russian, some in English, focus primarily on technical questions about the war: the equipment, the specifics of particular battles and the quality of leadership. But the young interviewers also ask about the soldiers' relations with the civilian populations, whether German, Hungarian, Polish, Romanian or others. The answers sometimes reveal that rape was at least recognised as an issue among a number of the veterans. Still, there is a great deal of denial of this problem in particular, while otherwise speaking frankly and uninhibitedly about other problematic issues during the war. Here are a few typical excerpts: "I should say there were some cases of pillage and rape in Germany" (Nikolai Safronov); "Our soldiers were not plunderers, but liberators" (Ivan Berkesh); "Our soldiers and officers related correctly to the Germans" (Iosif Vul); "The Russian soldier doesn't bear grudges" (Ivan Polianovskii); "There were incidents ... People are different; the circumstances were different" (Georgii Krivov); "Such excesses happened frequently" (Semen Ariia); "We did not disturb peaceful civilians" (Nikolai Kuzmichev).

Elka Sherstjannoi, a German expert on the Soviet military during and after the war, recently translated and published 161 letters home

(*Feldpostbriefen*) from Soviet soldiers to their relatives, friends and lovers from the end of the war to the beginning of the peace. These letters, located mostly in Russian archives, were subject to both military censorship and the self-censorship of their authors. Still, writes Sherstjannoi, "the letters from the period January to April 1945 are full of implicit indications of violent meetings" between German civilians and Soviet soldiers. Yet there is nothing explicit, which, she says, is the result of "an unwritten law of silence about the savagery of the battlefield" that continued into the postwar period. "This made it possible for the soldiers – and with them the society as a whole – to return to a normal civilian world." She rightly notes that this silence about atrocities is characteristic of soldiers at war everywhere.[46] One need only think about Japanese silence about rape in China during the Second World War or, for that matter, of the American proclivity to separate what Tom Brokaw called the "greatest generation", the Americans who fought in the Second World War, from atrocities in the Pacific against the Japanese and violence against the Germans after the major battles were over.[47]

At Greifswald University in the former GDR, an interdisciplinary team of scholars, led primarily by psychologists and social psychologists, have put together a project to interview surviving German women who had been raped by Soviet soldiers during and after the war. The launching of the project coincided with the opening of the film, *Anonyma, Eine Frau in Berlin*, demonstrating the way in which academic studies of memory in Germany, in particular, are closely linked to changes in public consciousness. After all these years, the leaders of the project assert, in somewhat exaggerated and self-satisfied language, these women have not had the opportunity to speak of their past trauma, especially since they became part of the Soviet Occupied Zone of Germany and German Democratic Republic, which did not allow the discussion of this topic.[48] These eighty-year olds can now speak freely about their experiences, as can the eighty-year-old Russian veterans in Moscow. Even in West Germany, for a long time there was an unspoken conspiracy of silence around the problem of rape, since it was bound up with issues of German identity as a perpetrator nation, with left–right politics, with conservatism in gender questions and even with interstate relations, since *Ostpolitik* meant not offending West Germany's eastern neighbours, including the Soviet Union.

Although both German women and Russian veterans can now relate their wartime experiences without external constraints, their stories about each other remain very different. The narrative of German women is one of unremitting rape and violence by Soviet soldiers, of the fear and of the shame that came from being helpless victims of sexual assaults. Although the stories are punctuated by references to good Russians and decent Soviet officers who offer help and succour, the women hold the Soviets soldiers accountable for their suffering rather than Hitler and the Nazis, who started and pursued the war to the end. At the same time, these stories are often told very matter-of-factly, without much emotion or coloured language. In that sense, the tone of the diary *Eine Frau in Berlin* is typical. Most German women, however, do not talk about having taken on Russian protectors as lovers, which probably occurred more often than they admit.

The Russian veterans tell their story differently. It was one of bravery and self-sacrifice, the victorious test of wills against the "Fritzes", and of romantic devotion to the motherland. In the post-Soviet period, there is more recognition in the accounts of veterans that German women were the objects of occasional violent attacks by their peers. But much more often there are references to loose and easy German women. In the newly published diary by Vladimir Gelfand, the young officer speaks about rape, but is much more taken with the extent to which German women fell all over him interested in sex.[49] Boris Slutskii in his memoirs talks about how embarrassingly easy it was to find love among the Germans.[50] Here, the borders blur between rape and prostitution, between German women freely selling sexual favours for protection, food and shelter, and being forced to do so.

More than fifty years after the war, the former Russian conquerors and their German female victims will not agree on a common narrative of the war and one should not expect them to. Both groups were victims and perpetrators in some senses; both overcame enormous odds to live long and fruitful lives after the most terrifying of total wars. But increasingly, there are signs that scholars and publicists from the two societies have been able to find a common ground for discussion, research and publication. The new century has brought with it in Eastern Europe a growing confrontation with the past that depends less on individual nations coming to terms with difficult issues of the Second World War and more on the clash of historical memories between different nations. The ongoing and increasingly sophisticated argument between Poles and Czechs on one side and Germans on the other over the *Vertreibung*, the forced deportation of Germans from Eastern Europe, is a good example. The rape issue also involves Russians and Germans in a particularly difficult conflict of memory and history. In the age of the Internet and, setbacks aside, of the growing integration of Russia into Europe, the argument can only improve the historical record.

Notes

1. For numbers see Norman M. Naimark, *The Russians in Germany: The History of the Soviet Occupation Zone, 1945–1949*, Cambridge, MA, Harvard University Press, 1995, pp. 132–3; Antony Beevor, *The Fall of Berlin 1945*, New York, Viking, 2002, p. 410; Jan Foitzik, *Sowjetische Militäradministration in Deutschland (SMAD) 1945–1949. Struktur und Funktion*, Berlin, Akademie Verlag, 1999, pp. 60ff.; Helke Sander, Barbara Johr, eds, *BeFreier und Befreite: Krieg, Vergewaltigung, Kinder*, 2nd edn, Munich, Verlag Antje Kunstmann, 1992, p. 54; Atina Grossmann, "A Question of Silence: The Rape of German Women by Occupation Soldiers", *October* 72 (Spring 1995), p. 46.
2. Theodore Schieder, ed., *Dokumentation der Vertreibung der Deutsdchen aus Ost-Mitteleuropa*, 3 vols., repr., Munich, Deutscher Taschenbuch Verlag, 2004. For criticism of the Schieder project, see Robert Moeller, *War Stories: The Search for a Usable Past in the Federal Republic of Germany*, Berkeley, University of California Press, 2001, pp. 51–87.
3. Edith A. Repogle, "'And Where Is Our Homeland?': The Reconstruction of Personal and National Identity in German Diaries from 1945", seinor thesis, Cambridge, MA, 1996, pp. 1, 9–14.
4. See Giles MacDonough, *After the Reich: The Brutal History of the Allied Occupation*, New York, Basic Books, 2007.
5. James Mark, "Remembering Rape: Divided Social Memory and the Red Army in Hungary, 1944–1945", *Past and Present* 188 (August 2005), p. 134. Mark estimates 50,000 women were raped. Other estimates are higher. See Peter Kenez, *Hungary from the Nazis to the Soviets: The Establishment of the Communist Regime in Hungary, 1944–1948*, New York, Cambridge University Press, 2006, pp. 43–5.
6. Wolfgang Mueller estimates the number of rapes of Austrian women by Soviet soldiers from April to August 1945 at between 100,000 and 400,000. Wolfgang Mueller, "Stalinismus und gesamteuropäisches Gedächtnis", *Transit* 38 (Winter 2009), pp. 96–109. See also Mueller's *Die sowjetische Besatzung in Österreich 1945–1949 und ihre politische Mission*, Vienna, Böhlau Verlag, 2005, pp. 112–15.
7. Boris Slutskii, *O drugikh i o sebe*, Moscow, Vagrius, 2005, pp. 99–105.
8. Naimark, *The Russians in Germany*, p. 72.
9. Naimark, *The Russians in Germany*, pp. 78, 114–15.
10. See Beevor, *The Fall of Berlin 1945*, pp. 32–3, and Catherine Merridale, *Ivan's War: The Red Army 1939–1945*, London, Faber and Faber, 2005, pp. 272–3.
11. Merridale, *Ivan's War*, p. 260.
12. In Robert Conquest's translation: cited in Naimark, *The Russians in Germany*, p. 73.
13. Lev Kopelev, *No Jail for Thought*, trans. and ed. Anthony Austin, London, Secker & Warburg, 1977, p. 10.
14. Wladimir Gelfand, *Deutschland Tagebuch 1945–1946: Aufzeichnungen eines Rotarmisten*, trans. Anja Lutter and Hartmut Schröder, Berlin, Aufbau Verlag, 2005, p. 28.
15. See Wendy Jo Gertjejanssen, "Victims, Heroes, Survivors: Sexual Violence on the Eastern Front during World War II", PhD dissertation, University of Minnesota, 2004, pp. 1–18.

16. Silka Satjukow, *Besatzer: "Die Russen" in Deutschland 1945–1994*, Göttingen, Vanderhoeck und Ruprecht, 2008, pp. 284–99.
17. Sander and Johr, eds, *BeFreier und Befreite*, p. 9.
18. Sander and Johr, eds, *BeFreier und Befreite*, p. 108.
19. Claudia Koonz, *Mothers in the Fatherland: Women, the Family, and Nazi Politics*, New York, St Martin's, 1987.
20. Gisela Bock, "Racism and Sexism in Nazi Germany: Motherhood, Compulsory Sterilization and the State", *Women and Violence* 8:3 (1983), p. 402.
21. Grossmann, "A Question of Silence", p. 49.
22. Richard W. McCormick, "Rape and War, Gender and Nation, Victims and Victimizers: Helke Sander's *BeFreier und Befreite*", *Camera Obscura* (September 2001), p. 2.
23. See Mikkel Dack, "Crimes Committed by Soviet Soldiers against German Civilians, 1944–1945: A Historiographical Analysis", *Journal of Military and Strategic Studies* 10:4 (Summer 2008), pp. 13–15.
24. Mark, "Remembering Rape", p. 143.
25. Anonymous, *A Woman in Berlin: Eight Weeks in a Conquered City. A Diary*, trans. Philip Boehm, New York, Henry Holt, 2005, pp. 63–4.
26. Hans Magnus Enzensberger, "Foreword", in Anonymous, *A Woman in Berlin*, p. xv.
27. Enzensberger, "Foreword", p. xi.
28. Jens Bisky, *Süddeutsche Zeitung*, 24 September 2003. See also "Eine Frau in Berlin", in *Neue Zürcher Zeitung*, 19 January 2004, that talks about Walter Kempowski's positive evaluation of the diary.
29. Evelyn Finger, private correspondence, 30 September 2008.
30. Hans Ulrich Treichel, *Der Verlorene*, Frankfurt, Suhrkamp Verlag, 2005, p. 140.
31. Joachim Kronsbein, "Tränen in rauchenden Trümmern", *Spiegel online*, 22 October 2008, p. l.
32. Merridale, *Ivan's War*, p. 6.
33. See Elena Senjavskaja, "Deutschlandbild und die Deutschen in den Augen", in Elke Sherstjanoi, ed., *Rotarmisten schreiben aus Deutschland: Briefe von der Front (1945) und historische Analysen*, Munich, K.G. Saur, 2004, p. 266.
34. Merridale, *Ivan's War*, p. 6.
35. M. I. Semiriaga, *Kak my upravliali Germaniei: Politika i zhizn'*, Moscow, Rosspen, 1995, pp. 186–93.
36. See Senjavskaja, "Deutschlandbild und die Deutschen", p. 258.
37. Leonid Rabichev, "Voina vse spishet", *Znamia* 2 (2005), pp. 163–6.
38. Oleg Budnitskii questions the veracity of Rabichev's account of this terrible incident. See his "The Intelligentsia Meets the Enemy: Educated Soviet Officers in Defeated Germany, 1945", *Kritika* 10:3 (Summer 2009), pp. 643–4.
39. David Samoilov, *Pedennye zapisi*, Moscow, Vremia, 2002. Slutskii, *O drugikh i o sebe*. For an analysis of these and other post-Soviet (mostly) Jewish officers' memoirs, see Budnitskii, "The Intelligentsia Meets the Enemy", pp. 629–83.
40. Nikolai Inozemstev, *Tsena pobedy v toi samoi voine: Frontevoi dnevnik*, Moscow, Nauka, 1995, pp. 190–1.
41. "Lies and insinuations", *Telegraph online*, 24 January 2002. The Russian translation of Beevor is E. Bivor, *Padenie Berlina. 1945*, trans. I. F. Mikhailov, Moscow: Izd. ACT, 2004.

42. Dmitrii Lyskov, "Germaniiu zastaviat 'vspomnit' 'nasil'nika-osvoboditelia'", *Pravda online*, 21 October 2008.
43. Nikolai Ivashov, "'Zhenshchina v Berline' kak mif o Rossii", 22 October 2008.
44. Gennadii Bordiugov, "Beregis! Russkie!", *RIANovosti*, 19 January 2009.
45. At www.iremember.ru.
46. Sherstjanoi, ed., *Rotarmisten schreiben aus Deutschland*, p. 216.
47. Tom Brokaw, *The Greatest Generation*, New York, Random House, 1998. For the violence in Europe, see MacDonough, *After the Reich*, pp. 227–50.
48. See Siobhan Dowling, "New German Study Looks at Rape Trauma 60 Years on", *Spiegel online*, 22 October 2008. Martina Rathke, "60 Jahre Schweigen", *Zeit online*, 20 October 2008.
49. Gelfand, *Tagebuch*, pp. 185–92.
50. Slutskii, *O drugikh i o sebe*, pp. 117–18.

Select Bibliograpghy

Abdo, Nahla and Lentin, Ronit, eds, *Women and the Politics of Military Confrontation. Palestinian and Israeli Gendered Narratives of Dislocation*, New York and Oxford, Berghan Books, 2002.

Abler, Thomas S., "Scalping, Torture, Cannibalism and Rape: An Ethnohistorical Analysis of Conflicting Cultural Values in War", *Anthropologica* 34.1 (1992), pp. 3–20.

Ahmed, R., ed., *Understanding the Bengali Muslims: Interpretative Essays*, Dhaka University Press, 2001.

Amnistía Internacional, "Cuerpos marcados, crímenes silenciados", 2004, www.amnesty.org/es/library/info.

Anonymous, *A Woman in Berlin: Eight Weeks in the Conquered City: A Diary*, New York, Henry Holt, 2005.

Aolain, Fionnuala Ni, "Sex-based Violence and the Holocaust: A Re-evaluation of Harms and Rights in International Law", *Yale Journal of Law and Feminism* 12 (2000), pp. 43–84.

Askin, Kelly Dawn, *War Crimes against Women. Prosecution in International War Crimes Tribunals*, Leiden, Martinus Nijhoff Publishers, 1997.

Audoin-Rouzeau, Stéphane, *L'Enfant de l'ennemi (1914–1918): Viol, avortement, infanticide pendant la Grande Guerre*, Paris, Aubier, 1995.

Baris, Tommaso, *Tra due fuochi. Esperienza e memoria della guerra lungo la linea Gustav*, Bari, Laterza, 2003.

Barrett, Richard Palmer and Little, Laura E., "Lessons of Yugoslav Rape Trials: A Role for Conspiracy Law in International Tribunals", *Minnesota Law Review* 88 (2003), pp. 30–85.

Bartov, Omer, Grosmann, Atina and Nolan, Mary, *Crimes of War Guilt and Denial in the Twentieth Century*, New York Press, 2002.

Bassiouni, Cherif and Marcia McCormick, *Sexual Violence: An Invisible Weapon of War in the Former Yugoslavia*, Chicago, International Human Rights Law Institute, 1996.

Bastick, Megan, Grimm, Karin and Kunz, Rahel, *Sexual Violence in Armed Conflict: Global Overview and Implications for the Security Sector*, Geneva Centre for the Democratic Control of Armed Forces, 2007.

Baxi, Pratiksha, "Rape, Retribution, State: On Whose Bodies?", *Economic and Political Weekly* 35.14 (2000), pp. 1196–1200.

Beck, Birgit, "Rape: The Military Trials of Sexual Crimes Committed by Soldiers in the Wehrmacht, 1939–1944", in Hagemann Karen and Schüler-Springforum Stefanie, eds, *Home/Front: The Military, War and Gender in Twentieth Century Germany*, Oxford, Berg, 2002, pp. 255–73.

Beck, Birgit, "Sexual Violence and Its Prosecution by Courts Martial of the Wehrmacht", in Roger Chickering, Stig Förster and Bernd Greiner, eds, *A World at Total War: Global Conflict and the Politics of Destruction, 1937–1945*, Cambridge University Press, 2005, pp. 317–31.

Beevor, Antony, *Berlin: The Downfall 1945*, London, Viking, 2002.

Benderly, Jill, "Rape, Feminism, and Nationalism in the War in Yugoslav Successor States", in Lois A. West, ed., *Feminist Nationalism*, New York and London, Routledge, 1997, pp. 59–72.

Bergen, Doris F., "Sexual Violence in the Holocaust: Unique or Typical?", in Dagmar Herzog, ed., *Lessons and Legacies*, vol. VII, Evanston, Northwestern University Press, 2006, pp. 179–200.

Beverly, Allen, *Rape Warfare: Hidden Genocide in Bosnia-Herzegovina and Croatia*, University of Minnesota Press, 1996.

Bougarel, Xavier, Duijzings, Ger and Helms, Elissa, eds, *The New Bosnian Mosaic: Identities, Memories and Moral Claims in a Post-War Society*, Aldershot, Ashgate, 2007.

Bourke, Joanna, *Rape: A History from 1860 to Present*, London, Virago, 2007.

Bracewell, Wendy, "Rape in Kosovo: Masculinity and Serbian Nationalism", *Nations and Nationalisms* 6 (2000), pp. 563–90.

Branche, Raphaëlle, "Sexual Violence in the Algerian War", in Dagmar Herzog, ed., *Brutality and Desire: War and Sexuality in Europe's Twentieth Century*, Basingstoke, Palgrave Macmillan, 2008, pp. 247–60.

Broken Bodies, Broken dreams: Violence against Women Exposed, Nairobi, OCHA, 2005.

Brownmiller, Susan, *Against Our Will. Men, Women and Rape*, New York, Simon and Schuster, 1975.

Buthalia, Urvashi, "A Question of Silence: Partition, Women and State", in Ronit Lentin, ed., *Gender and Catastrophe*, London and New York, Zed Books, 1997, pp. 92–109.

Cahill, J. Ann, *Rethinking Rape*, Ithaca and London, Cornell University Press, 2001.

Campbell, Kirsten, "The Gender of Transitional Justice: Law, Sexual Violence and the International Criminal Tribunal for the Former Yugoslavia", *The International Journal of Transitional Justice* 1.3 (2007), pp. 411–32.

Campbell, Kirsten, Starman, Hannah and Wastell, Sari, eds, *Testifying to Trauma: The Codification of Atrocity in Humanitarian Law*, London, Routledge Cavendish, 2011.

Capdevila, Luc, Rouquet, François, Virgili, Fabrice and Voldman, Danièle, *Sexes, genre et guerres (France, 1914–1945)*, Paris, Payot, 2010.

Carter, K. R., "Should International Relations Consider Rape a Weapon of War?", *Politics & Gender* 6 (2010), pp. 343–71.

Chang, Iris, *The Rape of Nanking: The Forgotten Holocaust of World War II*, New York, Penguin, 1997.

Chianese, Gloria, "Rappresaglie naziste, sacchegi e violenza alleata: alcuini esempi nel Sud", *L'impegno* 16.1 (1996), pp. 8–16.

Chiurlotto, Vania, "Donne come noi Marocchinate 1944–Bosniache 1993", *DonnaWomanFemme* 1 (1993), pp. 42–67.

Cockburn, Cynthia, "The Gendered Dynamics of Armed Conflict and Political Violence", in Caroline Moser and Fiona Clark, eds, *Victims, Perpetrators or Actors? Gender, Armed Conflict and Political Violence*, London and New York, Zed Books, 2001, pp. 13–29.

Cova, Anne, *Maternité et droits des femmes en France: XIXe–XXe siècles*, Paris, Anthropos-Économica, 1997.

Crawley, Heaven, "Engendering the State in Refugee Women's Claims for Asylum", in S. Jacobs, R. Jacobson and J. Marchbank, eds, *States of Conflict:*

Gender, Violence and Resistance, London and New York, Zed Books, 2000, pp. 87–104.
Crouzet, Denis, *Les guerriers de Dieu*, Paris, Champ Vallon, 1990.
Cyrulnik, Boris, *Autobiographie d'un épouvantail*, Paris, Odile Jacob, 2008.
D'Costa, Bina, "Coming to Terms with the Past in Bangladesh", in Luciana Riciutelli, Angela Miles and Margaret H. McFadden, eds, *Feminist Politics, Activism and Vision. Local and Global Challenges*, Toronto, Inanna Publications and Education, 2004, pp. 227–47.
Daqing, Yang, "Convergence or Divergence? Recent Historical Writings on the Rape of Nanjing", *The American Historical Review* 104.3 (1999), pp. 842–65.
Dara, Kay Cohen, *Explaining Sexual Violence during Civil War*, Proquest, Umi Dissertation Publishing, 2011.
Das, Veena, "National Honour and Practical Kinship: Of Unwanted Women and Children", in idem, ed., *Critical Events: An Anthropological Perspective on Contemporary India*, New Delhi, Oxford University Press,1995, pp. 55–83.
Das, Veena, *Life and Words. Violence and the Descent into the Ordinary*, Berkley, Los Angeles, London, University of California Press, 2007.
Delphy, Christine, *L'Ennemi principal*. I. *Économie politique du patriarcat*, Paris, Syllepse, 1998.
Delpla, Isabelle, "In the Midst of Injustice: The ICTY from the Perspective of Some Victim Associations", in Xavier Bougarel, Ger Duijzings and Elissa Helms, eds, *The New Bosnian Mosaic. Identities, Memories and Moral Claims in a Post-War Society*, Aldershot, Ashgate, 2007, pp. 211–34.
Delpla, Isabelle, "La preuve par les victimes: les bilans de la guerre en Bosnie-Herzégovine", *Le Mouvement social* 1 (2008), pp. 153–83.
Denich, Bette, "Of Arms, Men, and Ethnic War in (Former) Yugoslavia", in Constance R. Sutton, ed., *Feminism, Nationalism, and Militarism*, Association for FeministAnthropology/American Anthropological Association, 1995, pp. 61–71.
Devi, Mahasweta, "Draupadi", in idem, ed., *Breast Stories*, Calcutta, Seagull Books, 1997, pp. 19–38.
Devineau, Julie and Lacombe, Delphine, eds, "Violences envers les femmes", *Problèmes d'Amérique Latine*, special issue, 84.2 (2010).
Dombrowski, Nicole Ann, ed., *Women and War in the Twentieth Century: Enlisted with or without Consent*, New York and London, Garland, 1999.
Durham, Helen and Gurd, Tracey, ed., *Listening to the Silences: Women and War*, Leiden, Martinus Nijhoff, 2005.
El-Bushra, Judy, El-Karib, Asha and Hadjipateras, Angela, "Gender-sensitive Programme Design and Planning in Conflict-affected Situations", Research Report, Agency for Co-operation and Research in Development, 2002.
Engle, Karen, "Feminism and Its (Dis)contents: Criminalizing Wartime Rape in Bosnia and Herzegovina",*The American Journal of International Law* 99.4 (2005), pp. 778–816.
Enloe, Cynthia, *Manoeuvres: The International Politics of Militarizing Women's Lives*, Berkeley, University of California Press, 2000.
Epp, Marlene, "The Memory of Violence: Soviet and East European Mennonite Refugees and Rape in the Second World War", *Journal of Women's History* 9.1 (1997), pp. 58–87.
Ericsson, Kjersti and Simonsen, Eva, eds, *Children of World War II: The Hidden Enemy Legacy*, Oxford, Berg, 2005.

Farwell, Nancy, "War Rape: New Conceptualizations and Responses", *Affilia* 19.4 (2004), pp. 389–403.

Flaschka, Monika, "Race, Rape and Gender in Nazi Occupied Territories", PhD dissertation, Kent State University, 2009.

Forster, Cindy, "Violent and Violated Women: Justice and Gender in Rural Guatemala, 1936–1956", *Journal of Women's History* 11.3 (1999), pp. 55–77.

Freedman, Jane, *Gendering the International Refugee and Asylum Debate*, Basingstoke, Palgrave Macmillan, 2007.

Freedman, Jane, "Women's Right to Asylum: Protecting the Rights of Female Asylum Seekers in Europe?", *Human Rights Review* 9.4 (2008), pp. 413–33.

Gelfand, Wladimir, *Deutschland Tagebuch 1945–1946: Aufzeichnungen eines Rotarmisten*, Berlin, Aufbau Verlag, 2005.

Ginsburgs George, "Laws of War and War Crimes on the Russian Front during World War II: The Soviet View", *Soviet Studies* 11.3 (1960), pp. 253–85.

Godfroid, Anne, "Les relations franco-belges à la lumière des incidents rhénans de 1923", in *Actes du Congrès de l'Association des Cercles francophones d'Histoire et d'Archéologie de Belgique, Namur, 28–31 août 2008*, Presses universitaires de Namur, 2011, pp. 101–10.

Goldstein, Joshua S., *War and Gender. How Gender Shapes the War System and Vice Versa*, Cambridge University Press, 2001.

Green, Jennifer Lynn, "Collective Rape: A Cross-national Study of the Incidence and Perpetrators of Mass Political Sexual Violence, 1980—2003", Phd dissertation, Ohio State University, 2006.

Green, Jennifer Lynn and Granville-Chapman, Charlotte, *Rape and Other Torture in the Chechnya Conflict: Documented Evidence from Asylum Seekers Arriving in the United Kingdom*, London, Medical Foundation for the Care of Victims of Torture, 2004.

Gribaudi, Gabriella, *Guerra totale, Tra bombe alleate e violenza naziste Napoli e il fronte meridionale 1940–1944*, Turin, Bollati Boringhieri, 2005.

Grossman, Atina, "A Question of Silence: The Rape of German Women by Occupation Soldiers", *October* 72 (1995), pp. 43–63.

Guenivet, Karima, *Violences sexuelles: La nouvelle arme de guerre*, Paris, Michalon, 2001.

Guhathakurta, M., "Dhorshon Ekti Juddhaporadh" ("Rape Is a War Crime"), *Bulletin of Ain-O-Shalish Kendra* (February 1996), pp. 6–8.

Gullace, Nicoletta, "Sexual Violence and Family Honor: British Propaganda and International Law during the First World War", *American Historical Review* 102.3 (1997), pp. 714–47.

Harris, Ruth, "The Child of the Barbarian: Rape, Race and Nationalism in France during the First World War", *Past & Present* 141 (1993), pp. 170–206.

Hart, Janet, *New Voices in the Nation: Women and the Greek Resistance (1941–1964)*, Ithaca and London, Cornell University Press, 1996.

Heineman, Elizabeth D., "Sexuality and Nazism: The Doubly Unspeakable?", *Journal of the History of Sexuality* 11.1/2 (2002), pp. 22–67.

Heineman, Elizabeth, ed., *Sexual Violence in Conflict Zones: From the Ancient World to the Era of Human Rights*, Philadelphia and Oxford, University of Pennsylvania Press, 2011.

Helms, Elissa, "'Politics Is a Whore': Women, Morality and Victimhood in Post-War Bosnia-Herzegovina", in Xavier Bougarel, Elissa Helms and Ger Duijzings, eds, *The New Bosnian Mosaic*, Aldershot, Ashgate, 2007, pp. 235–53.

Helms, Elissa, "Justice et genre. Mobiliser les survivantes de guerre bosniaques", in Isabelle Delpla and Magali Bessone, eds, *Peines de guerre: La justice internationale et l'ex-Yougoslavie*, Paris, Editions de l'EHESS, 2010, pp. 249–65.

Héritier, Françoise, *Masculin/féminin. La pensée de la différence*, Paris, Odile Jacob, 1996.

Héritier, Françoise, ed., *De la violence*, Paris, Odile Jacob, 1996.

Herzog, Dagmar, *Sex after Fascism. Memory and Morality in Twentieth-century Germany*, , Princeton University Press, 2005.

Hobson, M., *Forgotten Casualties of War: Girls in Armed conflicts*, London, Save the Children, 2005.

Horne, John, "Corps, lieux et nation: La France et l'invasion de 1914", *Annales Histoire. Sciences Sociales* 1 (2000), pp. 73–109.

Horne, John and Kramer, Alan, *German Atrocities, 1914. A History of Denial*, New Haven and London, Yale University Press, 2001.

Human Rights Watch, *La guerre dans la guerre. Violences sexuelles contre les femmes et les filles dans l'est du Congo*, London, 2002.

Human Rights Watch, *Les soldats violent, les commandants ferment les yeux: violences sexuelles et réforme militaire en RD Congo*, 16 July 2009.

Independent Experts' Assessment on the Impact of Armed Conflict on Women and Women's Role in Peace-Building, UNIFEM, October 2002.

Kaffel, Hasebenebi, "Reintegration Programme for Demobilised Fighters: A Gender Prospect", *Conference on Gender, Armed Conflict and Political Violence, 10–11 June 1999*, World Bank, Washington, DC.

Kaplan, Alice, *The Interpreter*, University of Chicago Press, 2005.

Koenig, Dorean Marguerite, "Women and Rape in Ethnic Conflict and War", *Hastings Women's Law Journal* 5.2 (1994), pp. 129–41.

Krog, Antjie, *Country of My Skull: Guilt, Sorrow and the Limits of Forgiveness in New South Africa*, New York, Time Books, 1998.

Lagrou, Pieter, *The Legacy of Nazi-occupation. Patriotic Memory and National Recovery in Western Europe, 1945–1965*, Cambridge University Press, 2000.

Laviolette, Nicole, "Commanding Rape: Sexual Violence, Command Responsibility, and the Prosecution of Superiors by the International Criminal Tribunals for the Former Yugoslavia and Rwanda", *Canadian Yearbook of International Law* 36 (1998), pp. 93–149.

Le Goaziou, Véronique, *Le viol. Aspects sociologiques d'un crime*, Paris, La documentation française, 2011.

Le Huérou, Anne, and Régamey, Amandine, "Massacres de civils en Tchétchénie, Décembre 1999–février 2000", in *Online Encyclopedia of Mass Violence*, June 2012.

Le Naour, Jean-Yves, *Misères et tourments de la chair durant la Grande Guerre. Les mœurs sexuelles des Français 1914–1918*, Paris, Aubier, 2002.

Leiby, Michele L., "Wartime Sexual Violence in Guatemala and Peru", *International Studies Quarterly* 53 (2009), pp. 445–68.

Lentin, Ronit, ed., *Gender and Catastrophe*, London, Zed Books, 1997.

Lerner, Gerda, *The Creation of Patriarchy*, New York, Oxford University Press, 1986.

Les femmes et la guerre, 2/8 Violences sexuelles, Genève, Publications du CICR, 2001.

Liebman, Stuart, ed., "Berlin 1945: War and Rape 'Liberators Take Liberties'", *October* 72 (1995), pp. 42–63.

Lilly, J. R., *Taken by Force. Rape and American GIs in Europe during World War II*, Hampshire and New York, Palgrave MacMillan, 2007.

Lindner, Evelin Gerda, "Humiliation and History in Global Perspectives", *Social Alternatives* 25.1 (2006), pp. 56–61.

Loganathan, Bhawani, *Gendering Humanitarianism: An Annotated Bibliography on Gender and Capacity Building in Armed Conflict*, Colombo, International Centre for Ethnic Studies, 2000.

Luz, Piedad Caicedo, "Gravedad penal de la violencia sexual cometida en el marco del conflicto armado colombiano", www.humanas.org.co/html/doc/ponencias.

Mahmud, Nasreen, "Crimes against Honour: Women in International Refugee Law", *Journal of Refugee Studies* 9.4 (1996), pp. 367–82.

Mailander, Elissa, *Gewalt im Dienstalltag: Die Aufseherinnen des Konzentrations- und Vernichtungslagers Majdanek*, Hambourg, Hamburger Edition, 2009.

Margolin, Jean-Louis, *L'armée de l'Empereur, violences et crimes du Japon en guerre 1937–1945*, Paris, Armand Colin, 2007.

Mark, James, "Remembering Rape: Divided Social Memory and the Red Army in Hungary 1944–945", *Past and Present* 188 (2005), pp. 133–61.

Martin, Jean-Clément, "Femmes et guerre civile, l'exemple de la Vendée, 1793–1796", *Clio Histoire Femmes et sociétés* 5 (1997), pp. 97–115.

Martin, Jean-Clément, *Violence et révolution*, Paris, Seuil, 2006.

Mascha, Nina, Katjusha. Frauen in der Roten Armee, 1941–1945, Berlin, Deutsch-Russiches Museum-Karlshorst, 2002.

McDonough, Giles, *After the Reich: The Brutal History of the Allied Occupation*, New York, Basic Books, 2007.

McKale, Donald, "A Case of Nazi 'justice' – The Punishment of Party Members Involved in the Kristalnacht, 1938", *Jewish Social Studies* 35.3–4 (1973), pp. 228–38.

McKay, Susan, "The Effects of Armed Conflict on Girls and Women", *Journal of Peace Psychology* 4 (1998), pp. 381–92.

Merridale, Catherine, *Ivan's War: The Red Army 1939–1945*, London, Faber and Faber, 2005.

Mookherjee, Nayanika, "'My Man (Honour) is Lost but I Still Have My Iman (Principle)': Sexual Violence and Articulations of Masculinity", in R. Chopra, C. Osella and F. Osella, eds, *South Asian Masculinities*, New Delhi, Kali for Women, 2004, pp. 131–59.

Mookherjee, Nayanika, "'Remembering to Forget': Public Secrecy and Memory of Sexual Violence in Bangladesh", *Journal of Royal Anthropological Institute* 12.2 (2006), pp. 433–50.

Morris, Benny, *The Birth of The Palestinian Refugee Problem, 1947–1949*, Cambridge University Press, 1988.

Morris, Madeline, "By Force of Arms: Rape, War, and Military Culture", *Duke Law Journal* 45.4 (1996), pp. 651–781.

Moser, Caroline and Clark, Fiona, eds, *Victims, Perpetrators or Actors? Gender, Armed Conflict and Political Violence*, London and New York, Zed Books, 2001.

Mostov, Julie, "'Our Women'/'Their Women': Symbolic Boundaries, Territorial Markers, and Violence in the Balkans", *Peace and Change* 20.4 (1995), p. 515.

Mühlhäuser, Regina, *Eroberungen. Sexuelle Gewalttaten und intime Beziehungen deutscher Soldaten in der Sowjetunion 1941–1945*, Hamburg, Hamburger Edition, 2010, pp. 515–29.

Muravyeva, Marianna, "Seksual'nye prestupleniia v evropejskom voenno-ugolovnom prave rannego novogo vremeni", *Dialog so vremenem: Al'manakh intellektual'noi istorii* 29 (2009), pp. 248–70.

Murphy, Paul J., *Allah's Angels: Chechen Women in War*, Annapolis, MD, Naval Institute Press, 2010.

Murray, Jennifer, "Who Will Police the Peace-Builders? The Failure to Establish Accountability for the Participation of United Nations Civilian Police in the Trafficking of Women in Post-Conflict Bosnia and Herzegovina", *Columbia Human Rights Law Review* 2 (2003), pp. 475–527.

Nahoum-Grappe, Véronique, "Guerre et différence des sexes: Les viols systématiques (ex-Yougoslavie, 1991–1995) ", in Cécile Dauphin et Arlette Farge, eds, *De la violence et des femmes*, Paris, Albin Michel, 1997, pp. 159–84.

Nahoum-Grappe, Véronique and Allen, Beverly, *Rape Warfare: The Hidden Genocide in Bosnia-Herzegovina and Croatia*, University of Minnesota Press, 1996.

Naimark, Norman, *The Russians in Germany. A History of the Soviet Zone of Occupation, 1945–1949*, Cambridge, MA, Harvard University Press, 1995.

Narasimhan-Madhavan, Deepa, "Gender, Sexuality and Violence: Permissible Violence against Women during the Partition of India and Pakistan", *Hawwa* 4.2–3 (2006), pp. 396–416.

Notin, Jean-Christophe, *La campagne d'Italie. Les victoires oubliées de la France, 1943–1945*, Paris, Perrin, 2002.

Oxfam International, "La violencia sexual en Colombia. Un arma de guerra", 2009, www.oxfam.org/sites/www. oxfam.org/files.

Pasteur, Paul, "Violences et viols des vainqueurs: les femmes à Vienne et en Basse-Autriche, avril–aout 1945", *Guerres Mondiales et Conflits Contemporains* 198 (2000), pp. 123–36.

Podolsky, Anatoly, "The Tragic Fate of Ukranian Jewish Women under Nazi Occupation, 1941–1944", in *Sexual Violence against Jewish Women during the Holocaust*, Sonja M. Hedgepeth and Rochelle G. Saidel, eds, Hanover, University Press of New England, 2010, pp. 94–107.

Porzio, Maria, *Arrivano gli Alleati ! Amori e violenze nell'Italia liberata*, Roma-Bari, Laterza, 2011.

Poulos, Margaret, "Gender, Civil War and National Identity: Partisans during the Greek Civil War 1946–1949", *The Australian Journal of Politics and History* 46.3 (2000), pp. 418–27.

Power-Stevens, Tania, "Somalia Case Study", in B. Bridget, ed., *Gender, Conflict and Development*, BRIDGE–Development–Gender, report no. 35, vol. II, 1996.

Prochazkova, Petra, *The Aluminium Queen*, Lidove Noviny Publishing House, 2002.

Puar, J. K., "Abu Ghraib: Arguing against Exceptionalism", *Feminist Studies* 30.2 (2004), pp. 522–34.

Rehn, Elisabeth and Sirleaf, Ellen Johnson, *Women, War, and Peace: The Independent Experts' Assessment on the Impact of Armed Conflict on Women and Women's Role in Peace-Building*, UNIFEM, 2002.

Richter-Lyonette, Elenor, *Bibliography Gender, War & Justice: With Special Reference to the Balkan Wars 1991–1999*, the Coordination of Women's Advocacy, 2002.

Ringelheim, Joan, "The Split between Gender and the Holocaust", in Dalia Ofer and Lenore J. Weitzman, eds, *Woman in the Holocaust*, New Haven, Yale University Press, 1998, pp. 340–50.

Rittner, Carol and Roth, John, eds, *Rape: Weapon of War and Genocide*, Paragon, 2012.

Rivière, Antoine, "La quête des origines face à la loi du secret. Lettres d'enfants de l'Assistance publique (1900–1920)", *Revue d'histoire de l'enfance irrégulière* 11 (2009), pp. 77–96.

Roland, Charles G., "Massacre and Rape in Hong Kong: Two Case Studies Involving Medical Personnel and Patients Source", *Journal of Contemporary History* 32.1 (1997), pp. 43–61.

Rouquet, François, Virgili, Fabrice and Voldman, Danièle, *Amours, guerres et sexualité 1914–1945*, Paris, Gallimard, 2007.

Russell-Brown, Sherri L., "The Last Line of Defense: The Doctrine of Command Responsibility and Gender Crimes in Armed Conflict", *Wisconsin International Law Journal* 22 (2004), pp. 125–61.

Sanday, Susan R., "The Socio-cultural Context of Rape: A Cross-cultural Study", in Laura L. O'Toole and Jessica R. Schiffman, eds, *Gender Violence: Interdisciplinary Perspectives*, New York Press, 1997, pp. 52–66.

Sander, Helke and Johr, Barbara, eds, *BeFreier und Befreite: Krieg, Vergewaltigung, Kinder*, Munich, Antje Kunstmann, 1992.

Schmidt, David Andrew, *Ianfu: The Comfort Women of the Japanese Imperial Army of the Pacific War: Broken Silence*, Lampeter, Edwin Mellen Press, 2000.

Seifert, Ruth, "Rape in Wars: Analytical Approaches", *Minerva: Quarterly Report on Women and the Military* 11.2 (1993), pp. 17–32.

Seifert, Ruth, "The Second Front: The Logic of Sexual Violence in Wars", *Women's Studies International Forum* 19 (1996), pp. 35–43.

Sherstjanoi, Elke, ed., *Rotarmisten schreiben aus Deutschland: Briefe von der Front (1945) und historische Analysen*, Munich, K. G. Saur, 2004.

Shik, Na'ama, "Sexual Abuse of Women in Auschwitz-Birkenau", in Dagmar Herzog, ed., *Brutality and Desire. War and Sexuality in Europe's Twentieth Century*, London, Palgrave Macmillan, 2009, pp. 221–46.

Soucaille, Alexandre, "Le viol et la question du féminin", in B. Glowczewski and A. Soucaille, eds, *Désastre*, L'Herne, collection Cahiers d'anthropologie sociale, 2011, pp. 115–30.

Stanley, Penny, "Reporting of Mass Rapes in Balkans: 'Plus ça change, plus c'est la même chose?': from Bosnia to Kosovo", *Civil Wars* 2 (1999), pp. 74–110.

Stiglmayer, Alexandra, ed., *Mass Rape: The War against Women in Bosnia-Hercegovina*, Lincoln and London, University of Nebraska Press,1994.

Suarez, Natalia, "Le travail de résistance des femmes persécutées dans des situations de guerre: le cas de la Colombie", in Jane Freedman and Jérôme Vally, eds, *Persécutions des femmes, savoir, mobilisations et protections*, Paris, Édition de Croquant, 2007, pp. 273–86.

Tanaka, Yuki, *Japan's Comfort Women: Sexual Slavery and Prostitution during World War II and the US Occupation*, London and New York, Routledge, 2002.

Taylor, C., *Sacrifice as Terror: The Rwandan Genocide of 1994*, Oxford, Berg, 1999.

Teltumbde, Anand, *Khairlanji. A Strange and Bitter Crop*, New Delhi, Navayana Publishing, 2008.

Thapar-Björkert, Suruchi, "Women as Arm-bearers: Gendered Caste-violence and the Indian State", *Women's Studies International Forum* 29 (2006), pp. 474–88.

Thébaud, Françoise, *La femme au temps de la guerre de 14*, Paris, Stock, 1986.

Theidon, Kimberly, "Gender in Transition: Common Sense, Women, and War", *Journal of Human Rights* 6 (2007), pp. 453–78.

Thornill, Theresa, *Making Women Talk: Women Political Prisoners Talk about Their Lives*, Jerusalem, PASSIA, 1995.

Turshen, Meredith, "The Political Economy of Rape: An Analysis of Systematic Rape and Sexual Abuse of Women during Armed Conflict in Africa", in C. Moser and F. Clark, eds, *Victims, Perpetrators or Actors? Gender, Armed Conflict and Political Violence*, London and New York, Zed Books, 2001, pp. 55–68.

Van Boeschoten, Riki, "The Trauma of War Rape: A Comparative View on the Bosnian Conflict and the Greek Civil War", *History and Anthropology* 14.1 (2003), pp. 41–54.

Vervenioti, Tasoula, "Left-wing Women between Politics and Family", in Mark Mazower, ed., *After the War Was Over: Reconstructing the Family, Nation and State in Greece, 1943–1960*, Princeton and Oxford, Princeton University Press, 2000, pp. 103–14.

Vigarello, Georges, *Histoire du viol XVIe–XXe siècle*, Paris, Seuil, 1998.

Virgili, Fabrice, *Shorn Women: Gender and Punishment in Liberation France*, Oxford, Berg, 2002.

Virgili, Fabrice, *Naître ennemi. Les enfants nés de couples franco-allemands pendant la Seconde Guerre mondiale*, Paris, Payot, 2009.

Wilson, Amrit, *The Challenge Road: Women and the Eritrean Revolution*, London, Earth Scan, 1991.

Wishnia, Judith, "Natalisme et nationalisme pendant la Première Guerre mondiale", *Vingtième siècle. Revue d'Histoire* 45 (1995), pp. 30–9.

Wood, Elisabeth Jean, "Variation in Sexual Violence during War", *Politics and Society* 34.3 (2006), pp. 307–41.

Wood, Elizabeth Jean, "Sexual Violence during War: Toward an Understanding of Variation", in Ian Shapiro, Stathis Kalyvas and Tarek Masoud, eds, *Order, Conflict, and Violence*, Cambridge University Press, 2008, pp. 321–51.

Wood, Elisabeth Jean, "Armed Groups and Sexual Violence: When Is Wartime Rape Rare?", *Politics & Society* 37 (2009), pp. 131–61.

Yamamoto, Masahiro, *Nanking: Anatomy of an Atrocity*, New York, Praeger, 2000.

Žarkov, D., "War Rapes in Bosnia: On Masculinity, Femininity and Power of the Rape Victim Identity", *Tijdschrift voor Criminologie* 39.2 (1997), pp. 140–51.

Žarkov, D., "The Body of the Other Man: Sexual Violence and the Construction of Masculinity, Sexuality and Ethnicity in the Croatian Media", in C. Moser and F. Clark, eds, *Victims, Perpetrators or Actors? Gender, Armed Conflict and Political Violence*, New Delhi, Kali for Women, 2001, pp. 69–82.

Žarkov, D., *The Body of War: Media, Ethnicity, and Gender in the Break-up of Yugoslavia*, Durham, NC and London, Duke University Press, 2007.

Zawati, Hilmi, "Impunity or Immunity: Wartime Male Rape and Sexual Torture as a Crime against Humanity", *Torture* 17.1 (2007), pp. 27–47.

Zawati, Hilmi and Mahmoud, Ibtisam M., *A Selected Socio-legal Bibliographyon of Ethnic Cleansing, Wartime Rape, and Genocide in the Former Yugoslaviaand Rwanda*, Lewiston, NY, Edwin Mellen, 2005.

Zipfel, Gaby, "Ausnahmezustand Krieg? Anmerkungen zu soldatischer Männlichkeit, sexueller Gewalt und militärischer Einhegung", in Insa Eschebach and Regina Mühlhäuser, eds, *Krieg und Geschlecht. Sexuelle Gewalt im Krieg und Sex-Zwangsarbeit in NS-Konzentrationslagern*, Berlin, Metropol, 2008, pp. 55–74.

Index

CPSIA information can be obtained at www.ICGtesting.com
Printed in the USA
LVOW102125200613

339617LV00008B/62/P

9 780230 363991